Sana Haroon

Frontier of Faith

Islam in the Indo-Afghan Borderland

Columbia University Press
New York

Columbia University Press
Publishers Since 1893
New York

Library of Congress Cataloging-in-Publication Data

Haroon, Sana.
  Frontier of faith : Islam in the Indo-Afghan borderland / Sana Haroon.
    p. cm.
  Includes bibliographical references and index.
  ISBN 978-0-231-70013-9 (cloth : alk. paper)
  1. North-west Frontier Province (Pakistan)—Politics and government. 2.
Islam and politics—Pakistan—North-west Frontier Province. 3. Islam—Paki-
stan—North-west Frontier Province. I. Title.
  DS392.N67H379 2007
  954.91'2035—dc22
                                    2007020786

∞
Columbia University Press books are printed on
permanent and durable acid-free paper.
This book is printed on paper with recycled content.
Printed in India

c 10 9 8 7 6 5 4 3 2 1

References to Internet Web sites (URLs) were accurate at the time of writing.
Neither the author nor Columbia University Press is responsible for URLs
that may have expired or changed since the manuscript was prepared.

FRONTIER OF FAITH

For Zulfi, Raza and Rafay

CONTENTS

ACKNOWLEDGEMENTS

I have accumulated many debts of gratitude while working on this study. First, this research would not have been possible without a Research Student Fellowship and a fieldwork grant to consult the archives in Peshawar and Islamabad in 2001, both granted by the School of Oriental and African Sudies, and a fellowship grant from the Isobel Thornley bequest, granted through the Institute of Historical Research, in 2003. A post-doctoral fellowship grant from the Past and Present Society in 2004 made revision and completion of the manuscript possible.

My greatest intellectual and personal debt is to my adviser, Dr Avril Powell. Her advice and caution regarding source material and historical themes and her unfailing attention to detail corrected the course that this study would take early on. Professor Peter Robb at SOAS, Dr Mukulika Banerjee at UCL, Dr Sarah Ansari at Royal Holloway College, Professor Barbara Metcalf at University of California, Davis, Dr Alex McKay at the Wellcome Trust, Dr Robert Nichols at the University of Pennsylvania, Professor Andrew Porter at Kings College London, Professor Peter Marshall, and Dr Faisal Devji at the New School have provided valuable comments and suggestions, both in seminars and in conversation, over the last four years.

My thanks to Dr Andrew Cook, curator of maps at the British Library for his generosity with his time and his thoughts in introducing me to the map collection and considering ways to understand and 'read' these documents, and to Dr Sebastian Ballard who drew the maps for this book. Also, many thanks to Leena Mitford for her help with the Urdu collection, and to the rest of the staff at the Oriental and India Office Collection for their help and for making the working day there so much more pleasant. In addition, Zahra Reza at UCL provided valuable help in translating some key Dari documents.

In Peshawar, Humaira and Mustafa Kasuri, and Khalida and Gohar Zaman have my deepest gratitude for taking me in and making my research there possible. Zahirullah Khan Sahib and Bhatti Sahib at the Peshawar Archives, Mr Amjad Khan at the FC headquarters in Shabqadar, Professor Obaidur Rahman at Peshawar University, Salimullah Khan Sahib at the National Documentation Centre, Islamabad, and Wiqar Ali Shah Sahib at Quaid-e-Azam University rendered valuable assistance in tracing archival sources and personal collections. Abubakar Siddique proved a good friend and ally in Peshawar and his journalistic writings on the Tribal Areas put forward an important view about the region, its politics and its future. He introduced me to Agha Sahib Ghulam Nabi Chaknawari and my time spent with the latter hearing about his experiences and with his wonderful and affectionate family were the best part of my time spent in Peshawar.

The readings and responses of three people have been particularly important in the years over which I developed this study from a doctoral dissertation into a book. Professor Francis Robinson at Royal Holloway pointed out the presumptuousness of treating revivalism as the only religious discourse of note in the region; Professor Ian Talbot suggested ways in which a project of significance could emerge from the minutiae I painstakingly extracted from thirty years of political office records; and an anonymous reader at Hurst and Co. sent me a thorough and generous set of comments, questions and suggestions from which the book took on its current form and scope. I have benefitted enormously from their methodological critiques and their expertise in the field of modern South Asian Islamic history. In addition I would like to thank Michael Dwyer and Christopher Hurst for their editorial support and feedback. Any errors of fact or ommission are mine alone.

Thank you, finally, to my family and friends whose love, confidence and support has gotten me through these last few years, particularly

ACKNOWLEDGEMENTS

to Aassia, Saad and Nida, whose friendship, criticism and love is unrestrained; to Silvat and Rizvan Ali and Amna and Changez for their support and affection; and to Nadia, Lynn, Ahmed, Misbah, Obaid and Yasmeen for humouring me through years of being 'almost done'. My greatest debt is to my parents Tahirah and Mohammad Haroon and to Zulfi, who has stood behind me every step of the way, whose opinion and advice I have solicited every day and who made it possible for me to sustain the energy and momentum it has taken to write this. This book is dedicated to him and to our two sons Raza and Rafay.

ABBREVIATIONS

AINC	All India National Congress
BAR	Border Administration Report
BL	British Library
CC	Chief Commissioner
DC	Deputy Commissioner
DCOP	Deputy Commissioner's Office Peshawar
DOFCS	District Officer Frontier Constabulary Shabqadar
DRA	Democratic Republic of Afghanistan
ISI	Inter-Services Intelligence
JP	Jinnah Papers
JUH	Jamiyatul Ulama-yi Hind
JUI	Jamiyatul Ulama-yi Islam
JUS	Jamiyatul Ulama-yi Sarhad
MMA	Muttahida Majlis-i Amal
MPD	Mohmand Political Diary
NAI	National Archives Islamabad
NDC	National Documentation Centre (Islamabad)
NWFP	North-West Frontier Province
NWFPIBD	North-West Frontier Province Intelligence Bureau Diary
NWFPPD	North-West Frontier Province Provincial Diary
NWFPPA	North-West Frontier Province Provincial Archives
OIOC	Oriental and India Office Collection
PA	Political Agent
PO	Political Officer
PDPA	People's Democratic Party of Afghanistan
RBC	Rare Books Collection
SCNAI	Shaidai Collection, National Archives Islamabad
SRPORC	Saifur Rahman Papers, Obaidur Rahman Collection
TNSM	Tehrik-i Nifaz-i Shariat-i Muhammadi

NOTE ON TRANSLITERATION

Transliteration has been according to the rules laid down in the Library of Congress romanisation tables with some changes. The ' denoting the *ayn* has been omitted where it occurs in the middle of a word, as in the case of *jamaat*, but retained where it occurs at the beginning of a word, as in *'ulama*. All other diacritical marks have been omitted. With the exception of a few words, notably *'ulama* and *buzurgan*, plural forms are indicated by adding s to the singular of the word, as in *fatwas* rather than *fatawa*. In the case of some Arabic words adopted into Urdu, I have used the standard Arabic transliteration, as with *shari'a, hadith and madrasa*.

MAPS AND FIGURES

Maps
The Indian North-West Frontier *c.* 1900
The Tribal Areas *c.* 1930
Major tribal groups, roads and railways *c.* 1930

Figures
1. Dominant mullas among the eastern Pakhtuns during the late nine-teenth and early twentieth century
2. Mullas of the Akhund Ghaffur-Hadda Mulla line in the twentieth century
3. Shajarah of the Fazal Wahid Haji Turangzai engraved in marble. The plaque is displayed at the site of the Haji's masjid in Ghaziabad, Mohmand Agency.
4. The spiritual genealogy of the Tribal Areas mullas
5. Muhammad Ali Kasuri's Naqsha-yi Yaghistan.

1. The Indian North-West Frontier *c.* 1900

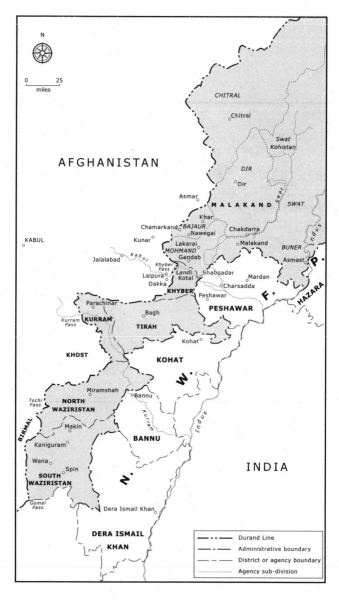

2. The Tribal Areas *c*. 1930

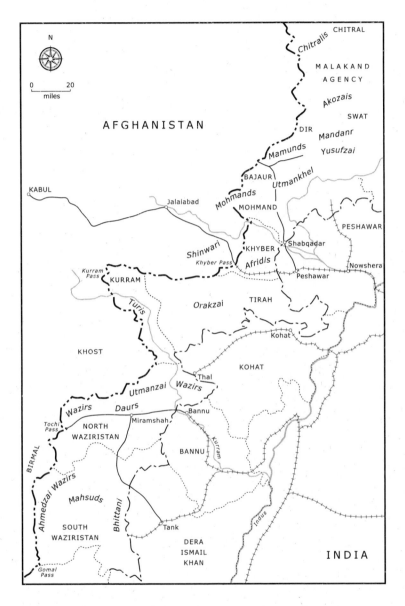

3. Major tribal groups, roads and railways *c.* 1930

INTRODUCTION

This book is an examination of religious organisation and mobilisation in the North-West Frontier Tribal Areas, a non-administered region on the border of Afghanistan with the North-West Frontier Province of what was British India, but is now Pakistan. The Tribal Areas were defined topographically as a strategic zone of defence for British India, but also determined to be socially distinct and hence were left outside the judicial, legislative and social institutions of greater British India. The cartographically defined region came to contain a distinct and separate sphere of organisation and became the location for a series of armed mobilisations led by the Pakhtun religious leaders—the '*mullas*'.

The creation and maintenance of the Tribal Areas region was based on both a theory of a natural topographic frontier, and the colonial identification and definition of the Pakhtun 'tribe'.[1] This study of Islam in the Tribal Areas is situated with reference to its unusual administrative situation in order to free the study of Pakhtun tribal Islam from the straightjacket of the debates centred on cultural predisposition and fanaticism. Rather, the history of the twentieth century suggests that the ethnographic and cartographic projects of the imperial and the nation states, and the complex interactions between Pakhtun frontier Islam and the discourses of Afghan and

---

1 Despite very important arguments that have been made against use of the term 'tribal', I have adopted the word in this book to refer to participants in the particular system of relations that dominated within the Tribal Areas and were the accepted basis for relations between the Tribal Areas and British India, Afghanistan and later Pakistan. Where there is a distinction to be made, I have opted for the use of the term 'clan', a tribal sub-group often in competition with other clans within the tribe, or the term 'community' to refer to the residents of just one of the villages which constitute the clan.

1

Indian Muslim nationalism were the basis for the religious revivalism that inspired *mulla*-led militant mobilisations across the region.

The practice of Islam among the highland Pakhtuns east of Jalalabad, Kandahar and Khost and west of Peshawar, Kohat, Bannu and Dera Ismail Khan was directed by *mullas* who were committed to the principles of Pakhtun tribal life and culture. These *mullas* were connected to one another by Sufi fraternities or *silsilas*. One *silsila* received particular attention from patrons in both India and Afghanistan, and came to dominate the areas which were simultaneously being cartographically carved out into an autonomous tribal buffer zone. The conditions of Tribal Areas autonomy, rooted in the segregation of the tribally organised Pakhtuns, accentuated the role and importance of *mullas* operating in the region, causing their social authority and the coherence of their regional network to rely on administrative alienation.

Mullas also participated in the national strategies of the actors to the east and west as empathisers and accomplices. Despite its great distance from the centres of political organisation in India and Afghanistan, the frontier proved a critical military organisation ground for both anti-colonial activists in India and for the Afghan amirate up till decolonisation of the Indian sub-continent in 1947. Greatly strengthened by their patrons, Tribal Areas *mullas* were articulators of a regional position, counselling members of the religious fraternity and consulting with tribes to act in a manner that would preserve the conditions of self government and prevent greater government controls, and leading tribal mobilisations to assert 'customary' principles of social behaviour such as honour and clan fraternity, and contributing to the maintenance of a regional tribal balance.

After independence and partition of the subcontinent in 1947, the Tribal Areas remained autonomous and maintained a status as a separated frontier in both the Afghan and the Pakistan national imaginations. Yet over the next half century this periphery played a part in crucial issues confronting each. Soon after independence, the Tribal Areas came to international attention as thousands of Pakhtun tribesmen invaded the princely state of Kashmir which had gone to India, and shortly thereafter Afghanistan championed a movement for the creation of an independent Pakhtunistan centred in the region. After the Soviet invasion of Afghanistan, the Tribal Areas became the epicentre of the resistance movement, linking the agenda of both Afghan religious nationalists and American-supported Pakistani military strategists in a decade-long campaign. After the Soviet withdrawal, support for the hardline religious revivalism of the Taliban regime of the 1990s was centred in and channelled through the Tribal Areas. And after the September 11 attacks in the United States and the Afghan war of 2002, it allegedly became the redoubt for dispersed Al Qaeda members, testimony to this organisation's resilience and popularity in the Pakhtun regions, and of the contradictions in Pakistan's position as accomplice to the War on Terror.

This hinterland of successive, contradictory *jihads* in support of Pakhtun ethnicism, anti-colonial nationalism, Pakistani territorialism, religious revivalism and anti-American imperialism generated, in turn, fluid and fluctuating political allegiances within the Tribal Areas. Only the claim to autonomy persisted unchanged and uncompromised, and within that claim the functional role of religious leaders as social moderators and ideological guides was preserved. From outside, patrons recognised and supported that claim, reliant in their own ways on the possibilities the autonomous Tribal Areas and its *mullas* afforded.

1
ETHNOGRAPHY, CARTOGRAPHY AND THE CONSTRUCTION OF THE NORTH-WEST FRONTIER TRIBAL AREAS

India, as cartographically defined by the twentieth century, was bounded in the north-west by a region that was described as an autonomous tribal zone. The small genealogically linked communities that populated the region were left outside the administrative structures of 'settled' India—the systems of land administration, policing, law, and politics of the Indian provinces. Instead, they were organised into five agencies—South-Waziristan, North-Waziristan, Kurram, Khyber and Malakand—which were controlled by the political department of the Government of India rather than the provincial government. The semi-autonomous status of the region, known as the Tribal Areas, suggested that the division was a sociological one - that the nature of the highland community was different from the nature of the peasantry of the agricultural region. The differentiation of the North-West Frontier Tribal Areas and the identification of the tribe were largely consequences of the strategic concerns expressed by, and the processes of, the imperial cartographic project. The process of creating 'region' was not just a depiction of a pre-existing political landscape, but was itself an instrument of change as the science of cartography was underlain by a series of administrative processes that circumscribed and rationalised a differentiated political space.

The western and north-western frontiers of India assumed importance for the British in India with the beginnings of Russian expansion in Central Asia in the 1830s. This early history, of the Great Game of imperial manoeuvring, stealthy expansion and the

careful confrontation between empires, led British India into a series of political alliances with and interventions in the north-west
Indian 'native' states of Kalat and Kashmir, and with the Afghan
amirate at Kabul. This 'forward' move was accelerated by the decline
and ultimate dissolution of the Sikh empire after 1839, leading to
the British annexation of Sindh in 1843, and the Punjab in 1849.
However extension of direct British authority towards Central Asia
was checked in 1842, when the bloody end of the First Afghan War
with the killing of British occupying forces in Afghanistan evidenced
the cost of a permanent garrison. As the new amir Dost Muhammad
Khan (1826-63) began to consolidate his authority, imperial policy
became the conciliation and maintenance of 'friendly relations' with
Afghanistan. Direct colonial authority extended through the agricultural plains of Jacobabad, Dera Ghazi Khan, and the Peshawar
area while Dost Muhammad Khan extended his influence through
to Jalalabad and Kandahar.

The processes of imperial consolidation in India and Afghanistan
left a number of highland communities and small polities between
them. This tract of land extended from the north-western and western most limits of the Maharaja of Kashmir's authority down to the
native state of Kalat and included groups of both Pakhtun and Baluch ethnicity. Contemporary Afghan, Indian and British observers
of the Pakhtun communities noted that they were village-based clans
that invested authority in a headman known as the *khan* or *malik*. It
was observed that clans mustered *jirgas* or councils consisting of all
the male members of the community, within which older members
had more clout than younger members. Clans participated in a wider
organisation of comunities to which they were linked ancestrally,
deemed to be a tribe, within which total unanimity was maintained
by a tribal *jirga* of representative males from the participant clans. A
number of separate tribes occupied the region and competed strongly
for natural resources and patronage of Afghan and Indian courts.
This system of internal tribal unanimity and inter-tribal rivalry was

understood to underlie the relations and concerns of all communities residing in the Pakhtun tribal tracts.

During the period 1849–76 British Indian frontier defence and policy towards the tribes were two separate issues. Afghanistan in the south and Bokhara and Kokand north of the Oxus river were the frontier buffer states for Britain and Russia respectively,[1] and the tribes between Afghanistan and British India were only of concern to the revenue generating districts of western Punjab. Hence tribal policy was marked only by a concern with settling and then protecting the revenues of the Peshawar and Dera Ismail Khan districts. The compacts struck with the north-western Pakhtun tribes were aimed at safeguarding roads, and preventing trespass by the tribes into the settled, administered districts of the Pakhtun north-west. If any member of the 'assured' tribes who had entered into treaty relations with the DCs of the administered districts committed murder or pillage in the administered districts or on the roads, or allowed such acts to be initiated from their territory, the *malik* of the offending tribe was expected to hand over the offending party and compensation.[2] Policy towards the tribes of this region was engineered to check and control criminality and ensure the safety of British subjects and interests in the administered districts. Tribalism was an internal, provincial concern, separate from the imperial consideration of frontier building.

This changed when Russia annexed Kokand and advanced on Herat in 1876.[3] Afghanistan's Amir Sher Ali Khan resisted British efforts to consolidate regional influence, and although he was ousted in the Second Afghan War which ensued, a new government in England and viceroy in India called for a more cautious, less expensive

---

1 Henry Rawlinson, 'Memorandum on the reorganization of the western and north-western frontiers', 28 July 1877. OIOC L/PS/18/A 17.

2 'Note covering the memorandum by Sir Robert Sandeman explanatory of the future policy to be pursued on the Baluchistan Frontier', January 1888. In OIOC Curzon Collection, MSS EUR F11/54.

3 Karl Meyer and Shareen Blair Brysac, *Tournament of Shadows* (Washington DC, 1999), p. 189.

frontier policy.[4] Hence the frontier retreated back to the borders of British India[5] and came to rely on British influence among the tribes of the Khyber, Kurram and Gomal passes. [6]

Encountering the tribe: ethnographic understanding of the Pakhtun north-west

British military and political exploratory missions into the north-west began with the occupation of Kandahar during the first Anglo Afghan War (1839-42), and the annexation of the Punjab in 1849.[7] These expeditions along with the settlement of the revenues of the Punjab in the districts of Hazara, Peshawar, Kohat, Bannu, Dera Ismail Khan and Dera Ghazi Khan inspired the first series of en-counters with the highland Pakhtuns.[8] Information on the nature of the 'Pathans', as they were called, was gathered from accounts of the tribes of Dera Ghazi Khan, Bannu, Kohat and Peshawar as prepared

---

4 See Brian Robson, *The Road to Kabul—the Second Afghan War 1878-1881* (London, 1986).

5 See G. J. Alder, *British India's Northern Frontier, 1865-1895* (Plymouth, 1963), pp. 58-72.

6 See the treaty of Gandamak, reproduced in Charles Aitchison, *A Collection of Treaties, Engagements and Sunuds Relating to India and Neighbouring Countries* (Calcutta, 1909).

7 Earlier surveys included Lieutenant Leech's 1837 'Description of the Khyber Pass and of the tribes inhabiting it', Captain J. Biddulph's 1865 'Tribes on the North-West Frontier of Punjab', and Surgeon Bellew's 1864 'Report on the Yusufzais' (noted in the Political and Secret Department Library List). Certain tribal genealogies were later compiled and published more comprehensively in government publications. See E. G. Hastings, *Genealogical Tree of the Peshawari Sardars of the Barakzai Family* (Lahore, 1880); E. G. Hastings, *Genealogical Tree of the Kandahari Sardars of the Barakzai Family* (Lahore, 1880); A. H. Mason, *Report on the Mahsud and Waziri Tribe* (Simla, 1893); Captain Swayne and Captain A. Nichols, *Tribal Tables of the Afridis, Orakzais, Mohmands and Akozai-Yusufzais* (Simla, 1897); Captain Swayne, *Tribal Tables of the Bunerwals and Neighbouring Tribes* (Simla, 1897).

8 *Punjab Customary Law—a selection from the records of the Punjab Government*, vol. I (Calcutta, 1881), p. 1.

by their respective Deputy Commissioners.[9] Expeditions against the frontier tribes further increased the Punjab government's knowledge of the Pakhtun communities outside the administered districts, and the total fighting strength of these communities. This information was compiled and published in popular accounts of expeditions in the north-west.[10] Historical interrogation by anthropologist-administrators evidenced that these Pakhtun communities were largely genealogically homogeneous and orally recorded their descent from a Pakhtun forefather.[11] Classical Pakhtun tribal genealogies produced in literary texts such as the *Makhzan-i Afghani*,[12] *Hayat-i Afghani*,[13] and *Khalid-i Afghani*,[14] and oral accounts of community descent were correlated to military and settlement surveys to describe community size, location, organisation, interlinkages and precedence among the 'border tribes'.[15] Hence the tribal genealogical tree became the format for the organisation of statistical data on the communities of the north-west highlands in 'tribal tables'.

The entire region from the Maharaja of Kashmir's dominions down to the native state of Kalat, and the border of the adminis-

---

9   Settlement reports of deputy commissioners were the basis for the sections on Hazara, Bannu, Peshawar, Kohat and Dera Ismail Khan in *Punjab Customary Law*. See vol. II, pp. 219-80.

10   See for example, Paget, *Record of the Expeditions against the North-West Frontier Tribes since the Annexation of the Punjab*.

11   C. M. Macgregor, *Central Asia: A Contribution towards the Better Knowledge of the Topography, Ethnography, Statistics and History of the North-West Frontier of British India*, vol. I (Calcutta, 1873), preface.

12   Parts of the *Makhzan-i Afghani* (or *Makhzan-i Islam*), written by the Akhund Darweza in the seventeenth century, were translated and printed in English as early as 1860 in Raverty, *Gulshan-e Roh* (London, 1860).

13   *Hayat-i Afghani*, a history of the Afghan people, was written by Muhammad Hayat Khan in the nineteenth century. An English translation of the work was published as early as 1865. See Henry Priestly, *Afghanistan and its Inhabitants* (London, 1874).

14   An English translation was first printed in 1875. See Trevor Plowden, *Translations of the Kalid-i Afghani* (Lahore, 1875).

15   As by H. W. Bellew in *Afghanistan and the Afghans: being a brief history of the country, and account of its people* (1879, reprint Delhi, 1982), p. 216.

tered districts to the passes through the Hindu Kush was surveyed jointly by the military and political departments. The survey reports produced both topographical descriptions of land and tribal tables describing tribe-clan genealogies. Tribal tables for important tribal groups including the Afridis, Wazirs and Mahsuds were prepared in 1893.[16] These tables noted the place of the tribe in the Pakhtun genealogy, the clans and sub-groups within the tribe, the number of men in each group, and the *malik* of each clan. The number of 'fighting men' in each clan, and the area that each group controlled were highlighted in these tabular ethnographic summaries. The tribal genealogies were drawn and connected, and then summarised in a *Dictionary of the Pathan Tribes of the North-West Frontier of India* in 1899 that listed the tribal structure as a six-tier system.[17] Each group described in the dictionary was listed as either under the classification of 'tribe', 'clan', 'division', 'sub-division of division', 'section of subdivision', or under 'other minor fractions'. This information was first represented comprehensively in the single-sheet map of Afghanistan published by the Survey of India in 1889, which contained both the topography and tribal groupings in a single representation of the region.[18] The

---

16 The more famous published vols of these genealogies are Merk's *Report on the Mohmands*; E. Howell, *Mizh: a Monograph on the Government's Relations with the Mahsud Tribe* (reprint Karachi, 1979); L. W. King, *Monograph on the Orakzai Country and Clans* (reprint Lahore, 1984); H. W. Bellew, *A General Report on the Yusufzais, 1864* (Lahore, 1994); and probably the most significant and widely known study of the tribes of the north-west frontier, Olaf Caroe's *The Pathans* (London, 1965). The military department and political agency records contained detailed genealogies of all the frontier tribes with notes on the formation of new clan units and included 'Tribal Tables of the Afridis, Orakzais, Mohmands and Akozai-Yousufzais', 'Tribal Tables of Bunerwals and Neighbouring Tribes', and 'Tribal Tables of the Mahsud and Wazir Tribes', compiled by J. E. Swayne, Intelligence Branch, and Captain A. Nichols (Simla, 1897). OIOC L/PS/20/B160-4.

17 Quarter Master General India in the Intelligence Branch, *A Dictionary of the Pathan Tribes on the North-West Frontier of India* (Calcutta, 1899).

18 Map of Afghanistan, published under direction of Colonel Thullier, Survey of India Office, Calcutta, 1889. OIOC W/L/PS/21/H22.

map provided with the dictionary showed the approximate location of tribal settlements.[19]

It was thus that the tribal organisation of the frontier region was mapped.[20] In the south, around the Zhob river, were the Zhob Joge-zai, Ahmedzai and Kakar Pakhtuns, who entered into treaty relations with the khanate of Kalat to guarantee their own political independence. These factions were later incorporated into the Baluchistan province. Above these were the Wazirs and Mahsuds, tribes of a common descent, but antagonistic to one another, hence recognised as separate tribes. The Wazirs and Mahsuds controlled the land north of the Zhob river and south of the Kurram road, including the Gomal and Tochi passes. Below the Khyber Pass were the Afridi and Orakzai tribes, of a common descent but differentiated among themselves by the fact that the Orakzais were Shia. The Khattak tribe lay east of the Afridis, while above the Khyber Pass and Kabul river lay the rough and dry Shinwari, Mohmand and Bajaur lands. Above and besides these tribal lands lay three states, each ruled by an authority that levied taxes and oversaw internal governance and dispute management. To the north-east was Swat, whose kings and later 'Mianguls' controlled the most fertile and productive lands in the region - those of the Yusufzai Pakhtuns. Dir was to the west of Swat, and its Nawab was struggling to consolidate his polity. In the far north was the Chitral valley ruled by a Mehtar whose authority was deeply contested.

Constructing the frontier

With the gradual retreat of the British from Central Asia and the identification of the Hindu Kush highlands as a zone of strategic

---

19 Intelligence Branch, *Map to Accompany a Dictionary of the Pathan Tribes on the North-West Frontier of India* (Calcutta, 1899).

20 Territorialisation of the clan identity is discussed in different terms in the anthropological work on descendency and inheritance relating to the late nineteenth century. See Paul Titus, 'Honour the Baloch Buy the Pashtun', *Modern Asian Studies* (Cambridge, 1998), p. 667.

defence, the latter 'tribally' inhabited regions were assigned the role of the Indian north-western frontier. Administrative and military policy in the region had two agendas: the preparation of the highlands for possible military mobilisation, and the conciliation and involvement of tribal groups as facilitators of frontier policy, not antagonists to it.

Because of budgetary concerns and the continued concern over the Anglo-Afghan relationship, organisation of a strategic frontier within the tribal region was not based on a policy of military garrisoning by regular troops. It developed rather as a forward zone through which troops, massed at Peshawar, Quetta, Dera Ismail Khan and Dera Ghazi Khan, could be mobilised to assume an offensive position in Jalalabad and Kandahar.[21] In 1880 a period of road, railway and telegraph construction through the frontier was begun as 'one of the measures to contain Afghanistan'.[22] Expenditure on railways and roads through the tribal regions (including Baluchistan) amounted to almost 8 million rupees over the period 1882-91. By 1890 there were 571 miles of metalled and unmetalled 'imperial' roads extending from Kohat, Peshawar and Dera Ismail Khan. About 200 miles of these roads were being worked each year, at a cost of about 200,000 rupees a year.[23] Between 1884 and 1900, over 100 million rupees were spent on extending the North-Western Railways up to the Tribal Areas to open up routes across the passes.[24] The North-Western Railway system was extended to the foot of the Khyber Pass at Fort Jamrud and the Punjab railway connected Attock to Dera Ismail Khan.[25] Surveys began for a railway crossing the Khyber, and a rail connecting Kohat and Thal.

---

21 Description of routes and positions on the north-west frontier. OIOC L/MIL/17/13/7/1-6.

22 Frederick Roberts, Commander in Chief Indian Army, 1885-93 in letter to Foreign Secretary India, 4 April 1880, quoted in Rajit Mazumder *The Indian Army and the Making of the Punjab* (Delhi, 2003), p. 55. For a brief history of the expansion of trans-Indus communications, see Mazumder, pp. 50-64.

23 Punjab Public Works Administration Records 1890-1 to 1898-9.

24 Mazumder, *The Indian Army*, p. 56.

25 Robert Sandeman, 'A note on the North-West Frontier and Our Policy in Afghanistan', 30 June 1887. OIOC L/PS/18.

Because the highlands were never occupied, development of the region as a forward zone emerged around a model of tribal governance.[26] By this scheme, the Pakhtun tribal communities that inhabited the highlands were paid allowances to protect the roads and to ensure the security of the inner border with the administered districts.[27] This model meant that frontier policy was tribal policy and *vice versa*.[28] The strategy of tribally managed frontier defence was referred to as the 'forward policy' and was largely put into effect through the District Commissioners (DCs) of Dera Ismail Khan, Bannu, Kohat, Peshawar and Hazara—districts which at this time were still part of the Punjab. These DCs negotiated monetary settlements with tribes near the border with the administered districts or settled near roads running through the Tribal Areas by which they allocated small allowances in return for which the tribes mustered militias or tribal 'levies' to police the region.[29] Payments to tribes for the protection of roads and the borders of the administered districts became the cornerstone of regional policy—a means of control without direct intervention.

Delimitation of the Durand Line and the separation of the 'British-side tribe' from Afghanistan

After the initial hostilities of 1878 were over, negotiations over the separation of Afghan and British-Indian strategic interests began. The first demand by the British was the renunciation of all Afghan

---

26 The architect of this scheme was Robert Sandeman who, as District Commissioner Dera Ghazi Khan in 1867 negtiated settlements with the Marri and Bugti tribes, granting them allowances and arms in return for mustering 'levies' to protect the roads and borders of the settled revenue generating districts.

27 Terence Creagh Coen, *The Indian Political Service* (London, 1971), p. 153.

28 Major General E. H. H. Collen, 'Memorandum—the Central Asian question and our future military policy' Simla, 1892. OIOC L/PS/18/A 26.

29 For example, an allowance of 1000 rupees per annum was allocated to the Aka Khel Afridis, who occupied territory near Peshawar, before 1867. See 'Statement showing Tribal Allowances in the North-West Frontier Province, 1931'. OIOC L/PS/12/3150.

claims to political authority over what was demarcated as the 'natural' Indo-Afghan frontier:

The Khyber and Michni passes leading from Jalalabad into the Peshawar district, and over the independent tribes inhabiting the territory connected with these passes. [Also,] the District of Kurram, from Thal to the crest of the Shutargardan pass, and the districts of Pishin and Sibi, will remain under the protection and control of the British government.[30]

These demands were ratified under the treaty signed between the British Agent to Afghanistan, Cavagnari, and the Afghan Amir, Yaqub Khan, at Gandamak in Afghanistan in 1879. Under the terms of the Treaty of Gandamak,

The British government [would] retain in its own hands the control of the Khyber and Michni passes, and all relations with the independent tribes of the territory directly connected with these Passes.[31]

In negotiations with the amir, Cavagnari treated the 'independence' of the Pakhtun tribes of the Michni and Khyber passes as an established phenomenon, and emphasised the British commitment not to occupy these 'independent' territories, but merely to maintain their longstanding autonomy.[32] Yet it was clear that this state of autonomy was largely a myth. Christine Noelle's work highlights the role of the eastern Pakhtuns in the Afghan state during the reign of Amir Dost Muhammad Khan.[33] She argues that the 'so-called border tribes' were tied to the Afghan state through an allowance system. Moreover, some groups identified as 'independent tribes', such as the Turis of Kurram, were already paying revenues to the Afghan state by 1850.[34] While it was true that the Khyber and Michni Passes were not highly profitable and had largely remained outside the tax net of

---

30 'Narrative of events in Afghanistan from August 1878 to December 1880, and connected correspondence', p. 53. OIOC L/PS/18/A 43.

31 Terms of the treaty of Gandamak, Article 9, ibid., p. 65.

32 Ibid., p. 62.

33 Christine Noelle, *State and Tribe in Nineteenth-Century Afghanistan* (London, 1997), pp. 163-90.

34 Ibid., p. 174.

the Afghan amirate, other connections existed between the authority in Kabul and the 'tribes' of the eastern highlands. One such connection was the tribal relationship with the Badshah of Kunar who possessed large land holdings in the area west of Bajaur and south of Chitral.[35] The revenue-paying Badshah of Kunar had acted as the amir's agent among the tribes of Bajaur and Mohmand.[36] Another tangible connection was through the Khan of Lalpura, the dominant Mohmand *khan* whose lands lay east of Kunar. The Khan of Lalpura's extensive land holdings and authority had led the amir to accord Lalpura the status of a small state, and the khan great personal privileges in return for military cooperation.[37] These privileges included the right to a quarter of the tolls collected on the Khyber Pass.[38] In return for these privileges, the amirate often interfered in the succession of the Lalpura title and *jagirs*.[39] The Hakim of Jalalabad would also call on the Khan to collect revenue from the outlying Shinwari villages.[40] The Khan of Lalpura managed a relationship between the amirate and the Mohmands who were described in the classic British ethnographic study of the tribe as being independent. Some of these independent Mohmands shared the privilege of collecting Khyber tolls on behalf of the amir, and were allocated allowances for services rendered to the amirate through the Khan of Lalpura. Amir Abdur Rahman was concerned with and oversaw the allowances paid by

---

35 The Badshah of Kunar was also recognised as a *pir* and enjoyed great spiritual repute in addition to his wealth and political position. His importance indicates that authority was exercised at multiple, often overlapping levels among the eastern Pakhtun communities. The Badshah was one of the only *pirs* of the eastern Pakhtuns with such significant and profitable land holdings, but because he curtailed his influence east of the Durand Line, his case is not discussed in chapter 2, although it is extremely interesting.

36 'Relations of the Amir of Afghanistan with the Khan of Lalpura and the Badshah of Kunar', Oban, 1882, p. 4. OIOC L/PS/18/A 47.

37 See Noelle, *Tribe and State*, p. 181.

38 W. R. Merk, *The Mohmands* (1898, reprint Lahore, 1984), pp. 46-50.

39 Noelle, *Tribe and State*, pp. 181-2.

40 Merk, *The Mohmands*, p. 46.

Lalpura to the more easterly Mohmands as a means of indirect control.[41]

In 1893 Mortimer Durand began negotiations with the new Amir Abdur Rahman Khan (1880-1901) over the delimitation of a border between the Indian north-west frontier and the Afghan Eastern and Southern Provinces. Creation of the frontier was represented to Amir Abdur Rahman as the constitution of a zone of 'neutral provinces' between Afghanistan and India,[42] entailing the amir's acceptance 'for the first time ... that independent border tribes have nothing to do with Afghanistan.'[43] When the amir questioned the idea of the tribal tracts as a 'neutral' region,[44] the theory of the traditional social and political autonomy of the independent tribes was put forward as a reasonable premise for the demand that the amir 'exercise no interference' in Chitral, Bajaur, Swat, Afridi territory, Kurram, Dawar, all Mahsud Waziri territory, almost all Darwesh Khel country and the Zhob and Chaghai regions which had been incorporated into the Baluchistan Agency to the south.[45] The language of the Durand Commission reports demanded a delimitation of the political interests and authority of the Afghan amir within a border. In negotiations with Amir Abdur Rahman, Mortimer Durand asked the amir for his commitment that he would define the extent of his 'sphere of influence' and his political suzerainty.[46]

To the north the dominions of the Mehtar of Chitral were already politically established as being outside Kabul's direct authority.

---

41 Ibid., pp. 57-9.

42 Sultan Mahomed Khan, *The Life of Abdur Rahman, Amir of Afghanistan*, vol. II (London, 1900), p. 159.

43 Viceroy of India to the Political and Secret Department, 18 Nov. 1893, p. 91. OIOC L/PS/3/332.

44 Abdur Rahman described Afghanistan's interests in developments in Chitral and Bajar, and scoffed at the British references to 'so-called neutral provinces', in Khan, *The Life of Abdur Rahman*, p. 159.

45 Viceroy of India to the Political and Secret Department, 18 Nov. 1893.

46 Durand to Lansdowne, Indiki 24 Oct. 1893. 'Letters of Durand to Viceroy India'. OIOC Durand Papers.

Below, in Mohmand and Bajaur, the division was harder. The exact location and definition of the 'independent' clans outside the sphere of the amirate's authority were debated with the amir, and settled on the basis of the amir's economic interests. So although Lalpura was maintained as part of Afghanistan on the basis that it was a revenue-generating region for the amirate, the amirates' social and political interest in the communities east of Lalpura was denied and the amir forced to sever ties with the eastern Mohmand clans. The lack of clarity or rationale behind the precise points of division of interests between Afghan and Indian Mohmand became a central issue during the later years of Amir Abdur Rahman's reign (1880-1901) and the early years of Amir Habibullah's reign (1901-19).[47] In 1895 Abdur Rahman asserted his right to the whole of the Mohmand tract. In 1905 Habibullah abandoned this claim but maintained the Afghan ownership of the Bohai Dag valley.[48]

Further south, the amir did not query the Anglo-Afghan border along Afridi, Turi and Orakzai territory. Waziristan however did present problems. Out of a concern to maintain the integrity of the tribal groups that surrounded the roads and passes, Durand drew the Waziristan border to accommodate the Wazir, Mahsud and Afridi tribal settlements within the Indian north-west frontier. However there was an existing relationship between the Wazirs of Wana and Tochi and the Afghan government at Khost. Durand argued for the separation of Waziristan from Khost on the premise that there was 'little population and wealth in the country' of the Wazirs that could benefit Afghanistan, while on the other hand keeping together all the Wazir clans in India would maintain the social integrity of the tribe and the region.[49] The genealogy of the Wazir tribe was used to demarcate the extent of the Tribal Areas on the border with Khost,

---

47 M. Monteath, 'Memo regarding the demarcation of the Durand Line in Mohmand Country' 1923. OIOC L/PS/18/A 198.
48 See Ludwig Adamec, *Afghanistan 1900-1923* (California, 1967), p. 79.
49 Durand to Lansdowne, Indiki 31 Oct. 1893, in 'Letters of Durand to Viceroy India'.

but this was a difficult ethnographic dissection owing to the proximity of 'Wazir' and 'Khostwal' settlements.

The amir did not dispute the reference to the Tribal Areas and its population as tribal and culturally distinct. In fact, he affirmed the 'unruliness' of the eastern Pakhtuns in a letter to the viceroy. But he questioned the British-imposed segregation of the Tribal Areas from Afghanistan, stating his authority over the 'tribes'.

If [these frontier tribes] were included in my dominions I should be able to make them fight against any enemy of England and myself, by the name of a religious war, under the flag of their co-religious Muslim ruler (myself)... I will gradually make them peaceful subjects and good friends of Great Britain. But if you cut them out of my dominions, they will neither be of any use to you nor to me.[50]

Resisting this circumscription of the 'influence' of the Afghan court, Amir Abdur Rahman attempted to represent his interests in this allusion to religion, but this was dismissed summarily with no real interrogation of the nature of the Afghan amirate's connections with the 'frontier tribes', except to consider it as political 'expediency' in his dealings with the British, and a greedy expansionism.

Still, Abdur Rahman refused to compromise on the delimitation of Waziristan on purely tribal lines. He pushed his claim to Birmal,[51] which Durand was unwilling to concede in order to maintain the integrity of the tribe.[52] Durand identified the amir's resistance as stemming from a point of honour; the amir had said that his interest in the Waziri lands was *nom*—name.[53] But Birmal was also a regional market place and a hub for commercial exchange. Trading communities from within Afghanistan came here to trade every year. The Afghan amirate's claim to Birmal asserted these interests above the 'cultural' policy of maintaining tribal integrity.

---

50 Khan, *The Life of Abdur Rahman*, p. 158.

51 Durand to Lansdowne, Indiki 1 Nov. 1893, ibid.

52 In his letter to to Lansdowne of 31 Oct. 1893, Durand wrote: 'I have told [the amir] that I have no authority to split up the Waziris.'

53 Durand to Lansdowne, 31 Oct. 1893, in 'Letters of Durand'.

In the case of Birmal, the amir's 'grand ideas' of honour were barely entertained by Durand until the amir indulged in what Durand patronisingly referred to in his personal correspondence with Lansdowne, Viceroy of India, as 'the sulks'.[54] It is of note that when Durand informed Lansdowne of this concession, he also stated that it was acceptable because 'tribes' from the 'Amir's side' occupied Birmal for half the year in any case, rationalising the concession on the basis of tribal occupation.[55]

Durand's suggested frontier line drew major communications features, roads and railways, and the passes, into the British 'sphere', as agreed under the Treaty of Gandamak. In the course of negotiations, disputes over the definition of Afghan strategic interests in the east also arose partly due to the incomplete and sometimes inconsistent mappings of the eastern Pakhtun areas. Percival Sykes observed in his *History of Afghanistan* that portions of the frontier had not yet been surveyed by 1893.[56] In one phase of the negotiations the amir brought his own map, on which a road was marked 'with two red crosses'—a road that had evidently not been featured on the British maps, but one the amir believed had to be considered a major geographic feature although it was not currently in use—it had been abandoned because of resistance by the people of Shartun who would regularly fire on the road leading from the river to Asmar.[57] The amir claimed Durand represented the region 'all wrong—I know. I have been to these places—your maps are guesswork.'[58]

The dispute over marking the border, in its many complexities, was about marking zones of economic interest and political involvement—definable spheres of influence. Durand denied Afghanistan's

---

54 Durand to Lansdowne, Indiki 4 Nov. 1893, ibid.

55 Durand to Lansdowne, Indiki, 30 Oct. 1893, ibid.

56 P. Sykes, *History of Afghanistan* (London, 1940), p. 176, quoted in J. R. V. Prescott, *Map of Mainland Asia by Treaty* (Melbourne, 1975), p. 181.

57 Durand to Lansdowne, Indiki 3 Nov. 1893, Letters of Durand to Viceroy India.

58 Durand quoted the amir in his letter to Lansdowne, ibid.

claim to areas where there was no palpable, engaged relationship between the communities resident in the region, and Kabul, or no identifiable strategic development of the region. At the conclusion of Mortimer Durand's talks with Amir Abdur Rahman, the implications of the delimitation were clear and accepted by Abdur Rahman, although grudgingly. At British insistence, all Afghan officials in the areas assigned to India were recalled, and British authority over the Tribal Areas was acknowledged.[59]

Afghan and British interests still overlapped the border. Kabul had traditionally collected its tolls at the Khyber, Gomal, and Shartun Passes. After the delimitation of the Durand Line, one Afghan customs officer was allowed to remain at Khyber to calculate the value of goods leaving India.[60] In addition, border communities on both sides were still connected by proximity, family ties, and trade networks, both legal and illegal. But the agreement was that the Afghans would not 'interfere' with the tribes across the Durand Line. This meant that the amir could not recruit across the border, pay any subsidies, or formally entertain representatives from clans or tribes on the British 'side'. The Durand Line treaty and the subsequent agreements regarding the demarcations of the border marked a transformation of Afghan state relations with the eastern tribes. The tribes of the Hindu Kush highlands were formally released from responsibility to the Afghan amirate.

The border necessitated a new system of settlements between communities politically divorced, but in close functional contact with one another. Amir Habibullah Khan (1901-19) highlighted a need for such a system by attaching a 125-page list of petitions received by the amirate since 1893 from tribes on the Afghan side of the border, asking for compensation from tribes on the British side of the border.[61] Before 1893 the *rais* of Khost, the Hakim of Jalalabad,

---

59 Khan, *The Life of Abdur Rahman*, p. 158.

60 Terms of the treaty of Gandamak, Article 9, quoted in 'Narrative of events in Afghanistan', p. 65.

61 Enclosure to letter from Amir of Afghanistan to the Viceroy of India, 22

the Badshah of Kunar or the Khan of Lalpura would have attempted to effect a settlement,[62] but the circumscription of their authority by the border now made this impossible. Instead a joint Indo-Afghan Commission was established in 1910 to settle disputes at the Kurram section of the Indo-Afghan border and at the Tochi-Khost border. Settlements of fines and penalties were first paid over by the respective British and Afghan commissioners, and then settled internally between the commissioners and the groups involved in the dispute.[63] This new system removed the frontier tribes entirely from any sort of direct Afghan authoritative influence.

In trying to circumscribe the authority and 'political sphere of control' of the amirate, the British called for a cessation to all Afghan payments and involvement with tribes on the British side of the border that might extend the amirate's political authority.[64] Payments in return for labour were however allowed to pass. It was only when the Afghan government invoked a moral, social or military connection to the 'independent tribes' that this was considered to be 'intrigue'.

The creation of the Tribal Areas

With the delimitation of the Durand Line, the north-west frontier was not just a system of defence against the Russians—it was equally being organised as a frontier against Afghanistan. The outer line conclusively separated the Pakhtuns of the Hindu Kush from Afghanistan and brought them into British India, and excluded Afghanistan as an arena for strategic defensive organisation. This delimitation necessitated a regularisation of the position of the tribes

---

July 1909. In 'North-West Frontier Joint Commissioner'. OIOC L/PS/10/37.

62　See Christine Noelle for the relationship between Afghan authorities in the Samt-i Mashriqi or Eastern Province, and the highland tribes, *State and Tribe*, pp. 163-94.

63　Letter from Roose-Keppel, Chief Commissioner, NWFP, to the Foreign Department, 2 Dec. 1910, in 'North-West Frontier Joint Commissioner'.

64　Terms of the treaty of Gandamak, Article 9, quoted in 'Narrative of events in Afghanistan', p. 65.

now within British India, and a consolidation of defensive positions through the area between the Durand Line and the border with the administered districts.

A system of imperial defensive management through further extension of allowances and tribal levies was first attempted in 1878, in the Khyber. The outbreak of the second Anglo-Afghan War necessitated the securing of supply lines to Kandahar, and the protection of passes into India. The DC Peshawar called on the Afridis in Khyber and Turis in Kurram to provide troops to protect the passes for the British and keep them open before the war even commenced—an effort that was managed by a Political Agent stationed at the Khyber Pass. Allowances were agreed for the Afridis amounting to about 38,000 rupees.[65] A tribal levy, named the *jezailchis*, later renamed the Khyber Rifles, was established under a Political Officer responsible to the District Commissioner of Peshawar.

In 1892 the Shia Turi tribes of Kurram were asked to raise a militia, on the same lines as in Khyber, to guard the Peiwar Kotal Pass.[66] In Waziristan agreements had been made with the Shirani, Mahsud and Darwesh Khel Wazir tribes to open passage through the South-Waziristan Gomal Pass—relations managed through a Political Agent established at Wana. In 1894 the government of India asked the Secretary of State for India for sanction to include Tochi in the British sphere of authority and received permission to send a Political Agent to the Tochi valley.[67] Orders were sent out for the establishment of garrisons at Wana and Spin consisting of battalions of native infantry but these regular troops were withdrawn by 1896 because the expense of occupation could not be justified. Finally tribal levies were established in their place in Tochi and Wana

---

65 See 'Statement of Tribal Allowances 1931'

66 See *Gazetteer of the North-West Frontier from Bajour and the Indus Kohistan on the north to the Mari Hills on the south*, vol. II (Simla, 1887), section on 'The Kuram Valley'. This expenditure was borne by the army rather than the Punjab Government.

67 Curzon, Confidential Memo on Present and Future Position in Tochi Valley, 19 June 1899. In Curzon Collection. OIOC MSS/EUR/F11/315A.

under the supervision of their Political Agents, along the lines of the Khyber militia. The primary responsibility of these militias was the protection of roads through the region.

Allowances paid to the *maliks* of the Tochi valley Darwesh Khel Wazir tribe, the Mahsud tribe in the Wana area, the Turis in Kurram and the Afridis in the Khyber were to be divided between clans contributing men to the scheme, in proportion to each clan's importance. Similarly, agreements were made regarding the financial liability of each clan if a 'criminal' transgression originated from the territories or was committed by the men of any clan within tribe. The distribution of allowances and the responsibilities of the tribes were overseen by the various Political Agents. The allowance system, based on a collective tribal responsibility accepted on behalf of the tribe by the *malik*, invoked both the genealogy of the tribe-clan, and the 'culture' of collective tribal action. However the payment of *lungis* demonstrated that the model rested on the conciliation of the Pakhtun elites rather than a culture of egalitarianism and consensus-driven action. *Maliks* and *khans* who accepted allowances were further rewarded with privileges that accrued to them personally. Of the total 885,000 rupees being paid annually in allowances in 1931, almost 65,000 rupees, or 7 percent of the total disbursements, were paid in 'special allowances' or *lungis* as personal allocations to *maliks* of assured tribes.[68]

The years 1892-97 marked great upheaval and final consolidation of the tribal regions. The ruler of Chitral, who had accepted the authority of and been controlled through the Maharaja of Kashmir, died. His successor Umra Khan joined with the ruler of Swat to attack Dir and cut off outside access to the British Agent in Chitral. The British were forced to take direct action, and moved in through Hoti Mardan and Peshawar through to Bajaur to lay siege to Chitral.[69] The need for direct intervention in the affairs of Dir, Swat and

---

68 Figures calculated from information represented in 'Statement of Tribal Allowances, 1931'.

69 Henry Newman, 'Umra Khan and the Chitral Campaign of 1895 --

Chitral made it obvious that these states could no longer be control-led through Kashmir. Hence, these polities entered the spectrum of tribal politics. In 1895, a Political Agent Malakand was established, responsible for the states of Dir, Swat and Chitral and answerable directly to the Viceroy's office, bringing the total number of tribal agencies to 5—South-Waziristan, North-Waziristan, Kurram, Khy-ber and Malakand.

In 1899 Curzon assumed viceroyalty in India and immediately turned his attention to the consolidation of an imperial frontier which was being compromised by budgetary concerns of the Punjab government. He also believed that 'the conduct of the external rela-tions with the tribes of the frontier should be more directly ... under the control and supervision of the Government of India'.[70] Hence in 1901 the five administered districts of Dera Ismail Khan, Bannu, Kohat, Peshawar and Hazara were separated from the Punjab and their respective Deputy Commissioners made to report to a new Chief Commissioner based in Peshawar. The five appendage tribal agencies of South-Waziristan, North-Waziristan, Kurram, Khyber and Malakand were combined into the Tribal Areas and their re-spective Political Agents also made responsible to the Chief Com-missioner Peshawar. Together, the five fully administered districts and the adjoining 'tribal tracts' or independent territories constituted a newly formed North-West Frontier Province.

The biggest change that this entailed was that expenditure on the frontier was part borne by the Indian Army but the remainder, some 60 percent, was now borne by the administered districts which com-prised the revenue-generating section of the province.[71] The regula-tory structures of the administered districts were not extended and the Tribal Areas were left as a non-administered region. Earlier features of the colonial relationship with the tribes of the Pakhtun north-west

---

compiled from the civil and military gazette'. (Lahore, n.d.)

70 Ibid.

71 'The Administrative Creation of the Frontier', NWFP Enquiry Committee 1922-4, Proceedings vol. I. OIOC V/26/247/1.

were confirmed and maintained within the modified organisation of the NWFP. The Punjab frontier system of raising 'tribal levies' and paying allowances to tribes for 'good behaviour' remained the mainstay of the relationship between the Chief Commissioner and the Pakhtun clans. Alongside this, the Frontier Crimes Regulation (FCR) enacted in 1872, which empowered the Deputy Commissioner to convene a *jirga* to hear a case 'in accordance with Pathan custom', remained in effect in the Tribal Areas.[72] The FCR restricted British interest in judicial administration in the Tribal Areas to such cases in which 'disputes or disagreements between the peoples on either side of the administrative border' arose.[73] In cases where administered-side interests were not involved, the colonial administrative system did not engage at all.

Colonial ethnography

Ethnographic understanding of the Pakhtun north-west had one crucial social implication: the strategy of frontier construction, the move forward and consolidation and mobilisation within the border was dependent on the social definition of population inhabiting the region as tribal. Yet the 'tribe' was not a natural and uncontested formation. Historical and anthropological scholarship on the concept of the tribe has already established this as a deeply problematic category. Terence Ranger links the tribal construct to the traditions 'invented' by the colonial government to facilitate governance.[74] In his work on the history of the Peshawar valley Pakhtuns, Robert Nichols points to the dangers of using colonial ethnographic tracts

---

72 Baha *NWFP Administration*, pp. 9-10.

73 H. N. Bolton, Secretary to the CC NWFP, to PA Khyber, 16 June 1910, in 'Combined *Jirga* Case Against and By the Afridis', Deputy Commissioner Office Peshawar (hereafter DCOP), File 140; 'Memorandum on Border Justice, 12 May 1910', by W. R. H. Merk, Chief Commissioner NWFP, in 'Combined *Jirga* Case Against and By the Afridis'.

74 Terence Ranger, 'The Invention of Tradition in Colonial Africa' in Terence Ranger and Eric Hobsbawm (eds), *The Invention of Tradition* (Cambridge, 1983), pp. 211-62.

and the 'segmentary lineage theory' as a system of social analysis and history writing since these 'non-historical static frameworks may lack the flexibility to reveal change over time, hierarchy and class, individual initiative and ecological imperatives'.[75] Akbar Ahmed on the other hand argues that although it was an intervention, British administration ultimately preserved the traditional, pre-modern order of Pakhtun tribal society and captured a sociologically 'pure' expression of tribal social structure and values.[76] An analytical position perhaps lies between these two arguments, in understanding 'tribal unanimity' and the genealogical order as a political construct,[77] yet accepting the currency of the discourse of tribe.

It is without doubt that the single dimensionality of the understanding of the frontier Tribal Areas was an inaccurate representation of social organisation of the Pakhtun highland communities. This was revealed by the clumsy accounting for non-genealogically linked groups in the region. Phenomena like the yearly passage of the Powindah traders from Bokhara across the Gomal pass into Dera Ismail Khan in the Punjab were understood and represented as nomadic tribal participation in the regional trading system.[78] However the very transit agreements negotiated between the Powindahs and tribes and clans along their trade routes, and the compacts and relationships these engendered, demonstrated that the Powindah tribe was not governed by the narrow and linear social and geographic relationships suggested by the tribal genealogy.[79] Similarly in cases where unrelated communities were settled with or near another ge-

---

75 Robert Nichols, *Settling the Frontier* (Karachi, 2001), pp. 6-9.

76 Akbar S. Ahmed, *Pakhtun Economy and Society* (London, 1980).

77 David Hart suggests this formulation in David Hart and Akbar S. Ahmed, (eds), *Islam in Tribal Societies* (London, 1984) introduction.

78 'The Powindah Trade' in 'Trade Routes to Afghanistan', Parliamentary Papers, 1874, p. 113. BL, RBC V/4 session 1874 v.49.

79 Waris Muhammad Wazir, *Afghanistan's Destiny and the Eastern Pashtuns* (Peshawar, 1998), p. 105. Wazir argues that the Powindahs were a protected group, whom most of the regional clans had pledged to protect and avenge in case of any harm coming to a member of their tribe.

nealogically homogeneous tribe these received only passing mention as 'vassals' or dependent settlers and anomalies within the system of tribe-clan social organisation, in the tribal genealogies drawn up by colonial administrators.[80]

An issue of greater political significance was that the transcribed tribal genealogies which identified individuals with representative authority for a tribe did not allow for dissent or re-negotitations of authority within tribal groups. Identified representative members of the tribes or clans were allocated large personal allowances which confirmed their authority. A letter to the Political Agent Khyber from two Zakka Khel *maliks* discussing their efforts to ensure tribal commitment suggests the sort of impact the colonial understanding of the tribal system had:

We collected all the Zakka Khel ... we held many *jirgas* with them and solicited and entreated them in every way, but for all the exertions that we made, they gave us a flat refusal ... we hope that, if men, cartridges etc are given to us, we will firmly occupy Bazaar and break the backbone of the Zakka Khel. The other Afridis will not take it ill, and the germs and causes of raids will be extirpated... When we, the Khyber *maliks*, had the Khyber Rifle Companies, with the government's help, and the allowances in our hands, we used to make a very good *sarishta* [agreement] of the Khusrogis and of all the Zakka Khel.[81]

As the Afridi representation demonstrated, the British categorisations of the tribes made hierarchies, which may otherwise have been subtle, absolute, and encouraged a coercive assertion of representative authority.

Incidents of dissent indicated the tensions created by the social and political model of the tribe. In the case of the some clans, 'settlements' with the British were not reached for many years. The Orakzai Sturi Khel in Tirah refused to take allowances initially, and

---

80 *Dictionary of the Pathan Tribes*, p. ii; Merk, *The Mohmands*, pp. 82-6.

81 'Letter from Maliks Jabbar Khan and Nur Ahmed Khan, Zakka Khels, to the PA Khyber, Tirah, 4 Oct. 1904' in Enclosures of a secret despatch to His Majesty's Secretary of State for India, 5 January 1905, Zakka Khel Affairs, p. 204. OIOC L/PS/10/45.

were only brought into the allowance system in 1899.[82] This refusal emerged in resistance to the British political and social model of the tribe. Some individuals deemed the idea of collective tribal responsibility to the British government as 'absurd'.[83] But others, most often those benefiting from the monetary rewards offered by the British, defended the model of the unanimous tribe and worked to ensure internal coordination and guarantee the actions of all members of the tribe.

Although the British conceptualising of tribe skewed social balances and misrepresented the social position of some regional groups, seeking the 'truth' of tribal social organisation outside of and untouched by colonial discourse is to an extent to start from the most basic prejudice of the colonial administrative system that envisioned a temporally and ideologically isolated tribal reality. There was no autonomous tribal mind. A dialogue was taking place between the British and the local Pakhtun population in the north-west. The definition of the tribe was not imposed—it was an acceptable model rooted in 'some reality of patrilineal kinship' groups that 'cooperated against external threat',[84] combined with the administrative techniques and discourse of frontier-building.

Production and reproduction of the Pakhtun genealogy through history had been inspired by religious, literary and political influences on tribal self-conception. The British ethnographic project was just another part of this history. As compilations of myths of descent and living memory of the time, the Pakhtun *shajarah* or genealogy formalised a system of membership in the Afghan or Pakhtun ethnic group. Seventeenth to nineteenth-century literary production of

---

82 Rs 1000 was sanctioned for the Tirah Sturi Khel in 1893 but the clan refused the allowances. See 'Statement of Tribal Allowances, 1931'. OIOC L/PS/12/3150.

83 Extract from Khyber Political Diary, 4 May 1907, in 'Attitude of Zaka Khels, discussions with *jirga* as to disposal of allowances, 1907' in North-West Frontier Zakka Khel Affairs, pp. 65-7. OIOC L/PS/10/45.

84 See Charles Lindholm 'Images of the Pathan: The usefulness of colonial ethnography' in Charles Lindholm (ed.), *Frontier Perspectives*, p. 15.

shajarahs in the eastern Pakhtun areas was focused on 'authenticating' a Pakhtun descent narrative, but were largely sponsored by, or linked to the interests of, the court at Delhi. The Mughal emperor Jehangir commissioned the very early work *Makhzan-i Afghani*, in 1613.[85] The Yusufzai Akhund Darweza's *Tazkirat-al Abrar wa Ashrar*, written around 1623, elaborated a Pakhtun descent narrative, focusing on lineage of the Yusufzai, with a view to morally and socially condemning the anti-Mughal movement of the Roshaniyyas.[86] One of the last texts of this variety was *Tarikh-i Pashtun*, a comprehensive annotated *shajarah* commissioned at the Bhopal court in the late nineteenth century as a tribute to the Pakhtun ancestry of the royal family.[87] The tribal genealogy was also commonly invoked in its oral form in which it was fluid as it was deeply influenced by the personal affiliations of the narrator. In addition to commemorating a history of settlement, the orally recited genealogies were romantic claims to a shared Pakhtun heroic past, and were often performed by poets such as Khushal Khan Khattak.[88] With the beginning of the British ethnographic project, oral recitation of the genealogy was used to claim clan legitimacy and recognition by District Commissioners.

British cartography-ethnography was simply another embodiment of the 'indigenous' narrative of tribal descent. The contributions of the frontier Pakhtuns to the colonial discourse of tribe and frontier is best evidenced in representations by 'tribes' to administrators in the Tribal Areas and Peshawar. These groups accepted the conceptual fraternity and organisational structure of the tribe to negotiate the

---

85 See Nichols, *Settling the Frontier*, pp. 25-33, for the production of an early eastern Pakhtun discourse of tribe and ethnicity.

86 The Roshaniyyas were a millenarian group led by Pir Roshan Baba in a stand off against Akbar's army near the end of the sixteenth century. See Nichols, *Settling the Frontier*, pp. 36-37, also see Khaliq Ahmed Nizami, *Akbar and Religion* (Delhi, n.d.), p. 68.

87 Sher Muhammad Gandapur, *Tarikh-i Pashtun* (Karachi, 1991).

88 Khushal Khan himself served as inspiration to a twentieth-century Pakhtun writer, Meera Jan Syal. Syal quotes Khushal Khan in his introduction to his compilation of Pakhtun genealogies.

terms of their autonomy within the parameters of the Tribal Areas administrative-ethnographic construction. To do this, genealogically linked clans organised representative *jirgas* to negotiate compacts with the administration. By participating in the system of adminis-tration, parties from within the Pakhtun region were contributing to the colonial definition of the tribe.[89]

An inadvertent arena—Yaghistan, 'land of the free'

References to the Tribal Areas as '*Yaghistan*' were made as early as 1868 in colonial literature.[90] Colonel Brazier Creagh of the Indian Army commented on the significance of this term when describing his travels of 1893-4:

when we went to the frontier it was called *Yaghistan* (plundering land); it was a forbidden land, and no Englishman had ever been there before … It was impossible to go [inside]; and if you did your bones would be left there.[91]

The word *Yaghistan*, derived ostensibly from *yaghi* that had di-verse meanings from oily or slippery, to uncontrollable or unman-ageable, was also in use in Afghanistan to mean the 'land of the rebellious' during the nineteenth century, in what Christine Noelle terms a 'dialectical confrontation' between the eastern Pakhtuns and the state.[92] Amir Abdur Rahman used the term in his memoirs also to refer generally to the 'unruly' eastern Pakhtun population who were to be divided between Afghanistan and British India.[93]

---

89 See Lal Baha on the agreements reached between the British and Mohmands, Afridis, Wazirs, etc., *N.W.F.P. Administration Under British Rule, 1901-1919* (Lahore, 1978).

90 Meer Moonshee Munphool, 'On Gilgit and Chitral' *Proceedings of the Royal Geographic Society of London*, 13, 2 (1868-9), pp. 130-3.

91 Denys Bray and Colonel Brazier-Creagh 'The Highlands of Persian Baluchistan: Discussion', *Geographic Journal*, 78, 4 (Oct., 1931), p. 340.

92 Noelle, *State and Tribe in Nineteeth-century Afghanistan*, p. 162.

93 Khan, *The Life of Abdur Rahman*, p. 159.

Between 1844 and 1900 the term began to be refined in Indo-Afghan literature to refer to the 'independent' tribes of the Hindu Kush, a political designation of 'tribal type' that was beginning to correspond to the political-strategic identification of the highland-frontier.[94] While the Afghan use of the term had clearly not been so specific, the British negotiation of the Pakhtun ethnic bloc determined the highland Pakhtuns to be the *yaghis*. The drawing of the Durand Line demanded the Afghan definition of the same tribes as the *yaghis*—those outside the amirate's sphere of direct authority and control. In his 1899 article in the *Geographic Journal*, Colonel Raverty of the Indian Army further refined the term *Yaghistan* to refer to those Pakhtuns who resided specifically within the tribal tracts.[95] The geography of Tribal Areas separation was inherently coloured by the myths of warrior tribes and the impossibility of administration in the region, reinforced, no doubt, by the publication of Winston Churchill's account of the battles between the British and the Mad Mulla in Malakand in 1898.[96]

Loose accommodation of the region within the borders of a rapidly changing twentieth-century British India may have consolidated a frontier but it did little to dispel possibilities for armed mobilisation within the region. The discourses that had created this region and made it an imperial frontier also circumscribed it in a manner that deeply influenced religious, political and military organisation over the century to come.

---

94   Charles M. Macgregor, *Central Asia* Part I, vol. 2 (Calcutta, 1873), p. 126; quoted in Noelle, *State and Tribe*, p. 162.

95   H. G. Raverty, 'The Geographical Terms "Tirah" and "Afghanistan"', *Geographical Jounrnal* (1899), pp. 83–4.

96   Winston Churchill, 'The Malakand Field Force' (1898) reprint in *Frontiers and Wars* (New York, 1995).

2

ISLAMIC REVIVALISM AND SUFISM
AMONG THE TRIBAL PAKHTUNS

Underlying the ethnic-tribal continuum that was consolidated into the frontier and the Tribal Areas at the end of the nineteenth century was a network of religious functionaries, the *mullas*. This was the *pirimuridi* line of Akhund Abdul Ghaffur, unified by the chain of transmission of knowledge passed down from the spiritual-religious instructor, the *pir*, to his devotees, the *murids*. The transformation of the line under the influence of reformist ideology during the nineteenth and twentieth centuries was concurrent with the political processes converting the eastern Pakhtun highlands into the frontier of British India, and the pedagogy and politics of members of this *pirimuridi* line came to dominate religious organisation in the autonomous Tribal Areas.[1]

---

1 A very important study of this *pirimuridi* line has already been written by the anthropologist David Edwards, *Heroes of the Age: Moral Faultlines on the Afghan Frontier* (California, 1996). Edwards' exceptional study of the Hadda Mulla's spiritual life and his *murids*—primarily those who remained on the Afghan side of the border after the delimitation of the Durand Line—recounts instances of the Hadda Mulla's magical and temporal powers and influence to explore religious belief as a 'lived reality'. In his more recent study, *Before Taliban—Genealogies of the Afghan Jihad* (California, 2002), Edwards applies his understanding of the Hadda Mulla's spiritual life and social position in late nineteenth century Afghanistan to gain better understanding of religious politics posed in opposition to the Soviet invasion. My understanding of the Hadda Mulla and the centrality of his spiritual line and legacy in Tribal Areas religious organisation is deeply influenced by Edwards'compelling descriptions of this elusive character.

Discourses of authenticity: the tazkirah and the Sufi silsila

Systems of Sufi religious practice in Afghanistan and northern India were varied and widely dispersed. The Naqshbandiyya-Mujaddidiyya *silsila* or Sufi order of the nineteenth and twentieth century Pakhtun regions was one of many Sufi *sisilas* in the region. Naqshbandiyya-Mujaddidiyya *tariqa* or method was based on the teachings of the seventeenth-century north-Indian Sufi philosopher Sheikh Ahmed Sirhindi, also known as Mujaddid Alf Sani (1564-1624), and developed further by his spiritual and methodological successor, Shah Wali Ullah (1703-1762)[2] whose writings elaborated Sheikh Ahmed Sirhindi's emphasis on *shari'a* as the basis for social practice.[3] Naqshbandiyya-Mujaddidiyya thought presented a means for confronting the 'crisis of Islam', meshing Sufism with a return to the text of the Quran, *hadith* and authoritative commentaries in order to re-introduce principles of individualised religious practice and de-emphasise the role of the *pir* as spiritual mediator. It was rare however, in the Pakhtun regions, for Naqshbandiyya-Mujaddidiyya *tariqa* to be practised exclusively. Qaderiyya, Suhrawardi and Chishtiyya thought intermigled with the Naqshbandiyya-Mujaddidiyya in the oral transmission of *tariqa*, which was itself open to innovation by the sages within the order. Because of the secrecy surrounding the substance of Sufi pedagogy, the fact of adherence by *murids* to their *pirs* was more socially evident than the content of their spiritual learning. In its social, economic and political context, the *pirimuridi* line was as important as a social institution as an ideological trend.

The line of the oral transmission of knowledge from *pir* to *murid* was expressed in the production of *tazkirahs* or compilations of biographies of religious authorities. *Tazkirahs* traced the pedagogic lineage of religious authorities in a highly formalised narrative crucial

---

2 See Sayyid Athar Abbas Rizvi, *Muslim Revivalist Movements in Northern India in the Sixteenth and Seventeenth Centuries* (Delhi, 1965).

3 See Marcia K. Hermansen's excellent translation of this important work - *The Conclusive Argument from God: Shah Wali Allah of Delhi's Hujjat Allah al-Baligha* (Leiden, 1996).

to establishing the authenticity of spiritual authority within *silsilas*. The strength of the line of transmission of knowledge was the mark of interpretive authority - a varying degree of emphasis was placed on spiritual intuitiveness and supernatural power to complement that spiritual authenticity. [4]

The organisation of the *pirimuridi* line of Akhund Ghaffur in the eastern Pakhtun highlands provided a living account of the substance of religious formations outside the highly intellectualised and rationalised *tazkirah* form. The *silsila* was a crucial point of cohesion within the spectrum of eastern Pakhtun Islam given the many different bases for religious status and identity across the region. Some religious categories such as *sayyid* and *miyan* described personalities said to descend from the Prophet Muhammad. British records describe these as 'caste' categories within the social landscape of the tribe. *Qazis* were legal functionaries of the Afghan state, often trained in *madrasas*. *Akhund* and *hazrat* were terms of respect reserved for pious people who may or may not have also possessed qualities that *sayyids*, *miyans* and *qazis* possessed. The use of the term *badshah* implied that the religious leader was descended from, or himself possessed, temporal power. This last category was not reserved for religious functionaries, but certain religious functionaries could possess this title. It is impossible to generalise the function or status of all religious leaders, given these distinctions between them. However, very different personalities came together under the ideological umbrella of a Sufi *silsila*.

Study of the evolution of Islam in the Tribal Areas is hampered by the absence of literary production by which to trace religious interpretations or the precise nature of religious practice in the Pakhtun areas. But the *tazkirah* form provides a template by which to consider the structures of religious organisation in the Tribal Areas—the chain of transmission of knowledge. This basic principle of the *silsila* formation—the transmission of religious knowledge from *pir* to

---

4   Arthur Buehler, *Sufi Heirs of the Prophet: the Indian Naqshbandiyya and the Rise of the Mediating Sufi Shaykh* (South Carolina, 1998).

murid and the assertion of this pedagogic line—joined the religious functionaries of the Tribal Areas in a *pirimuridi* fraternity. Coupling colonial intelligence information with hagiographic literature makes it possible to trace the genealogy of this *shaakh* of the *silsila* and the fraternal compacts between the '*mullas*' of the Tribal Areas who came to dominate religious organisation in those areas.

Pirs *and Sufis among the Pakhtuns up to the nineteenth century*

The Pakhtun communities of the north-west frontier had settled in Swat, Bajaur and the Peshawar valley during the Yusufzai migrations in the early sixteenth century. Religious functionaries were clearly part of a political and social landscape from the beginning of these migrations. Pir Roshan or Bayazid Ansari (1525-60) who later staged a revolt against the Mughal Akbar; Sayyid Ali Ghawwas Tirmizi (d. 1583) and Hazrat Akhund Panju Baba (d. 1630), all came to prominence among the Yusufzai or Mandanr clans soon after the Peshawar valley was settled, establishing bases where they could practise and train their *murids*. In some cases the clan-patrons of *pirs* were more generous than others, as in the case of Shaikh Adam Milli who was granted lands by the Yusufzai-Mandanr clans in the Hashtnagar-Peshawar Area in the early sixteenth century.[5] Miangul Jahanzeb of Swat recollected in his memoirs that the Yusufzais had granted permanent, privately-owned lands to the 'religious families' when they settled the Peshawar valley, while land tenure was fixed at only ten years for tribal land owners.[6] This was because Pakhtun communities had accorded a mediatory role to *pirs*, who often acted as neutral arbitrators in disputes.[7]

Mughal accounts suggest that emperors took advantage of the organisation of society around these *pirs*, vesting an amount of au-

---

5 In Ijazul Haq Quddusi, *Tazkiray Sufya-yi Sarhad* (Lahore, 1966), pp. 53-4, quoted from Akhund Darweza's *Tazkirat-ul Abrar Wa Ashrar*.

6 Miangul Jahanzeb and Frederik Barth, *The Last Wali of Swat* (Oslo, 1985), p. 24.

7 Quddusi, *Tazkiray, p.* 439

thority in them as the eyes and ears of the imperial government in outlying and politically volatile regions. The *Jehangir Namah* gives some insight to the nature of Mughal patronage of a religious leader in the Pakhtun areas. Jehangir, a faithful patron of the Naqshbandi-yya order, granted allowances to several *pirs* in return for their 'particular love and loyalty' to himself as Mughal Emperor.[8] Aurangzeb also appealed to *pirs* in the Pakhtun areas, using them as a means of asserting state control.[9] Without a functioning machinery of state in the region, organisation and mobilisation of society was effected through local religious functionaries.[10] State patronage of *pirs* in the Pashtun areas reinforced their social authority and personal wealth, making it possible for these *pirs* to build up large *waqf* properties and dominate regional religious organisation.

The arbitrator-role was formalised by the Afghan state, which accorded a juristic role to *pirs* in the creation of the 'modern' state, during the eighteenth and nineteenth centuries. Ahmed Shah Abdali (1723-73) engaged the Naqshbandiyya *madrasa*s through Kunduz, Tashkent, Kokand and Balkh, in the eighteenth century, in opposition to Chinese penetration in Turkestan.[11] During Amir Dost Mu-

---

8 Khwaja Qasim, Shaykh Pir and Mulla Asiri were some of the religious men honoured with Jehangir's attentions. See Wheeler Thackston's translation of the *Tuzuk-i Jahangiri* (Washington, DC, 1999), pp. 145, 205, 273.

9 Quoted from 'Munaqib Haji Bahadur Sahib Kohati' in Quddusi, *Tazkiray*, p. 373. Khushal Khan Khattak, a Pakhtun *Malik* and poet philosopher, was invited to serve the Mughal emperor Aurangzeb in return for *jagirs* of land. Khattak believed himself slighted by Aurangzeb and rejected his authority, resigning his *jagirs* and refusing to serve the emperor, and was subsequently imprisoned. See *Mutakhi'bat Khushal Khan Khattak, ba Urdu Tarja'mah*, introduction by Doctor Sayyid Anwar-ul-Haq (Peshawar, 1956). Also see Khushal Khan's poem, *Keh Tum Samjho keh Yeh Duniya Kya Hai*, in *Mutakhi'bat* pp. 174-91. Pir Haji was warned by his friend not to go to Delhi, but he insisted that he would, to represent the truth at any costs.

10 Muhammad Ibrahim Ata'i, *Dictionary of Pashtun Qabaili Law and Punishment* (Kabul, 1978), quoted in Wazir, *Afghanistan's Destiny*, p. 105, 124.

11 See Robert McChesney, 'Waqf at Balkh: A Study of the Endowments at the Shrine of 'Ali Ibn Abi Talib' (PhD thesis, Princeton University, 1973), p. 300; and Jos Gommans, *Rise of the Indo-Afghan Empire* (Delhi, 1999), pp. 64-6.

hammad Khan's reign (1826-63), religious authorities were brought into a state-monitored domain, in part to regularise a legal code for the nascent and fragmented Afghan state.[12] In the absence of mechanisms of state governance and a strong central command, the Dost Muhammad Khan regime depended on village-level religious functionaries to create and implement laws, to register births, deaths and marriages, and to act as the mouthpiece of the state. It also used religious leader to mobilise militarily the far reaches of the eastern Pakhtun lands. Amir Dost Muhammad had abolished taxes for the eastern Pakhtuns. Instead, the state paid allowances to the clans in the Khyber region and in the Peshawar valley, in return for which the tribes were required to provide military assistance in men and logistical support to the Afghan Government. The loose structure of the early nineteenth-century Afghan state and its reliance on religious leaders meant that civil administration in small outlying villages was in the hands of local religious leaders, giving them the freedom and the authority to dispense justice individually, without reference to precedence or a legal code.[13] These religious leaders made decisions on matters of law and inheritance, and were most numerous in the Eastern and Southern Provinces where shortage of farm-land made clerical occupation the most popular form of livelihood. Even Amir Abdur Rahman who was committed to bringing *waqfs* under state supervision allocated 126,000 Afghan rupees to religious figures as *wazifa* in Kandahar alone in 1877-8.[14] Because *pirs* often took on the patronage of the state and became invested with the authority of the ruler, the substance of religious authority extended beyond the pedagogic and divine-intercessionary mandate of Sufi *tariqa* and became linked to temporal power.

---

12   Olivier Roy argues that the Afghan state's drive towards legitimisation and modernisation led Amir Dost Muhammad (1835-63) to employ *'ulama* and impose *shari'a* as a means of rationalising state control and curtailing tribalism. *Islam and Resistance in Afghanistan* (Cambridge, 1986), p. 15

13   Senzil Nawid, *Religious Responses to Social Change in Afghanistan 1919-1929* (California, 1998).

14   Noelle, *State and Tribe*, p. 278.

Abdul Ghaffur (1793-1878), son of a Safi-Mohmand clansman from upper Swat, received his first training in *Sufi tariqa* from the Hazrat Ji of the Kabul-Mujaddidiyya line, in Peshawar in the early part of the nineteenth century. Abdul Ghaffur's training with Hazrat Ji was cut short when he was accused of not following the *tariqa* closely enough.[15] He then went to Akhund Muhammad Shoaib, a *pir* who had taken *bait* in the Qaderiyya order, but also in the Naqshbandiyya, Suhrawardi and Chishtiyya orders.[16] Abdul Ghaffur received his most rigorous training from Akhund Muhammad Shoaib and took on multiple *silsila* affiliations, taking *bait* in the Naqshbandiyya[17] as well as the Qaderiyya *silsila*.[18] Multiple *silsila* affiliation was commonly a feature of Indian Sufi teaching. [19] Muhammad Shoaib himself taught all four *tariqas* to his students and Abdul Ghaffur 'refined and practiced' this intermingled teaching after his *pir's* death in 1819.[20] The multiplicity of *silsila* affiliations was unified by the charismatic personality of the *pir* and transmission of knowledge through his person.

Abdul Ghaffur attained the title of *akhund* as a mark of his learning and mastery of *tariqa*. Popular accounts of Abdul Ghaffur's life described his dedication to prayer and his ascetic lifestyle until 1835 when the Afghan Amir Dost Muhammad Khan began an offensive against the Sikh kingdom of Ranjit Singh (1780-1839) with its capital in Lahore. Amir Dost Muhammad appealed directly to religious authorities to sanction his rule, referring to the campaign against the

---

15 Muhammad Asif Khan, 'Introduction', in Miangul Abdul Wudud Khan, *The Story of Swat* (Peshawar, 1963), p. xliii.

16 Quddusi, *Tazkiray*, p. 559.

17 Khan, introduction, *The Story of Swat*. p. xliii. Khan quotes a British military-political officer, Bellew, stating that Abdul Ghaffur took *bait* in the Naqshbandiyya order.

18 Ibid., p. 551.

19 This trend was generally recognisable across North India at this time. Claudia Liebeskind notes that the *sajjada nashin* of the Khanqah-yi Karimiya passed on initiation into multiple orders. See *Piety on its Knees* (Delhi, 1998), p. 141.

20 From *Hayat-i Afghani*, quoted in Quddusi, *Tazkiray*, p. 559.

Sikhs as a '*jihad*' and sent appeals to the Yusufzai *pirs* to rally *lashkars* to his aid.[21] Akhund Ghaffur was recruited into this effort, and he brought 'many *ghazis* and students' to the battlefield at Peshawar.[22] It was after his political engagement with and assistance to Dost Muhammad Khan that Akhund Ghaffur attained his greatest prestige and importance.

In return for his assistance to Amir Dost Muhammad Khan, Abdul Ghaffur was awarded lands in Swat, Lundkhwar and Mardan among the Yusufzai.[23] These rewards were considerable—the Akhund's *langarkhana* (a combination of an open community kitchen, entertaining quarters and almshouse) at Saidu in lower Swat fed 500 men a day and his wealth was sufficient to provide for the running of the state of Swat established 70 years later by his grandson Miangul Abdul Wudud.[24] Abdul Ghaffur's reputation attracted devotees from great distances, turning Saidu into a thriving city whose economy revolved around the *langarkhana*. The *langarkhana* and the Akhund's reputation were supported by the sale of *ghee* from the Akhund's large herds of livestock.[25] During these years Abdul Ghaffur conferred on a scheme for a united throne of Swat and selected a candidate for it.[26]

In 1849 Akhund Abdul Ghaffur nominated Sayyid Akbar Shah, a Sayyid in the line of the Pir Baba, as the amir of an Islamic state of Swat.[27] Sayyid Akbar Shah, a descendant of Pir Baba of Swat, had served under Sayyid Ahmed of Rai Bareilly as a secretary, so he brought knowledge of administration and Islamic jurisprudence

---

21 Noelle, *State and Tribe*, p. 15.

22 *Hayat-i Afghani*, pp. 209-11, quoted in Quddusi, *Tazkiray*, p. 559.

23 Ibid., p. 560.

24 Khan, *The Story of Swat*, p. 1.

25 Muhammad Asif Khan, *Tarikh-i Riyasat-i Swat* (Lahore 1958, reprint, Swat 2001), p. 83.

26 *Hayat-i Afghani*, pp. 209-211 in Quddusi, *Tazkiray*, p. 559 and Khan, *The Story of Swat*, p. lviii.

27 Quddusi, *Tazkiray*, p. 553.

with him.[28] Yet Sayyid Akbar was a weak ruler and produced no capable heirs, at least in the opinion of the Akhund. Akhund Sahib financed and propped up his candidate for eight years until Sayyid Akbar Badshah's death in 1857 when the Akhund assumed control himself.

The development of Akhund Ghaffur's *pirimuridi* line was not only the result of Afghan patronage and the emergence of the Swat state; its establishment and development were deeply tied to ideological influences on him. Ahmed Shah Abdali had induced descendants of Mujaddid Alf Sani to move to Kabul after his raid on Delhi in 1748. On their arrival and with patronage from the courts of Ahmed Shah and later Timur Shah (1772-93) and Shah Zaman (1793-1800), they gained pre-eminence at the Afghan court. They were also granted lands in Kabul, Kohistan, Jalalabad, Kandahar and Herat where the influence of the Naqshbandiyya-Mujaddidiyya line grew to its strongest. [29] The Mujaddidiyya *silsila* in Afghanistan produced three major lines - the Hazrats of Shor Bazaar based in Kabul, the Hazrats of Karrokh in Herat, and the Hazrats of Charbagh in Jalalabad.[30] These personalities were deeply invested in inter-tribal competitions for power, and performed the *dasturbandi* (the coronation or, literally, tying of the turban) ceremonies at the succession of the title of amir.[31] Akhund Ghaffur maintained close links with the Kabul-based religious leader Hafiz Ji, a Kabuli Mujaddidiyya and the *mir waiz* (head preacher) of Kabul, and his son, also known as Hafiz Ji, who together were central definers of Amir Dost Muhammad Khan's religious policy both during the 1835 Sikh war, and after.[32] Hafiz Ji had solicited Akhund Ghaffur's assistance in the Afghan

---

28 Khan, *Tarikh-i Riyasat-i Swat* , p. 64.

29 Ibid., pp. 279-81; and Nawid, *Religious Responses*, pp. 15-6.

30 Nawid, *Religious Responses*, p. 16.

31 Ibid., p. 17.

32 Noelle, *State and Tribe*, pp. 15, 56; see also Nawid, *Religious Responses* pp. 20-1.

mobilisation against the Sikh kingdom and greatly strengthened the latter's reputation by his patronage.

The second great ideological influence on Akhund Ghaffur was the incorrectly termed 'wahhabi' movement led by Sayyid Ahmed of Rai Bareilly.[33] This movement, initiated in the 1820s, was a militant interpretation of Shah Wali Ullah's call to social and political reform. The 'wahhabis', led by Shah Ismail, Shah Wali Ullah's grandson, and Shah Ismail's student and close friend, Sayyid Ahmed of Rai Bareilly, led campaigns against both the Sikh kingdom, and recalcitrant local Pakhtun tribes in order to create a space in which Shah Wali Ullah's vision could be realised. The movement culminated in the Battle of Balakot in 1831 in which Sayyid Ahmed was killed. Many of Sayyid Ahmed's *mujahidin* remained on at Buner in the south of Swat under the protection of Akhund Ghaffur and began a new insurrection against the British in 1862 under his leadership.[34] This movement was termed the movement of the 'Hindustani fanatics' by the British and widely advertised by the wahhabi trials, and then in Hunter's book *Our Indian Musalmans*.[35] It is clear that during his time in the Pakhtun areas Sayyid Ahmed had also struck up a close relationship with the Akhund of Swat Abdul Ghaffur while promoting the tenets of Shah Wali Ullah's philosophy among the Pakhtuns.[36] The movement for the promotion of these principles, termed 'Tariqa-yi Muhammadiyya', called for strict adherence to the word of the Quran and authenticated *hadith*, and observance of the individualised ritual practices of the faith such as prayer and fasting, instead of the reliance on the *pir* as mediator between the individual

---

33   See Qeyamuddin Ahmad, *The Wahhabi Movement in India* (Calcutta, 1966).

34   *List of Leading Persons in Afghanistan 1888* (Simla, 1888). OIOC L/PS/20/26.

35   See Janab Maulana Muhammad Jaffer Thanesseri *Kala Pani* (Lahore, 1981) for an account of the trials and Thanesseri's subsequent deportment and internment at Malta. Also see W. W. Hunter, *Our Indian Mussalmans*, 1872 (reprint Lahore, 1964).

36   Ghulam Rasul Mehr, *Sarguzasht-i Mujahidin* (Lahore, 1956), p. 336.

and God. Sayyid Ahmed conferred and colluded with Akhund Abdul Ghaffur in pursuit of religious reform of the Pakhtun communities in line with these principles.[37] Akhund Ghaffur strongly supported the revivalist principles and instructed his *murids* in the tenets of revivalism, as well as asking them to promote these tenets through travel, preaching and personal example. These religious functionaries and their revivalist imperative established the dominant face of Islam in the eastern Pakhtun areas.[38]

The pirimuridi line of Akhund Abdul Ghaffur: institution and ideology

As was tradition, Akhund Abdul Ghaffur took on a number of *murids* who pledged their allegiance at his hand and were entrusted with a social mission of reform and revitalisation of Islam - an imperative to which the Akhund was said to have devoted his life. A trusted few *murids* were appointed as *khalifas* whose services to their *pir* included those of scribes and of official representatives. The *khalifas* was trusted enough to represent their *pir's* authority and spirituality to the layman in the *pir's* lifetime and were entrusted with taking forward his teachings after his death.[39] Akhund Ghaffur still taught his *murids* the particulars of Sufi religious practice according to the secrecy and rigour of Sufi *tariqa*, but he also tried to make the teachings of Islam general and accessible. Sufi pedagogy was no longer simply confined to a close circle - the focus changed to making knowledge available and disseminating it widely. In its new form Islam existed outside the confines of the Sufi *dargah* and the rigours of *tariqa*. Its driving imperative was to engage the local Pakhtun populations in revivalist religious practice, and de-emphasise the place of the shrine and the Sufi *pir* as intercedents between man and God.

---

37 Mehr, *Sarguzasht-i Mujahidin*, pp. 335-7.

38 Khan, *Tarikh-i Riyasat-i Swat*, p. 64.

39 Ibid., pp. 90-1.

The innovation in Akhund Ghaffur's pedagogy created a network of his deputies who took the practice of religion to the village level. Of his many *murids* some of the most important were the Mulla Najmuddin in Hadda Sharif (d. 1901); the Sartor Faqir Saadullah Khan (1824-1914) from Buner who was involved in Swat politics; Mulla Atkar of Khost (active in 1888); Mulla Babra in Bajaur (active 1882); the Hazrat Abdul Wahab of Manki Sharif (d. 1904); Mulla Khalil (active in 1888) and the Haji Sahib Bedmani (d.1883) in Mohmand; Wali Muhammad Khan in Tirah (d. 1887); and Sayyid Akbar who became the *amir-badshah* of Swat.

Akhund Abdul Ghaffur had not simply affected the ideological bent of regional religious personalities, but brought about the relocation of his *murids* as in the case of Hazrat Abdul Wahab who moved to Manki Sharif after participating in the Akhund's 1862-3 *jihad*.[40] Mulla Abubakar Akhunzada from Ghazni moved to Makhrani in Swat as the Akhund's *murid*.[41] The Akhund appeared to send away those who fell out of favour as well. When a dispute arose between Mulla Khalil and Haji Sahib of Bedmani, the Akhund forced Mulla Khalil out of Swat.[42] Akhund Ghaffur's greatest conflict was with Hazrat Sayyid Maruf Bey, the Kotah Mulla who had moved to upper Swat-Kohistan from Swabi and participated in Sayyid Ahmed's movement as well. The Kotah Mulla was a supporter of Shah Shuja, the British sponsored Afghan Amir who briefly held the throne of Kabul from 1839 to 1843.[43] The Kotah Mulla had opposed the Dost Muhammad Khan faction in 1835 and provided the British with information that led to the Akhund's defeat and flight from the battlefield at Peshawar in 1835. Akhund Ghaffur focused efforts on undermining and excluding the Kotah Mulla from the domain of religious leadership in Swat. He referred to the Kotah Mulla as the disciple of the sixteenth-century

---

40 Quddusi, *Tazkiray*, pp. 584-91.

41 *List of Leading Persons in Afghanistan 1888.*

42 Ibid.

43 Quddusi, *Tazkiray*, p. 563.

apostate, Bayyazid Roshan Baba, and the practitioner of heretical rituals.[44]

Akhund Ghaffur's exclusion and discrediting of the Kotah Mulla demonstrates the manner in which the former consolidated and promoted his own presence in Swat by asserting interpretive authority. [45] He also threatened supporters of the Kotah Mulla with armed attacks if they did not evict the latter from Buner. Akhund Ghaffur finally managed to convince the Bunerwals to push the Kotah Mulla out of the village where he was hosted.[46] This incident demonstrates Akhund Ghaffur's will to consolidate and regularise regional religious authority. Competitors could not be tolerated, or even allowed to remain in Swat. Hence, the dominance of his line in the late nineteenth century was engineered by Akhund Ghaffur by effort rather than by chance.

The Akhund's regional influence, in no small part stemming from his alliance with Dost Muhammad Khan and the great fortune he received after 1835, was represented by and exercised through his *murids*. Akbar Badshah was the most obvious example of this, but the *murid* who came to great prominence later was the Hadda Mulla Najmuddin who had served as a *khalifa* to Sayyid Ahmed of Rai Bareilly.[47] All of Akhund Ghaffur's *murids* brought their own influence to their relationship with Akhund Abdul Ghaffur, creating a composite that would dominate the Pakhtun Tribal Areas well into the twentieth century.

The Hadda Mulla Najmuddin

Swat and the Akhund's great fortune went to his children, Abdul Hanan and Abdul Khaliq. Miangul Abdul Hanan ruled until his death in 1887 after which his brother Miangul Abdul Khaliq took the throne. Neither ruled for long enough to consolidate a following,

44 Ibid., p. 572.

45 Ibid., pp. 561-73.

46 Ibid., p. 573.

47 Muhammad Ali Kasuri, *Mushahidat-i Kabul wa Yaghistan* (Karachi, 1970), pp. 41-2.

nor with the same charisma as their father, and therefore neither was an effective ruler. Miangul Abdul Khaliq, the more spiritually inclined of the two, studied religion under the Haji Sahib of Bedmani for some years before he died in 1892. But Abdul Ghaffur's political power and his mantle were inherited by his *murid*, the Mulla Najmuddin of Hadda. The Hadda Mulla Najmuddin arrived in Saidu Sharif after receiving his training in the Shilgarh and Ghazni area, south-west of Jalalabad, and received instruction from Akhund Ghaffur after he took *bait* in the Qaderiyya *silsila* alongside the Karboghay Mulla Sahib and Miyan of Manki Sharif, among others. After a period of training, the Hadda Mulla was appointed a *khalifa* or emissary of Akhund Ghaffur, and it was in this capacity, both during the Akhund's lifetime and for a further ten years after his death, that the Hadda Mulla consolidated and extended the Akhund Ghaffur's pedagogic line as the dominant one through the eastern Pakhtun region.[48]

Swabi	Hadda	Bajaur/Mohmand	Waziristan
Kota Mulla Sahib	Hadda Mulla Najmuddin	Gujjar Mulla d. 1915	Mulla Hamzullah
		Hazrat Masood Sahib	Karboghay Mulla Sahib
		Haji Sahib Bednani d. 1883	Masood Mulla
		Mulla Khalil d. 1888 (approximately)	
Tirah	**Swat**	**Khost**	**'Punjabi' areas**
Mulla Mahmud Akhunzada	Mulla Abubakar Akhunzada	Mulla Atkar of Khost	Haji Mulla Akbar
Mulla Sapri	Sandaki Mulla		Qazi Sahib Gujarat
Mulla Sayyid Akbar	Spinkara Mulla		Hazrat Miyan
	Pir Manki Sharif		
Dir	**Unknown**	**Other**	
Palam Mulla	Quddus Mulla	Abdur Rahim Sahib	
Shah Babu Sahib	Faiz Muhammad Akhunzada		

Fig.1 Dominant mullas among the eastern Pakhtuns during the late nineteenth and early twentieth century[49]

---

48   Quddusi, *Tazkiray*, pp. 579-82.

49   This table is a compilation of data derived from three particular sources: British intelligence reporting on *mullas* compiled in *Lists of Leading Persons in Afghanistan*, the *Who's Who NWFP, 1914*, and recorded in the NWFP Provincial Diaries from 1901-30; Ijazul Haq Quddusi's *Tazkiray Sufya-y Sarhad*; and hagiographic accounts of the lives of Mulla Sahib Chaknawar, Haji Sahib Turangzai and the Babra Mulla Sahib.

Akhund Abdul Ghaffur's death and Hadda Mulla's succession in 1878 coincided with the beginning of Amir Abdur Rahman's reign (1879-1901) - a period of consolidation of Afghan state authority. The religious leadership no longer had the administrative, legal and military independence it had earlier.[50] Instead a central bureaucracy and army began to emerge. Afghan state authority began to intrude into the eastern Pakhtun tribal regions from the west at the same time that the British forward movement was being initiated from the east. The Hadda Mulla's major efforts were focused on resisting these pressures and encroachments on his regional authority. A large part of the Hadda Mulla's effort was to oppose Abdur Rahman Khan and his assertions of authority in any way possible. Abdur Rahman explained the Hadda Mulla's particular antagonism to himself in a letter to the Superintendent Peshawar in 1897:

Just as in the old days of Europe the popes used to profess to be the sole dis-
posers of heaven and hell, and the people also accepted the word of worth-
less priests, so too these *mullas* claim to possess the same power and during
these last few years they have stirred up my own Afghan subjects to rebel
against me ... there is a village called Hadda which is inhabited by *chammars*
or leather tanners but because it is the residence of this mischievous Mulla
Najmuddin, his disciples have named this impure village Hadda Sharif, that
is to say, Hadda the noble, and his pupils and disciples regard him as a
prophet. What calamities are there that they have not suffered and what
blood is there that they have not shed by his senseless commands? ... Every
mulla for many years denounced me in various ways as a *kafir* and at their
bidding their disciples fought against me and their houses were destroyed
and they themselves were killed. For fourteen years they raised every part
of Afghanistan against me, both in the plain country and in the hills, till
thousands of men perished on both sides and several of the *mulla* agitators
themselves were killed with thousands of the disciples of these turbulent
priests.[51]

---

50 Noelle, *State and Tribe*, p. 278.

51 'Letter from Amir Abdur Rahman to Commissioner and Superintendent
Peshawar Division dated 18 Aug. 1897', in 'Papers Regarding British Relations
With the Neighbouring Tribes on the North-West Frontier of India and the
Military Operations Undertaken Against them During the Year 1897-1898'.

The Hadda Mulla also mobilised in response to the British campaign in Chitral in 1893, and he spoke out against the penetration of the region by railway lines and cantonments past Peshawar.[52] Joined by other *mullas* of the Pakhtun Areas (Abdul Karim Chamarkandi explained, 'because the Hadda Mulla Sahib Ghazi himself was an enemy of the *kafir*, hence some—rather all—his *murids* were enemies of the *farangi*'[53]) the Hadda Mulla rose to real prominence in the battle of Malakand (1897-8) against the British, observed by Winston Churchill.[54] Saadullah Khan or the Sartor Faqir, also called the 'Mad Mulla' by the British, together with the Hadda Mulla, organised the Bunerwals and Mohmands in an attack on the British post at Chakdarra and the Malakand Pass.[55] In a letter to 'all the *mullas* and elders of the Afridi and Orakzai tribes' Hadda Mulla said:

The *kafirs* have taken possession of all Muslim countries, and owing to the lack of spirit on the part of the people are conquering every region. They have now reached these countries of Bajaur and Swat, but though the people of these places showed want of courage in the beginning, they have now realised their mistake and having repented and become ashamed of their former deeds, they attack them (the *kafirs*) day and night and have quite confounded them. I have myself informed the people of Laghman and Kunar and the Mohmands, Ningraharis and Shinwaris and they are all prepared to take part in the fighting. ... I have deputed Mulla Abdullah, Akhunzada of the Mohmand country to attend on you [the *mullas* and elders], and, God willing, he will reach you. Please let me know whatever decision you may unanimously arrive at. So that it may be acted upon. If you decide to send for me there, I am willing to come, but if you wish to come here, I also agree. If you choose to commence fighting there, and desire me to fight in this direction, I am ready to do so but it is necessary to fix the

---

BL RBC, Balfour Papers 1-9.

52 See 'Letter of the Mullah 'Adda to all Mullahs and Elders of the Afridi and Orakzai Tribes, n.d.', ibid.

53 Abdul Karim Chamarkandi, *Sarguzasht-i Mujahidin* (Lahore, 1981), p. 34.

54 Churchill, 'The Malakand Field Force', *Frontiers and Wars*, p. 66.

55 'Telegram from Viceroy to Secretary State India 11 Aug. 1897', in 'Papers Regarding British Relations with the Neighbouring Tribes on the North-West Frontier of India.'

time and day of fighting so that by the grace of God the work may be accomplished.[56]

Because the Hadda Mulla's moblisations and his rhetoric were anti-British, he has been largely read as a reactive leader opposing the tools and appearance of the modern state and 'forces of change'.[57] But it is important to see his efforts as more than just a backlash against colonial encroachment - the Hadda Mulla was consolidating the Akhund's network of religious leaders across the areas mutually agreed between the Afghans and British as being autonomous –Swat Chitral, Dir, Tirah, Mohmand, Bajaur, and to a lesser extent, Waziristan. This interpretation is supported by events in 1890 during which the Hadda Mulla, along with other regional religious leaders, supported Umra Khan's attack on and seizure of power in Dir; in 1895 when he supported Umra Khan's failed claim to the throne of Chitral;[58] and in 1897 when the Hadda Mulla sent the Sartor Faqir to take over the Pir Baba's shrine in Upper Swat, to incorporate the region into his sphere of influence.[59] In 1893, 1897 and again in 1899, he initiated mobilisations against the British in the newly formed Tribal Areas, targeting communications lines and militia posts in Malakand.

Alienated by the Hadda Mulla's anti-British stance, and under pressure from the British supported Nawab of Dir who felt threatened by the Miangul-Hadda Mulla alliance, it was in this period that the Swat Mianguls under the young Miangul Abdul Wudud Khan began to break from the Hadda Mulla's line. Miangul Abdul Wudud had initially joined the Sartor Faqir's attacks on Malakand

---

56 Letter From Mulla Adda to all Mullas and Elders of the Afridi and Orakzai Tribes (n.d.).

57 Mahon and Ramsay, *Report on the Tribes of Dir, Swat and Bajour together with the Utman-Khel and Sam Ranizai*, pp. 9-10.

58 Henry Newman, *Umra Khan and the Chitral Campaign of 1895* in 'Correspondence relating to Chitral', BL RBC B.P.13/41 (1) vol. II.

59 'Major Deane to PA Dir, Swat, Chitral 21 July 1897, p. 65. OIOC L/ PS/20/Memo 20.

and Chakdarra, but then backed off, blaming the Bunerwals for inciting the people. He claimed he was 'losing hold of people owing to the [Sartor] Faqir's miracles'.[60] Distancing himself from the Akhund's line, the Miangul chose the Pir Baba of Swat's shrine in Manki Sharif as his family's spiritual affiliation and appointed the Passani Mulla, *murid* of the Pir of Manki Sharif who differed with the Hadda Mulla on points of religious interpretation and had not taken part in the 1893 and 1897 mobilisations, to manage the shrine.[61] While they continued to revere Akhund Ghaffur both as their *pir* and ancestor, Miangul Abdul Wudud and his descendants split from the Akhund's spiritual line that now pivoted on the personality of the Hadda Mulla.[62] This event marked the end of the possibility of a Swat amirate controlled by the Hadda Mulla and a religious base in that area. But the Hadda Mulla still managed to successfully consolidate his authority in the Tribal Areas, inspite of losing the political and financial legacy of the Akhund Ghaffur. And he did so by organising his fraternal counterparts in the *pirimuridi* line in support of his mobilisations.[63]

The structure and formation of the *pirimuridi* line begs examination for the mechanisms by which it brought a conscious commonality of purpose and self-representation to an otherwise highly differentiated group of leaders. Some of the Akhund Ghaffur's *murids* had alternate lineages through the Hazrats of Charbagh, Badshahs of Islampur and Butkhak and the Shahzadas of Rehankot in Dir. These were legacies of great significance for the *murids* as they were

---

60 Khan, introduction, *The Story of* Swat, pp. 30-1; 'Correspondence relating to Chitral'.

61 *Whos Who NWFP 1914.*

62 Quddusi, *Tazkiray*, p. 59.

63 'Letter from Sufi Sahib to the Mulla Sahib of Siah, the Mulla of Aka Khel (Sayyid Akbar), Badshah Sahib, Malik Amin Khan, Malik Sher Muhammad Khan, Maliks Yar Muhammad Khan, Khawas Khanm Samandar and the *maliks* of Kamar Khel, Aka Khel and other Maliks and People of Tirah, 7 Rabius Sani 1315 [5 September 1897]' in 'Papers Regarding British Relations with the Neighbouring Tribes on the North-West Frontier of India'.

in possession of *waqf* properties that had come down through their own direct family lineages.[64] Moreover, sometimes direct descendents of *pirs* such as the Akhund's own sons who inherited his lands in Swat and Mardan chose not to actively promote the line.[65] Social difference was inevitable because of the economic disparities between different members. Some members were poor village preachers with no personal wealth. Others, like the Hazrats, came out of the Kabul Mujaddidiyya line and were widely recognised in Afghanistan. The Shahzadas of Rehankot were an old religious line based in the Dir area, while the Badshah of Kunar owned vast tracts of land on the Afghan side of the border, west of the Durand Line. Others were successful traders, like the Mulla Chaknawar who imported and distributed sugar and wheat in the Tribal Areas.[66] Meanwhile proof of ideological conformity between members of the Akhund Ghaffur-Hadda Mulla line cannot be extrapolated from the substance of *muridi* training because of the wide variation in the sort of training received by different *murids* in Akhund Ghaffur's line and the different influences on them.[67]

Members of the Akhund Ghaffur-Hadda Mulla *pirimuridi* fraternity were connected to that line and to one another only by the fact of the *bait* - the undertaking of the *murid* to his *pir* to devote himself to instruction by the latter.[68] Membership of the *silsila* was conferred by the *bait* itself, irrespective of the social, cultural, economic or political circumstances of the *murid*, and so this device was the instrument of creation and extension of the *pirimuridi* line. As the tool of induction into the *pirimuridi* line, the mechanism of its perpetuation,

---

64 Nawid, *Religious Responses*, appendix.

65 Khan, *The Story of Swat.*

66 Interview Ghulam Nabi Chaknawari, Peshawar, 8 Feb. 2002.

67 Peter Hardy coins the term 'ideological class' to understand Muslim religious social organisation and unanimity in north India in 'Ulama in British India', *Journal of Indian History*, Jubilee vol. (1973), pp. 821-45. This structure of analsis cannot however be applied to the *mullas* of the Pakhtun regions.

68 Richard Eaton, *Sufis of Bijapur* (Princeton, 1996), p. xxvii.

and the guarantee of its solidarity, the *bait* gave the *pirimuridi* line its coherence. The significance of the *pirimuridi* line was in the solidarity of its members, in its persistence, in the spread of its fame, and the extension of its influence. The *pirimuridi* line of the Akhund Ghaffur-Hadda Mulla, unified by the *bait* and directed by the Hadda Mulla into the twentieth century, became the vehicle for the dissemination of a revivalist ideology of religious practice through the eastern Pakhtun regions, and, with its creation, the Tribal Areas.

The Hadda Mulla in turn went back to Hadda and settled there after the death of Akhund Abdul Ghaffur. Acknowledged and respected as a *pir* in his own right, and having attained wide renown for his *jihad* against the British, the Hadda Mulla drew prospective *murids* to himself. Some learning was evidently imparted at the Hadda Mulla's *muqam* or base. It appears however that most *murids* learned through apprenticeship—the Hadda Mulla was said to have up to 200 *murids* and *khalifas* at a time who would travel everywhere with him until such a time as they were ready to go forward as representatives of the Hadda Mulla's will.[69] Other *murids* of the Hadda Mulla such as the Butkhak Hazrat Sahib, Mulla Babra, and the Sartor Faqir Saadullah (1824-1916), the Hazrat Sahib Charbagh (d. 1919), Mir Sayyid Jan Badshah of Islampur, the Sarkanri Miyan Sahib, Sufi Alam Gul and Mulla Sahib Tagao were reported to have received similar initiation into the Hadda Mulla's line.[70]

The regional dominance of the Akhund Ghaffur-Hadda Mulla line and its revivalist message was not uncontested. The prescriptions of religious thought and practice promoted by the Akhund Ghaffur-Hadda Mulla line were challenged both from within the Akhund Ghaffur's line, as in the case of the Pir of Manki Sharif's opposition to the Hadda Mulla's religious method, and from without, as exemplified by the Kotah Mulla's opposition to Akhund Ghaffur. Tensions between the Hadda Mulla and the Pir of Manki Sharif led to a split in the Akhund Ghaffur's *pirimuridi* line itself with some

---

69 Chamarkandi, *Sarguzasht-i Mujahidin*, p. 34.
70 Javed, *Haji Sahib Turangzai*, p. 41.

claiming the Sufi legacy of the Pir of Manki Sharif, and others that of the Hadda Mulla. However it was the Hadda Mulla's spiritual antecedents who were the more prominent in the twentieth-century Tribal Areas. His *murids* were widely established at villages across the Pakhtun non-administered regions where they continued to promote the Hadda Mulla's teachings. The pattern of their settlement centred around the Tribal Areas and into the Ningrahar-Jalalabad-Kabul triangle to the west.

It was thus that the legacy of the Hadda Mulla was extended by his *murids* in Mohmand and Shinwari, Bajaur, Swat, Tirah, Khyber Orakzai and in Waziristan. These *murids* of the Hadda Mulla took forward his agenda of social reform as inspired by the revivalist school in the areas where they settled. On the next is a table of known *mullas* of the twentieth century who promoted his teachings, listed by district and noting their *pirs* in parentheses. 'Mapping' the geographic distribution of these affiliated *mullas* describes the regional influence and reach of the Akhund Ghaffur-Hadda Mulla line.[71]

Haji Turangzai and the perpetuation of the Hadda Mulla's line

Of the Hadda Mulla's successors, Fazal Wahid (1842-1937), from a small village in the Pakhtun Utmanzai area, was the most important. Fazal Wahid, who came to be known as the Haji Sahib Turangzai, had started his education with Mulla Abubakar Akhunzada, one of Akhund Abdul Ghaffur's *murids*, at an early age. He studied the Quran and Farsi literature with Mulla Abubakar up to the age of 14. After this he was admitted into an 'Islami *madrasa*' at the nearby village of Tehkal, in which he studied for six years. This *madrasa* was closely connected to the Naqshbandiyya-Mujaddidiyya revivalist movement inspired by Mujaddid Alf Sani and furthered by Shah

---

71 This table has been compiled using the following sources: the Peshawar District *Whos Who 1930*; *Whos Who NWFP 1914*; Quddusi, *Tazkiray*; Mehr, *Sarguzasht-i Mujahidin*; and NWFP Intelligence and Provincial Diaries for the period 1915-1930.

Malakand	
Mohmand	**Bajaur**
Haji Turangzai (Hadda Mulla)	Babra Mulla (Hadda Mulla)
Akhund Muhammad Shoaib (Haji Turangzai)	Jan Sahib Doda (Babra Mulla)
Sufi Sahib Burhanuddin (Hadda Mulla)	Kama Mulla (Hadda Mulla)
	Spin Miyan (Unknown)
Spinkara Mulla (Akhund Swat)	Maulvi Ibrahim Kama (Hadda Mulla)
Chaknawar Mulla (Hadda Mulla)	**Swat**
Butkhak Mulla (Hadda Mulla)	Spinkara Mulla (Hadda Mulla)
Mulla Sahib TT (Hadda Mulla)	Sartor Faqir (Hadda Mulla)
Gud Mulla (Hadda Mulla)	Sandaki Mulla (Hadda Mulla)
Muhammad Ayub (Haji Turangzai)	Gujjar Mulla (Hadda Mulla)
Shalour Mulla (Haji Turangzai)	Mulla Abubakar Akhunzada (Akhund Swat)
Sarkanri Miyan (Hadda Mulla)	Abdul Jabbar Badshah (Akhund Swat)
Miyan Kasai (Haji Turangzai)	Maulvi Pakhli (Haji Turangzai)
Mulla Buzurg (Haji Turangzai)	Gujjar Mulla II (Haji Turangzai)
	Pacha Mulla (Haji Turangzai)
	Dir
	Mulla Shahu Baba (Hadda Mulla)
	Shahzada Rehankot (Haji Turangzai)
Waziristan	**Tirah, Orakzai and Khyber**
Lala Pir Khost (Akhund Swat)	Mulla Mahmud Akhunzada (Akhund Swat)
Mulla Hamzullah (Akhund Swat)	Faqir Alingar (Sandaki Mulla)
Mulla Powindah (Mulla Hamzullah)	Sayyid Asghar (unknown)
Karboghay Mulla Sahib (Akhund Swat)	Naib Mulla (Sufi Alam Gul)
Mulla Hissamuddin (Karboghay Mulla)	Haji Abdul Haq (Miyan Manki)
Dildar Mulla of Musakki(Karboghay Mulla)	Nazian Mulla (Hadda Mulla)
Shaikh Ghulam Sarwar (Karboghay Mulla)	Sufi Sahib Drabgai (Sufi Sahib Butkhak)
Maulvi Makhfi in Salarzai Daur (Haji Turangzai)	Mulla Sayyid Akbar (Hadda Mulla)
Tor Mulla of Ispinki Tangi (Haji Turangzai)	Mulla Hayat Khan (Sayyid Akbar)
Masai Mulla (Hazrat Charbagh/Lala Pir)	Sayyid Wazir (Sayyid Akbar)
Shew Mulla (Karboghay Mulla)	Qazi Ghulam Habib (Mulla Sayyid Akbar)
	Mulla Abdul Manan (Mulla Sayyid Akbar)
Khost	
Mulla Atkar (Akhund Swat)	Sahibzada Fazal Ilahi (Mulla Sayyid Akbar)
Masai Mulla (Hazrat Charbagh)	Sayyid Almar (Mulla Sayyid Akbar)
Kandahar-Ningrahar-Jalalabad	
Hazrat Sahib Charbagh (Hadda Mulla)	**Mardan**
Mulla Tsappri in Gandamak (Hadda Mulla)	Maulvi Ismail (Kama Mulla)
Tagao Mulla (Hadda Mulla)	Shahzada Maulvi (Haji Turangzai)
Akhunzada Tagao (Tagao Mulla)	
Pacha Mulla (Hadda Mulla)	
Ustad Hadda Sharif (Hadda Mulla)	
Sayyid Abbas Badshah (Badshah Islampur/Hazrat Charbagh)	
Badshah Tirgarhi (Hadda Mulla)	
Sufi Sahib Bedmani (Butkhak Mulla)	
Mir Sayyid Jan Badshah of Islampur (Hadda Mulla)	

Fig.2 *Mullas* of the Akhund Ghaffur-Hadda Mulla line in the twentieth century

Wali Ullah, and taught his principles. Haji Turangzai's *khalifa* and biographer claimed that this early education and its revivalist bent was to influence the Haji for the rest of his life.[72] In 1878, Fazal Wahid travelled to Deoband. He stayed at the Darul Ulum long enough to strike up a deep friendship with the chancellor there, Maulana Mahmudul Hasan. When he discovered that a group of *'ulama* of Deoband were travelling to Mecca to undertake Haj, he decided to join the party, and went on to perform *haj* with Maulana Mahmud. In Mecca, Fazal Wahid was introduced to Haji Imdadullah, a member of the so-called wahhabi movement. After the *haj*, Fazal Wahid took the title of Haji, and became popularly known as Haji of Turangzai, a title comprised of the title granted to one that performs the *haj*, and the name of the town to which he belonged. [73]

In Mecca, Haji Turangzai took the *bait* at Haji Imdadullah's hand, and promised that he would take up Sayyid Ahmed of Bareilly's mission, kept alive by Haji Imdadullah, and promote revivalism and opposition to the British among the Pakhtuns.[74] When he returned to the Pakhtun north-west, he went in search of a *murshid*—a spiritual teacher—and found one in Hadda, in the Mulla Najmuddin. Here Fazal Wahid did *bait* at the hand of the Hadda Mulla, committing himself to Akhund Ghaffur's *pirimuridi* line and to his mission to spread Shah Wali Ullah's revivalist message among the Pakhtun tribes.[75] The Haji's double *bait*, first at the hand of Haji Imdadullah and then the Hadda Mulla, marked the Haji Turangzai's two allegiances—to revivalism, and to the spiritual line of the Hadda Mulla Sahib. When the Haji took position as the local *mulla* at Lakarai in Mohmand, and control of the land allotment, *masjid* and *hujra* associated with this position, he used his placement to fulfil his commitments to both the revivalist cause and his *pirimuridi* line.[76]

---

72 Aziz Javed, *Haji Sahib Turangzai* (Lahore, 1981), pp. 39-40.

73 Ibid., p. 42.

74 Ibid., pp. 42-3.

75 Ibid., pp. 40-1.

76 Ibid., p. 54.

Alongside the Haji Turangzai, the three other *mullas* rose to great prominence within the *pirimuridi* line, and in the Mohmand agency—these were the Mulla Chaknawar, Mulla Sandaki and Mulla Babra. The Mulla Chaknawar (1884-1930) was from Ningrahar, near Kabul. He studied briefly under the Hadda Mulla in the Qaderiyya *tariqa*, and after the Hadda Mulla's death in 1903 continued his education in '*tariqa* and *tajdid*' (method and elucidation) under the Hadda Mulla's *murid* and *khalifa*, the Butkhak Hazrat Sahib, Abdul Shakoor Al Mujaddidi. Although his base was in Ningrahar in Afghanistan, he traded, travelled and preached among the Mohmand tribes, and became a close supporter of the Haji Turangzai,

Fig.3 Shajarah of the Fazal Wahid Haji Turangzai engraved in marble. The plaque is displayed at the site of the Haji's *masjid* in Ghaziabad, Mohmand Agency.

gaining prominence within the Tribal Areas. [77] Mulla Sandaki was a *murid* of the Akhund Ghaffur and was from Sanda in upper Swat. He had forged links with his *mujahidin* at Asmast in the south of Swat during the Akhund Ghaffur's mobilisation against the British. After the movement was disbanded, Mulla Sandaki organised the Swatis in contests for the throne of Swat and Dir, and also established a base for himself among the Shinwaris in Tirah. The Mulla Babra had been a *murid* of the Akhund Ghaffur.[78] He had also found his introduction to regional politics in Buner, and had participated in

---

77 Meera Jan Syal, *Nomyali Ghazi Chaknawar Mulla Sahib* (Peshawar, 1999), p. 20.

78 Hussain Ahmad Madni, *Tehrik-i Reshmi Rumaal* (Lahore 1966), pp. 160-6.

the mobilisations in Dir.[79] After the Akhund's death Mulla Babra swore *bait* at the hand of the Hadda Mulla Najmuddin and established himself at a base in Bajaur.[80]

Amr-bil maruf – mobilising the revivalist agenda

Islamic reform encapsulated in Naqshbandiyya-Mujaddidiyya thought was beginning to erode Sufi practices and to 'exert pressure on Sufism and its institutions, both from within and without'.[81] Akhund Ghaffur and the Hadda Mulla were not alone in this as Sufi thinkers across north India and at other Qaderiyya and Naqshbandiyya *khanqahs* in the Pakhtun and northern Punjabi regions had also come in contact with Mujaddidiyya thought, both through the efforts of Shah Ismail and through other personalities, and were beginning to show greater interest in *hadith* literature and Quranic study. Different Sufis acknowledged and responded to revivalist imperative in different ways, some taking on its discourse and others maintaining traditional rituals unchanged. The engagement of the Akhund Ghaffur's line with the revivalist Mujaddidiyya thinking was not unique, but it was a more extreme and wholesale response to the revivalist imperative than that of many other Sufis who came in contact with Shah Wali Ullah and Abdul Aziz's thinking. The traditional Sufi method of *bait* and the chain of transmission of pedagogy continued to give coherence to the Akhund Ghaffur-Hadda Mulla line, but this pedagogy took on the imperative of social and religious reform as a guiding principle. This revivalist imperative in the Akhund Ghaffur-Hadda Mulla line took the title of *amr-bil maruf wa nahi anal munkir*, the movement for 'the promotion of virtue and prevention of vice'—a social mission that was to give the line its greatest cohesion and form its primary agenda in the twentieth century.

---

79 Government of India, 'Who's Who Afghanistan, 1888'.

80 Kasuri, *Mushahidat*, p. 43, and Barkatullah Bhopali quoted in Mehr, *Sarguzasht-i Mujahidin*, p. 186.

81 Liebeskind, *Piety on its Knees*, p. 251.

Spiritual Genealogy of the Tribal Areas Mullas:

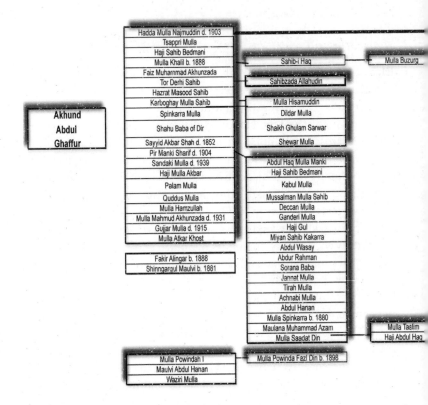

Fig. 4 The spiritual genealogy of the Tribal Areas *mullas*. (Compiled from colonial intelligence sources, Deobandi writings, and Quddusi's *Tazkiray Sufya-yi Sarhad.*)

The Akhund Ghaffur-Hadda Mulla Line

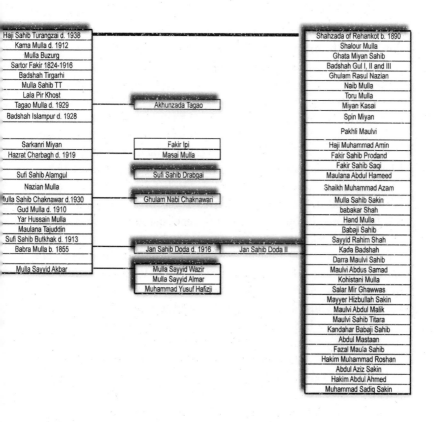

Haji Sahib Turangzai d. 1938		Shahzada of Rehankot b. 1890
Kama Mulla d. 1912		Shalour Mulla
Mulla Buzurg		Ghata Miyan Sahib
Sartor Fakir 1824-1916		Badshah Gul I, II and III
Badshah Tirgarhi		Ghulam Rasul Nazian
Mulla Sahib TT		Naib Mulla
Lala Pir Khost		Toru Mulla
Tagao Mulla d. 1929	Akhunzada Tagao	Miyan Kasai
Badshah Islampur d. 1928		Spin Miyan
		Pakhli Maulvi
Sarkanri Miyan	Fakir Ipi	Haji Muhammad Amin
Hazrat Charbagh d. 1919	Masai Mulla	Fakir Sahib Prodand
		Fakir Sahib Saqi
Sufi Sahib Alamgul	Sufi Sahib Drabgai	Maulana Abdul Hameed
Nazian Mulla		Shaikh Muhammad Azam
Mulla Sahib Chaknawar d.1930	Ghulam Nabi Chaknawari	Mulla Sahib Sakin
Gud Mulla d. 1910		babakar Shah
Yar Hussain Mulla		Hand Mulla
Maulana Tajuddin		Babaji Sahib
Sufi Sahib Butkhak d. 1913		Sayyid Rahim Shah
Babra Mulla b. 1855	Jan Sahib Doda d. 1916 Jan Sahib Doda II	Kada Badshah
		Darra Maulvi Sahib
Mulla Sayyid Akbar	Mulla Sayyid Wazir	Maulvi Abdus Samad
	Mulla Sayyid Almar	Kohistani Mulla
	Muhammad Yusuf Hafizji	Salar Mir Ghawwas
		Mayyer Hizbullah Sakin
		Maulvi Abdul Malik
		Maulvi Sahib Titara
		Kandahar Babaji Sahib
		Abdul Mastaan
		Fazal Maula Sahib
		Hakim Muhammad Roshan
		Abdul Aziz Sakin
		Hakim Abdul Ahmed
		Muhammad Sadiq Sakin

The Naqshbandiyya-Mujaddidiyya influence in the Pakhtun regions was re-enforced by a second great influence on the twentieth
century Tribal Areas. This was the *madrasa* Darul Ulum Deoband
in Saharanpur in the United Provinces which had been set up by
thinkers both initiated in Naqshbandiyya-Mujaddidiyya *tariqa* and
trained in the Islamic sciences, and who sought to promote Shah
Wali Ullah's teachings. The influence of the *madrasa* on the practice and teaching of Islam in the Tribal Areas was exerted through
students who moved to the Pakhtun north-west after completion of
their training. The son of the Baray Mulla Sahib of Charsadda in
Peshawar District, Abdul Aziz, who came to be known as the Pakhli
Maulvi, was educated in the Darul Ulum Deoband. Fazal Rabbi of
Hazara went to study at Darul Ulum Deoband and then moved to
Peshawar and then to the Tribal Areas after finishing his training.[82]
Taj Muhammad from Mardan who received some religious education and then forged connections with Deoband, became a secondary school teacher in Peshawar Islamia college where he met Haji
Turangzai.[83] The most important of these Pakhtun Deobandis was
Maulana Saifur Rahman, a Pakhtun from Mathra who had studied
in the Darul Ulum Deoband, then moved to teach in a *madrasa* set
up by Obaidullah Sindhi in Fatehpur near Delhi.[84] Saifur Rahman
brought many Pakhtun students to Fatehpur to study with him. In
1914, he returned with these students to his home town of Mathra
in Peshawar District, and then moved on to Mohmand in the Tribal
Areas.[85]

Religious practice had once been dominated by Sufi ritual, enacted
within the arena of the *dargah*. Revivalist influence meant that religious practice was shifting away from Sufi *tariqa* towards a standard

---

82 'Maulvi Fazal Rabbi alias Pakhli Maulvi, March 1922-1923'. OIOC L/
PS/11/217 file 3096.

83 Abdul Ghaffar Khan, *Meri Zindagi aur Jaddo Jehed* (Lahore, n.d.), p. 53.

84 Ibid., p. 60; 'Papers Regarding Recent Activities Among Wahabis, 1916'
OIOC L/PS/11/111.

85 'Papers Regarding Recent Activities Among Wahabis 1916'.

Quranic teaching. The progression of this trend was obvious in Akhund Ghaffur's own family. Akhund Ghaffur's younger son, Miangul Abdul Khaliq, pursued religious learning after the Akhund's death in 1877. He took *bait* at the hand of the Haji Sahib of Beg Manai (a *murid* of Akhund Ghaffur) and devoted himself to study under the Haji Sahib.[86] Anecdotal accounts about Miangul Abdul Khaliq suggest that he was deeply influenced by revivalist thought. He paid *zakat* every year and supported *shaikhs* trained in principles of *shari'a* in order to adjudicate disputes and decide punishments on the basic of scriptural law.[87] Yet he maintained his father's *langarkhana*—the mark of the Sufi *pir*—drawing devotees to him.[88]

Miangul Jahanzeb, great grandson of Akhund Ghaffur who received his earliest religious education under a local *mulla* who taught him the Quran, and then went on to study under a *maulvi* at the Islamia Collegiate School, said that 'the religious tradition from ... the Akhund of Swat, continued by my grandfather, was lost; though the influence deriving from our descent from such a saint and scholar continued.'[89] Accounts of religious pedagogy in the region all note *madrasas* aimed at imparting a formal Quranic education. The centrality of *tariqa* to the pedagogy of the Akhund Ghaffur-Hadda Mulla line began to diminish. Akhund Ghaffur's line was moving out from the teaching of a close and guarded Sufi *tariqa* that could only offer an intercession between the common man and God, towards a revivalist Islam that was being taken from village to village, and person to person. Shahzada Maulvi from Charsadda who visited the Haji Sahib Turangzai in Lakarai in the Tribal Areas claimed to have performed his *bait* and been deputed as a *khalifa* after only a single day of training. His mission as a murid was to 'work for the

---

86 Khan, *The Story of Swat*, p. lxv.

87 Barth, *The Last Wali of Swat*, pp. 23-4.

88 Khan, *The Story of Swat*, p. lxix.

89 Barth, *The Last Wali of Swat*, pp. 16, 33-40.

improvement of society through *amr-bil maruf wa nahi anal munkir* ... and remain involved in the teaching of Islam.'[90]

Like the Hadda Mulla, the Haji Turangzai, Mulla Chaknawar, Sandaki Mulla and Babra Mulla maintained large retinues of *murids*, *talibs* and *khalifas*.[91] Many members of these retinues were armed, and served to enhance the *mulla's* profile, to protect the *mulla*, and often help him enforce his religious directives among the Pakhtun tribes.[92] But it seemed that under the Haji Turangzai at least, *murids* did not necessarily receive long instruction in the intricacies of Sufi *tariqa*. While many *murids* spent years of their lives in the service of the Haji Turangzai during which time they may well have been introduced to Sufi *tariqa* in its complexities, Haji Turangzai also clearly introduced the possibility of *murids* receiving only the initiation in and the obligation to promote simple revivalist principles. This was a distinct shift in the pedagogy of the line from Akhund Ghaffur's time when the Hadda Mulla Najmuddin and Miyan Manki had been required to reside for a number of years with Akhund Ghaffur to receive instruction in both Sufi *tariqa* as well as Shah Wali Ullah's mission.

The *pirimuridi* line had become a vehicle for the dissemination of principles of individualised religious practice derived from Shah Wali Ullah's thought without necessarily also imparting either the full philosphical strucure of Shah Wali Ullah's Naqshbandiyya-Mujadidiyya Sufi thought, or the accompanying systems of Qaderiyya practice that Akhund Ghaffur's *murids* had been initiated in. The *muridi bait* at the hand of his *pir* was still the marker and tool of inclusion into the *pirimuridi* line, but under the influence of Naqshbandiyya-Mujaddidiyya revivalism, the line was expanding rapidly

---

90 Transcript of interview of Shahzada Maulvi with Aziz Javed, Javed, *Haji Sahib Turangzai*, appendix pp. 515-6.

91 Interview Ghulam Nabi Chaknawari, Peshawar, 3 Feb. 2002; Mohmand Political Diaries (henceforth MPD followed by date) 1926; NWFP Provincial Diaries (henceforth NWFPPD followed by date), 1915-21.

92 See MPD 1920-9; NWFPPD, 1915-30; Javed, *Haji Sahib Turangzai*, p. 452. The *mulla's* use of the *lashkar* will be discussed in detail in the last section of this chapter.

and its pedagogy had changed sufficiently to transform the *pir* from a spiritual intermediary to a conductor of and adviser in matters of religious ritual and belief.

This transition was reflected by the fact that by the end of the nineteenth century, titles like *akhund* and *pir* were being supplemented by, and in some cases discarded for, the title '*mulla*'. While this term has pejorative connotations in the contemporary period, it did not seem to have such implication at this time among the tribal Pakhtuns—it was rather used as a catchall term for religious leaders, whether they were *akhunds, sayyids, hazrats, Sufis, sheikhs, miyans* or *faqirs*. I suggest, without putting too fine a point on it, that the transition to the general term '*mulla*' conveyed a transition in religious pedagogy towards a more generalised and dispersed, village-based form of religious practice and emphasis on the individualised model of revivalist Islam.

The Hadda Mulla's line in the Tribal Areas

Although the Hadda Mulla's death and the failure of the 1897-8 mobilisation was followed by the separation of the Tribal Areas, his successors kept the *pirimuridi* fraternity together and brought it to dominate religious organisation in the newly formed administrative region. In 1908, the Sufi Sahib of Butkhak mobilised a *lashkar* of 5,000 Mohmands in an attack on Shabqadar, the British-occupied fort on the border with the administered districts. The *lashkar* included 2,000 Mohmands from the Afghan side of the border, and was supported by the Mir Sayyid Jan Badshah of Islampur in Kunar, the Sarkanri Miyan, the Sartor Faqir, the Miyan Sahib of Tsappri, and Mulla Sayyid Akbar. It was said that the *lashkar* had been primarily encouraged by elements at the Afghan court who hoped to compromise the British position and secure concessions from the colonial government.[93] But the Mohmands later used their participation to impress their importance upon the colonial government

---

93 Note, 21 May 1908, in 'Frontier disturbances, diary of events, April-May 1908'. OIOC L/PS/18/A 167.

and secure tribal recognition and allowances in their own right. This effort by the Hadda Mulla's supporters and devotees addressed regional autonomy and organisation in a new way—seeking to enter and not to undermine the new order of the Tribal Areas.

The vague motives and quick withdrawal of support from Afghanistan meant that this short-lived mobilisation marked the last major movement by the Hadda Mulla's contemporaries and direct accomplices. The heavy losses sustained by the *lashkar* had perhaps impressed upon the religious figures and the participating clans that this was a futile and dangerous endeavour. The British response had not been trifling—2 cavalry and artillery units and 2,600 soliders had met the Mohmand advance, out of a total field force of almost 13,000 men.[94]

The Hadda Mulla's efforts to undermine Abdur Rahman's authority and British encroachment in the north-west had dominated his political efforts through his lifetime. His successors refined his agenda to continue to revitalise religion and purge Pakhtun society of un-Islamic practices, but to do so having recognised the British design of the Tribal Areas and the tribal reliance on colonial allowances. The *mullas* integrated their mission with the now pervasive idea that communities of the Tribal Areas were socially and culturally distinct. Haji Turangzai who had been deeply involved in providing religious training through the establishment of 150 *madrasas* in the administered districts of the North-West Frontier Province abandoned his land and commitments in the administered areas to move to the Tribal Areas in 1914. He, along with his *pirimuridi* 'brothers', the Babra Mulla, the Sandaki Mulla and the Mulla Chaknawar as well as many other less known *mullas*, lived out the rest of their lives in the service of Tribal Areas Pakhtun society.[95]

---

94 'Frontier disturbances', appendix B composition of columns and appendix C composition of the Malakand Field Force.

95 Javed, *Haji Sahib Turangzai*; Interview Dr Ahmed Yousuf, 14 Feb. 2002, Interview Senator Ghulam Nabi Chaknawari, 3 Feb. 2002.

3

RELIGIOUS AUTHORITY AND
THE PAKHTUN CLANS

Analysis of social leadership in Pakhtun tribal communities began with the political anthropologist Frederik Barth's work, which was ground breaking for its systematic consideration of tribal interrelations and oppositions. Barth's analysis of the ancestrally derived tribal line resulted in his hypothesis that Sufis or 'saints' were 'outsiders' to the Pakhtun *jirga*-style political assemblies and asserted no political power there.[1] Subsequent anthropological and historical studies of Pakhtun political relationships were strongly affected by his compelling appraisal of the cultural order of human and collective social action represented as the 'segmentary lineage theory' to explain the social and political rivalries that dominated through the region. But in accepting his theory wholesale, resarchers have maintained Barth's extrapolation that individuals who were not participant in the tribal genealogy were not significant members of tribal society. [2] Akbar Ahmed suggests that the actual structure of the tribe did not involve religious authority in any form except in opportunist seizure of power in situations where 'traditional' *maliki* authority weakened.[3]

---

1 Frederik Barth, *Political Leadership among Swat Pakhtuns* (London, 1965), p. 17.

2 The most important of these is Christine Noelle's unequalled work on the history of *State and Tribe in Afghanistan*, p. 155. See also Louis Dupree, 'Tribal Warfare in Afghanistan and Pakistan: A Reflection of the Segmentary Lineage System' In Akbar Ahmed and David Hart, *Islam in Tribal Societies* (London, 1984), and Cherry Lindholm, 'The Swat Pakhtun Family as a Political Training Ground' in Charles Lindholm *Frontier Perspectives* (Karachi, 1996).

3 Akbar S. Ahmed, 'Tribe and State in Waziristan'. in Richard Tapper (ed.),

Christensen's work on the late nineteenth-century north-west frontier suggests that religious leadership was inspired by millenarian sentiments and opportunistic motives and completely separate from and opposed to 'secular authority' in the region.[4]

These understandings of history and society, reliant on oral and transcribed genealogies which described homogeneous clans and tribes of communities descended from a common mythical forefather Qais Abdur Rashid, cannot accommodate the membership of *mullas* in Pakhtun society as their participation was functional and not genealogical. By such reasoning, reinforced by the fact that organisation of the *silsila* and *shajarah* were rooted in separate myths of lineage, systems of representation and sources of patronage, *mullas* have been understood to have been a mere 'clients' of the tribal system and incidental to its functioning. Yet in the space of the non-administered Tribal Areas, religious practice, deeply influenced by Naqshbandiyya-Mujaddidiyya revivalism and the village and community-based activities of the *mullas*, gives little evidence of real distinctions between tribal social organisation and motivation, and the activities of the *mullas*. *Mullas* participated in village based community living: trading, interacting and inter-marrying within the clan unit. In almost all cases *mullas* were ethnically Pakhtun, and in many cases were originally from the clan that they served.

It is difficult to reconcile the moral and judicial authority of the *mullas* with the more 'secular' council or *jirga* that heard cases and punished the guilty on similar points of conduct if secular authority and religious authority are considered in opposition to each other. They must be understood as concurrent and overlapping realms that turned to each other for legitimisation. The *mulla* was participant in the tribal *jirga* and was often asked to dispense justice on the basis of the established

---

The Conflict of Tribe and State in Iran and Afghanistan (London, 1983).

4 R. O. Christensen, 'introduction', in McMahon, *Report on the Tribes of Dir, Swat and Bajour together with the Utman-Khel and Sam Ranizai* (Peshawar, 1981).

and indisputable principles of *shari'a*.[5] The village *mulla* was participant in *maliki* and *jirga* management as he would attend *jirgas*, read prayers before, and finally approve the decisions of a *jirga* at the conclusion of a meeting. He was open to affect the decision making process and offer advice according to his assessment. The *mulla* could also himself initiate proceedings against an individual or suggest strategy towards other clans or the British by approaching the *malik* and clan *jirga*. Real distinctions between *maliki* and *mulla* authority are hard to identify, undermining the thesis that these were essentially conflicting and competing forms of authority. In an equitable exchange of support, *mullas* confirmed *maliki* authority and the institutional integrity of the *jirga* while the *maliks* legitimised the *mulla's* directives.

Religious authority affirmed and strengthened the structures and coalescences of the tribal structure in the politics of clan-tribe representation to the colonial authorities as well, demonstrating their engagement with not only community practices but with the contemporary discourse and representation of the tribe.[6] In addition, the long standing relationship between the Kabul court and the *maliks* of the eastern Pakhtun regions fostered the engagement of *mullas* with the tribal structure. The amirate would use *mullas* to rally the eastern Pakhtun clans. *Mullas* would identify the leaders of communities, the *maliks*, and send them ahead to Kabul, Jalalabad or Kandahar as re-

---

5 Kasuri, *Mushahidat*, p. 55. Kasuri claims the *mulla* was head of the village council—a claim not substantiated by any other accounts. His description makes at least this much clear: that the *mulla* was a fully integrated member of the village or clan-level council although he was not considered to be a blood member of the tribe itself.

6 In several instances, *mullas* helped try to secure good terms of 'settlement' between the clan and the Political Agent. In one case the Faqir of Alingar wrote to the Political Officer Mohmand on 'behalf' of the Safi clan to allay tensions between the community and the authorities and to secure allowances for them. In a different sort of case, Mulla Mahmud Akhunzada started a massive campaign against the Shia Orakzai to punish them for asking the Deputy Commissioner Peshawar for territorial recognition and allowances as a tribe, trying to prevent them, as Shias and as adversaries of his own favoured clans, from getting this status. The Mulla Mahmud Akhunzada's movement against the Shia Orakzai is discussed in greater detail in chapter 5.

quired to receive instructions and allowances, thereby strengthening both the profile and the finances of the *maliks*. *Mullas* were not capable of undermining the social hierarchies and structures of tribal existence, as has been pointed out by many anthropologists, but it is important to note that they did not seek to do so.

Mullas of the Akhund Ghaffur-Hadda Mulla line saw themselves as culturally engaged with Pakhtun society and participant in *pakhtun-wali*, the unwritten cultural code of Pakhtun tribesmen that held the preservation of honour and exacting of revenge as its primary social principles. The mutual affirmation, influence and constraining of the *mullas* and Pakhtun tribal culture lay in the fact that *mullas* acted as custodians of *pakhtunwali*, and used their religious authority to pass binding judgements rooted in *pakhtunwali* in the arena of the tribal *jirga*.[7] 'Islamic inclinations and Pakhtun culture' came together in the definition and management of honour, crime, and morality.[8] In situations where murder had been committed, *mullas* would oversee the payment of blood money or put the murderers to death on the spot, as required under the tribal code.[9] It should be noted that while the payment of blood money had historically been practiced in Muslim societies other than the frontier and was a generally accepted point of *shari'a*, the *mullas* advocated and supported many other uniqely tribal customs as long as they were not expressly forbidden in the Quran, or *hadith*. One important example of such a practice was the burning of the house and possessions of criminal offenders. In one particular instance, a murder committed by a member of the Gullai Mohmand clan undermined the truce that had been crafted by the Haji Turang-zai. In response, Haji Turangzai raised a *lashkar* to burn down houses

---

7 This synchronicity has been examined by Nawid in *Religious Responses*, p. 98 and Akbar S. Ahmed in 'Religious Presence and Symbolism in Pakhtun Society', Akbar Ahmed and David Hart (eds), *Islam in Tribal Societies* (London, 1984).

8 Muhammad Dawi, an Afghan writer and poet, about the Mulla Sahib Chaknawar. Syal, *Nomyali Ghazi*, p. 48.

9 In 1923 the Karbogha Mulla oversaw the execution of Wattizai murderers of members of the Koedad Khel clan. See NWFPPD, May 1923.

in the Gullai village and applied a fine that was payable by the clan as a whole.[10]

Despite this balancing of religious and cultural principles, and *mulla* and *maliki* authority, tensions did often arise where the application of religious precept by the *mulla* and the cultural practices preferred by the community could not be reconciled. In one case Mulla Babra demanded the execution of alleged rapists, but his proposed punishment was rejected by one of the clans involved.[11] In many other instances, when the *mullas* of the Hadda Mulla line enforced points of social reform ordained under *amr bil maruf* such as eliminating the payment of bride-price and forbidding dancing boys at weddings, the *mullas'* punishments were very unpopular and strongly criticised. These tussles between religious and cultural interpreters could go either way, depending on the resources and persuasiveness of the particular *mulla* involved and there were instances where clans entirely rejected the directives of *mullas*. But it is incorrect to extrapolate that in such situations Islam retreated from the mainframe of society. Religious leadership was not merely spontaneous and opportunistic—the *mullas'* authority and agendas emerged from the social and political circumstances of the twentieth century Tribal Areas and were sustained by the combined will and efforts of the *mullas* themselves. In situations where their directives were contested, the *mullas*, like all other groups in the Tribal Areas, fought fiercely to protect their interests—sometimes succeeding and sometimes failing. But the reality of the *mullas'* participation in village and tribal life remained and underlay the relevance and impact of the Hadda Mulla's *pirimuridi* line to politics and society in the twentieth century Tribal Areas.

The mullas' authority and village-based religious practice

The Mulla Chaknawar's son emphasised that the village *masjid* was the primary basis for social participation by the Hadda Mulla's

---

10 NWFPPD, 9 March 1918.
11 NWFPPD, diary 32 1915.

murids in Pakhtun tribal community life, saying: '*masjids* had a very important role in the movement—this is where Pakhtun culture and Islamic culture met.'[12] It was as managers and maintainers of *masjid*, leaders of congregational prayers and commentators on questions of scripture that *mullas* claimed a place and stake within the homogeneous and insular clan unit. Their daily functions and places of residence were in the *masjid*, and their income was from religious alms giving in the *masjid* and from produce from the lands attached to that structure.

It was through the institution of the *masjid* and its attached *langarkhana* or almshouse that the Haji Sahib Turangzai was able to settle in the Tribal Areas and to forge a relationship with the independent Pakhtun clans. When the Haji moved to the Tribal Areas in 1915, he toured the frontier and had several offers from villages in need of *mullas* for their *masjids*.[13] He ultimately accepted an offer from the Safi Mohmands to move to Lakarai to manage the old Gud Mulla's *masjid*.[14] The Haji later accepted lands from the Safi Mohmands—an estate he named Ghaziabad—placing him outside the limits of the Safi villages and according him some autonomy of status, however he maintained a presence in village *masjids* of the Mohmands, visiting these regularly and even establishing a new *masjid* in Gandab in 1918 in order to establish a connection with the Halimzai Mohmand clans in this area.[15] Similarly, the Mulla Chaknawar built a *masjid* and established a *langarkhana* at Lalpura and Dakka,[16] then built one at Sorab in Gandab.[17] He kept a close eye on the maintenance and management of the *masjids*, providing

12 Interview Senator Ghulam Nabi Chaknawari, Peshawar, 3 Feb. 2002.

13 Javed, *Haji Sahib Turangzai*, p. 251.

14 'Haji Sahib of Turangzai and his Connections in Tribal Territory'. NWFP Provincial Archives (hereafter NWFPPA) Special Branch, file 979.

15 Javed, *Haji Sahib Turangzai*, p. 278.

16 Khyber Political Diary (hereafter KPD), 10 June 1922.

17 'Diaries and Reports on the Mulla Chaknawar's Activities 1924-7'. in NWFPPA, files of the Deputy Commisioner's Office Peshawar (henceforth DCOP) 'Miscellaneous Reports and Diaries 1924-7'.

money for their upkeep, and closely monitoring the subordinate *mullas* in charge of these interests.

The *mullas'* social participation was deeply dependent on the patronage of Pakhtun clans. Without guaranteed independent sources of income or claims to land, *mullas* needed their host clans to invite them to live in their villages and pledge monetary support as well as guarantee to protect the *masjids* and their *mullas* against attack or robbery.[18] But the *mullas'* management of this space also meant that they were in charge of a functional, inclusive and vibrant arena of male village life which gave them authority and power over its members. Relevance of the *masjid* to daily life in the village was great because of the daily and weekly communal prayers performed at the *masjid*. Worshippers would remain to eat at the *langarkhana* and would meet visitors and exchange news in the *hujra*. The *masjid* and its parts constituted a social space within the village.[19] Maintaining the *hujra* and making provisions for meals for guests were the direct responsibility of the *mullas* and the funds for this came out of their own budgets.[20] Host villages were expected to provide a quantity of food, but making up a shortfall fell to the *mullas* who extended hospitality to all worshippers.[21]

---

18 Pashto folklore tells of faqirs and *mullas* who claimed seats at village mosques, and received food and clothes after proving their spiritual powers. See F. H. Maylon, 'Story of the Tirah Faqir', *Pushto Folk Stories* (London, 1911, reprint Islamabad, 1980).

19 Makhdum Tasadduz Ahmad explains that every Yusufzai village had a mosque, and every *masjid* had a *hujra*. His descriptions relate particularly to the Yusufzai of Swat, but hold true across Malakand and Mohmand. In *Social Organization of Yusufzai Swat* (Lahore, 1962).

20 Aziz Javed describes the *langarkhana* as being an absolute prerequisite to the mobilization of and political authority over the Pakhtun peoples. He argues that in order to bring tribesmen together and to reach a political consensus among them, they had to be brought to one central location and housed and fed there. *Haji Sahib Turangzai*, p. 46.

21 Aziz Javed notes that the abundance of the Haji Turangzai's *langar* was a point of prestige. *Haji Sahib Turangzai*, p. 46. Muhammad Ali Kasuri's very important account of his travels in the frontier Tribal Areas describes the food he was fed at the Haji Turangzai's *langarkhana* in Chamarkand in great detail

Frequent congregation within its domain meant that the *masjid* was also a location for the exchange of information, stories, rumours or more general gossip.[22] This sort of exchange was made more significant by the fact that information was hard to come by in the Tribal Areas. A combination of social and administrative segregation and difficult terrain meant that newspapers were rare. In addition, few Pakhtun residents of the Tribal Areas could read well enough in Pashtu, leave alone Urdu or English, to make sense of newspapers when they did see them. *Mullas* on the other hand were often both able to read Urdu and Pashtu, and were well placed to receive bearers of news through networks of *murids* and travellers who were sent or directed to them by colleagues in Afghanistan and India. The Mulla Powindah was said to run his own *dak* network between '*faqirs* of the Mahsud clans, the *raees* of Khost, and the cities of Lahore and Peshawar', while the Haji Turangzai's son maintained a more informal system of sending and receiving messages through travellers,[23] ensuring reliable communications with colleagues. Other *mullas*, including the Haji Turangzai, Mulla Chaknawar and Mulla Babra were part of *tabligh* networks, passing regularly from village to village within the Tribal Areas, the administered districts and Afghanistan, and bringing news back with them to their host villages.[24] In addition, newspapers received from Afghanistan and India like the *Sirajul Akhbar*, *Zamindar*, *Al Hilal*, *Pioneer* and *Soul*[25] would be

---

and explains the importance of the *mulla's mehmandari*. *Mushahidat*, p. 47. Also see Miyan Akbar Shah, *Azadi Ki Talash* (Islamabad, 1989), p. 57.

22 Martin Sokefeld describes 'gossip' as one of the primary indicators of the tenuousness of colonial control in his study of the Chitral region, 'Rumours and Politics on the Northern Frontier: The British, Pakhtun Wali and Yaghestan', *Modern Asian Studies* 36, 2 (2002), pp. 299-340'.

23 'Diary Book of Frontier Constabulary Mir Hamzah 1922/23'. NWFPPA, Special Branch file 459.

24 Hakim Muhammad Karim, the son of Haji Sahib Turangzai's Khalifa Hakim Muhammad Abdul Ahad, said that much of Haji Turangzai's time was spent either going on '*doras*' (preaching missions) or receiving travelers on *doras* themselves. Transcript of interview appendix to *Haji Sahib Turangzai*, p. 514.

25 Kasuri, *Mushahidat*, p. 53.

read out in *masjids*,[26] and travellers would bring their stories there. Carrying news into the Tribal Areas was dangerous. Anybody caught delivering letters to or carrying letters or newspapers from the Tribal Areas to British India, or *vice versa*, was suspected of aiding the anti-British movement there and subject to arrest.[27] But there was a great demand for news—about on-going wars, the nationalist movement in India, colonial governance, and intrigue at the Afghan *darbar*, and events across the Tribal Areas.[28] There was little discrimination over the sources of information. Gossip and rumour were reported with the same authority as substantiated news and the teller assumed the right to embellish his reports, such as those of German advances, garnished with the declaration that the Turks were coming to liberate India and that all of Germany had embraced Islam.[29]

As the administration in Peshawar made the delivery of news-papers more difficult in order not to 'ignite' the sensibilities of the volatile frontier population during and after the years of the First World War, the value of information and the importance of the bearers of news only increased. When Muhammad Ali Kasuri, who travelled to the Tribal Areas in 1919-20, led the prayers and gave a *vaz* or sermon on the occasion of the eid prayers when he arrived in Chamarkand, he claimed that people came 'in great numbers, walking many miles' to hear him speak because they knew he was going to bring 'news of the situation in India, and the war'.[30]

When the religious congregation gathered, it received both spiritual and political tuition. Channelling outside information that impacted on local opinion and decision-making, the *masjid* was at once

---

26 NWFPPD 1915-7 contain frequent mentions of the dissemination of 'hostile propaganda' in *masjids* in the frontier.

27 Note on arrest of Shahzada Barkatulla's messenger in 'Chamarkand Colony 1936'. NWFPPA, Political Officer Mohmand, file 46.

28 The *Sirajul Akhbar*, *Zamindar* and *Sarhad* were the most popular newspapers being sent to Tribal Areas.

29 NWFPPD, 1914-8.

30 Kasuri, *Mushahidat*, p. 48.

a spiritual centre and a political vehicle. The *mullas'* main socially interactive and authoritative function extended their pedagogic role to the discussion and representation of political issues. Because the religious congregation demanded political direction and information, *mullas*, as leaders of congregations, were in positions to comment on issues of particular interest, and were encouraged to do so. Hence they could use the traditional Friday sermon to comment on the content of news and its implications for the local population, and to push an agenda in relation to the Afghan and British governments as well as local powers.

By virtue of their roles as caretakers of *masjids* and—by extrapolation—of village religious practice, *mullas* also had the ability to excommunicate members of the clan from the religious community on moral grounds. They could refuse to allow transgressors to participate in prayers in the *masjid*, refuse to perform a *nikah* or death rites for such transgressors, and could insist that anybody seen to have relations of any sort with them, whether personal or even commercial, would have to endure the same fate.[31] Ostracism was swift and absolute, and was rarely challenged on the threat of further punishment. The son of the Mulla Chaknawar explained:

Removal from society [was a terrible punishment] ... because the transgressor would for ever live alone. If someone died in his family no one else could help him bury [the dead]. If there was a wedding no one would attend. If anyone did attend he would be ostracised as well. [The ostracised] would not be treated as a member of society, [and would eventually seek forgiveness] because he could not live comfortably within the Tribal Areas without such a reconciliation.[32]

A traveller through the 1920s Tribal Areas described an incident when a renowned *malik* of a Bajauri clan died. Haji Sahib Turangzai was invited to perform the *janaza* which the *khan* of the neighbouring Jar clan could not attend because he and his clan had been ostracised

---

31 Interview Ghulam Nabi Chaknawari, Peshawar, 8 Feb. 2002; Kasuri, *Mushahidat*, p. 53.

32 Ibid.

by the Haji Sahib. The *khan* used the occasion to beg the Haji Sahib's forgiveness and promised never to cross him again, whereupon he was allowed to attend the *janaza* and once again freely mingle with other clans.[33]

Religious excommunication also meant that *mullas* would refuse to conduct political negotiations on behalf of 'wrongdoers'. In cases where entire clans were shunned, as was Malik Anmir's Gandab Halimzai clan in 1927, they would have no access to the arbitration and reparations system in effect through the *mullas*. If the village was raided or attacked, *mullas* would not effect a return or compensation for property lost or damaged.[34]

The level of interdependence of society made religious excommunication a particularly brutal punishment. There was no life for the Pakhtun clansman in the Tribal Areas outside the clan system. Personal safety as well as access to roads, water, oil, food and help were provided through the tribal system and found with difficulty outside it. Clans and villages in the Tribal Areas were religiously homogeneous, a feature of society that required all members to participate in the established rituals of religion. The religious community that the *mulla* directly influenced was, by definition, the entirety of male society. Hence the *mullas'* spiritual authority translated into social control that, because it encompassed all publicly active members of the clan, was far-reaching.[35]

---

33 Shah, *Azadi ki Talash*, p. 58.

34 The Halimzai stand off against the Malik Muhasil Kuda Khel, a *malik* strongly supported by Haji Sahib, was strongly criticized by the Haji Sahib. When they Halimzais wished to make terms with Malik Muhasil, they had to go through the Babra Mulla because the Haji Sahib would not hear their case. The Babra Mulla then refused to intervene on behalf of Malik Anmir which resulted in a continuation of the hostilities for months and no compensation being won by Malik Anmir. NWFPPD, January-Feb. 1915.

35 The relationship of the mulla to the *masjid*, and of the *masjid* to public male society was not, of course, restricted to the Tribal Areas. This was a reality in any Muslim community, whatever its administrative state, whether Pakhtun or otherwise. This section considers the relevance of excommunication from that public space given the particular administrative circumstances of the

The mullas *and tribal inter-relations*

The dispersed clans and tribes that made up the Tribal Areas were largely independent of each other. Subsistence-level agriculture in the villages meant that there were few integrated markets and social interactions, including marriage, were restricted by tribal genealogy. Polities were at the same time closely connected by resources such as land, water and roads.[36] Tensions created by geographic proximity coupled with social and economic confinement gave rise to a complex system of inter-village and inter-tribal relationships marked by intense competitions between clans, even those of the same lineage, which often turned violent and sparked blood feuds that could go on for generations. Cultural concern with the defence of honour underlay these tensions. Neglecting to avenge the death of a kinsman was to lose face permanently, and suggest to other tribes that the clan was unable to defend itself. No participant in a feud could ever afford to lay down his weapon when he was in the inferior position—such cowardice would have been an unacceptable and dangerous admission of weakness. This meant however that the cycle of violence between what were often neighbouring villages could potentially last for ever, bringing all commercial and productive activity to a halt until all male members of both kinship groups had been eliminated. In the interests of progress and the preservation of life, opposing parties would enter into brokered 'truces' to halt feuds without losing face. In the situation that the opposing clans were from the same tribe, they might have recourse to a common *jirga*. But more often than not, the only arbitrator acceptable to two opposed parties was a *mulla*.

Tribal Areas.

36   Leon Poullada, drawing on 1950s and 1960 anthropological literature, names women as another of these 'competition generating' resources. However, the utility of this suggestion is limited as the later anthropological theory can hardly be corroborated from early twentieth-century colonial and Afghan sources. See Leon B. Poullada, *Reform and Rebellion in Afghanistan 1919-1929* (Ithaca, NY, 1973), p. 23.

Once a *mulla* had accepted and been accepted at a *masjid*, he and his successors were deeply attached to the tribe with which they were affiliated. This primary relationship, generally handed down from *pir* to *murid*, connected certain lineages of *pirs* to particular clans, and often led *piri* families to marry into the communities they served.[37] But despite their greater commitment to their host clans, *mullas* prided themselves on, and were recognised for, their political neutrality and primary commitment to upholding *shari'a*. They maintained affiliations with villages and clans other than their hosts either as visiting preachers or through the *pirimuridi* fraternity. This meant that *mullas* could command authority over different clans, even if these clans were at odds with one another, and they tended to be acceptable arbitrators to all concerned parties in situations where truces needed to be created between warring parties, or reparations exacted from criminal offenders. Religious renown was, as an early traveller to the Tribal Areas, Miyan Akbar Shah, described it, 'no less than a passport to all of *Yaghistan* and Afghanistan'.[38] Haji Turangzai worked directly in Mohmand villages and Shinwari villages in Bajaur, but through the *pirimuridi* network made appearances in Afridi areas, Swat Yusufzai villages, and Dir. Mulla Sahib Babra was primarily active among the Mamunds in Charmung, and the Chaknawar Mulla had influence over most Mohmand and some Shinwari clans. The Faqir of Alingar, based in Alingar, was primarily influential among the Shinwaris, but made appearances among the Yusufzai and Mohmands as well.

Miyan Akbar Shah's memoirs of his travels through the frontier described the violence of blood feuds and the agency of *mullas* in resolving them. His entry into Doburjon in Bajaur was met with the chilling spectacle of streets empty of men; here, it was said, men did not die natural deaths—they died by the bullet of an enemy. So terrible was the enmity that whenever fighting broke out, the Haji Sahib would be summoned immediately to create a *tigah* or truce

---

37 Interview Ghulam Nabi Chaknawari, Peshawar, 3 Feb. 2002.
38 Shah, *Azadi ki Talash*, p. 60.

between the hostile parties, and until that time every man would remain hidden in his house to avoid being the next casualty.[39] In such roles *mullas* were facilitators and pivots of inter-group and inter-personal relations in the Tribal Areas, essential to the maintenance of normalcy.

Most prominent *mullas* of the twentieth-century Tribal Areas were documented as having spent significant amounts of their time travelling to scenes of disputes, and offering binding solutions to the parties involved.[40] Haji Turangzai spent a majority of his time travelling from village to village through Mohmand and Bajaur effecting new settlements and patching up old ones between Mohmand factions.[41] The various groups involved were constrained to accept his decisions, whatever they might be, and would enter into pacts to that effect before he would even hear the cases.[42] Then the disputes would be presented, the transgressors identified, and suitable compensation for the wronged parties decided.[43]

In situations where random and sporadic fighting was taking place between two rival factions, *mullas* had a slightly different role. Rather than merely ascertaining who was to blame and fining the guilty party, they would set terms for a cease-fire, mapping the boundaries between villages, and systems for access to shared resources such as water. Finally they would decide an amount payable as a fine by ei-

---

39 Ibid., p. 56.

40 NWFPPD, 1915-30, specifically note the diplomatic initiatives of Mulla Mahmud Akhunzada and Mulla Sayyid Akbar among the Afridis, Mulla Fazal Din in Waziristan and the Babra Mulla, Mulla Chaknawar, Sandaki Mulla, and Haji Sahib Turangzai in Malakand Bajaur and Mohmand. Mentions are made of several lesser known *mullas*, but these were invariably connected with the better known *mullas*.

41 MPD, 1923.

42 Interview Ghulam Nabi Chaknawari, Peshawar, 8 Feb. 2002.

43 The office of the Chief Commissioner NWFP reported Mulla Mahmud Akhunzada's involvement in brokering a truce and deciding the amount of blood money that had to be paid to the family of a murdered Aka Khel Afridi. Later Mulla Mahmud also brokered a truce between Kambar Khel and Malikdin Khel. NWFPPD 1915-6.

ther party breaking the peace. These cease-fires had a limited life and had to be reviewed, renewed and patched up periodically, demanding a long-term engagement and that the *mulla* be familiar with the situation. Haji Sahib Turangzai, who brokered the cease-fire and truce between the Yusufzai and Kandahari Mohmands, was expected to oversee its effectiveness and re-establish the truce when it was broken.[44]

It was almost impossible for opposing factions to approach each other through any other means than *mulla*-led arbitration. The inclusion of only some clans in the British system of regulation meant that political agents could not be effective arbitrators within the region. Hence even those tribes who accepted British allowances and had refused *mullas* who had advocated opposition to the British, were dependent on the same *mullas* to initiate dialogue with clans outside the allowance system.[45] This dependency on *mullas* as arbitrators was so great that when the village of Utmanzai in the administered districts was raided by Mohmands from the Tribal Areas, the citizens of Utmanzai opened negotiations through the Haji Sahib Turangzai who secured the return of their stolen sheep.[46] In the most dramatic instance of recognition of religious authority, Colonel Bruce of the Indian army contacted Mulla Mahmud Akhunzada when a British girl, Molly Ellis, was abducted by Ajab Khan, an Afridi. Without any other means of opening a dialogue with the captors, Colonel Bruce asked the Mulla to arrange a meeting between British representatives and Ajab Khan who was a devotee of Mulla Mahmud, so that a settlement could be reached and the girl released unharmed.[47] The negotiations, which were conducted at Mulla Mahmud's home,

---

44 MPD, 1926.

45 NWFPPD, 20 Jan. 1916.

46 The Burhan Khel asked Haji Turangzai to force the Isa Khel to return their stolen sheep. MPD, 3 May 1924.

47 Interview Naik Muhammad Ghazizuay, son of Ajab Khan Afridi, 10 Aug. 2002. A copy of the letter from Colonel Bruce is in the possession of Naik Muhammad Ghazizuay. Molly Ellis' kidnapping is discussed in greater detail in chapter 6.

established that the *mulla* was the only reliable and universally accepted agent of diplomacy between the Pakhtun clans.[48]

The position of the *mulla* was guaranteed by the fact that there was no other form of inter-party organisation or government. The son of Chaknawar mulla described what this meant:

> In Afghanistan there was an existing *hukumat*. But in the *ilaqa-yi ghair* there were no police, no influence of state. It all went by the *rivaj* of the nation and the man and the *mullas*. There were internal oppositions—enmities and friendships—but they all accepted the decision of the *mulla*.[49]

In the absence of a government, there were no institutionalised legal or political systems in the frontier Tribal Areas. British political agents and Afghan authorities each had some authority over some tribes, but because no single authority extended over the different groups and their interactions in the Tribal Areas, these administrators could not arbitrate between clans—even informally. It was this power vacuum that the *mullas* were able to fill. The condition of the tribe, defined by and relegated to the non-administered region, necessitated the involvement of the *mullas*.

Unanimity among the mullas

Coherence and unity of the *pirimuridi* fraternity of *mullas* evoked a practical solidarity between *mullas*. This was expressed in regular conferences between *mullas* about their religious and diplomatic activities on behalf of their tribes in order that they could maintain a consistent approach among themselves. Regular meetings of *mullas* took place at Hadda and Jalalabad in eastern Afghanistan.[50] In a few cases this consultation was aimed at deciding on a standard

---

48 Interview Ghulam Muhammad Din of Gandab Halimzai, 13 Aug. 2002.

49 Interview Senator Ghulam Nabi Chaknawari, Peshawar 8 Feb. 2002.

50 NWFPPD 1914-30 have frequent mentions of congregations of *mullas* meeting at Hadda or at the Chamarkand base. Some of these are as follows: 3 April 1915, 29 Jan. 1916, *jirgas* for regional *mullas* held at Hadda; 28 Oct. 1916, Haji Turangzai issues a *firman* calling for support to the Turkish Caliphate at a *jirga* in Hadda.

punishment for collaborators with the British who undermined the interests of other tribes or clans.[51] In another case, when the Mulla Chaknawar had failed to prevent the Musa Khel Mohmand clan from accepting British allowances, a meeting was convened to support him and advise him on a future course of action.[52] Even the Haji Turangzai reluctantly supported Mulla Mahmud Akhunzada's political directives which he disagreed with in the interests of maintaining indisputable religious authority. The *mullas'* belief in their unanimity was demonstrated on an occasion when the Babra Mulla was unable to attend a large *jirga* meeting of Mohmands at Bagh at which he was expected and so trusted Haji Turangzai to appear in his stead to hear and decide the grievances of the Mohmand clans.[53] This sort of organisation meant that the *mullas* were more than a group of loosely connected leaders—they were a coherent and self-aware leadership group whose internal cohesion was understood to be crucial to its success.

Location affected the way in which *mullas* organised, and there were stronger and more consistent exchanges of information and agenda between those *mullas* in closer proximity to one another. The Lala Pir of Khost met more regularly with the Mulla Powindah and Mulla Hamzullah in Waziristan than with the Mohmand and Bajaur *mullas*;[54] and similarly Mulla Sayyid Akbar in Tirah met regularly with Mulla Mahmud and other Tirah *mullas*, working with them on the resolution of local disputes and punishments for Afridis.[55] In Swat, Bajaur and Mohmand the Mulla Sandaki, the Mulla Babra,

---

51 NWFPPD, 22 July 1916.

52 The *jirga* of *mullas* advised the Mulla Chaknawar not to worry, and not to try to punish the Musa Khels and suggested that he instead use *amr-bil maruf* to influence the Musa Khel's behaviour in 'Diaries and Reports on the Mulla Chaknawar'. NWFPPA, DCOP, Miscellaneous Diaries and Reports 1924-7.

53 'Confidential Mohmand Reports 1915-16'. NWFPPA, Political Officer Mohmand, file 106.

54 Lala Pir calls for unity in *jihad*. NWFPPD, 18 March 1916, and NWFPPD, 19 Feb. 1916.

55 KPD, 26 May 1923.

Mulla Chaknawar and Haji Sahib Turangzai formed the primary nexus between themselves.[56] Within their respective regions, *mullas* maintained the coherence of the wider *pirimuridi* fraternity, either reconciling or excommunicating those who differed from the Hadda group's interpretations in the manner that the Lala Pir had forcibly reconciled the antagonistic Mulla Hamzullah and Mulla Powindah to one another,[57] and that Mulla Sandaki excommunicated Sayyid Abdul Jabbar Shah in Swat on the basis of an accusation that he was secretly a Qadiyani.[58]

The *mullas*' unanimity extended to their interests in regional politics. The Haji Turangzai's support of the Khan of Nawegai was taken up by his *pirimuridi* brothers. When the Mulla Chaknawar threatened to start a campaign of house burnings when the Musa Khel *jirga* refused to take his advice regarding British policy, he was promised complete moral support from Haji Sahib Turangzai, Mulla Sandaki and Mulla Babra who committed to applying pressure on the Musa Khels to force them to come to an appropriate understanding with the Mulla Chaknawar.[59] In one case the Faqir of Alingar, *murid* of the Sandaki Mulla, called repeatedly for a mobilisation against the British at a time when the Haji Turangzai was not willing to agree to it. The Haji advised him against the *jihad*, going so far as to refuse him help.[60] When the Faqir finally decided to undertake an attack on the British at Shabqadar on his own, the Haji joined it at the last minute, despite his misgivings.[61] The *mullas* chose to present a unified political front, as was made clear by group attendance of Mo-

---

56 Javed, *Haji Sahib Turangzai*; Kasuri, *Mushahidat*; The Haji Turangzai, Babra Mulla and Sandaki Mulla jointly sent out letters to encourage *jihad*. NWFPPD, 24 March 1917.

57 The Mulla Hamzullah was the Mulla Powindah's *pir*, but differences had arisen between them. Reported in *Who's Who NWFP, 1914.*

58 'Letter from Mulla Sandakay to Haji Turangzai and other Maliks and Mullas in NWFP'. Reproduced in NWFPPD, 24 March 1917.

59 'Diaries and Reports on the Mulla Chaknawar'.

60 NWFPPA, DCOP, Mohmand Reports 1915-16; MPD 1927, pp. 6-7.

61 MPD, 1927, pp. 6-7.

hmand, Afridi, Swat and Bajaur *mullas* at the amir of Afghanistan's *jirga* at Jalalabad in 1923,[62] then again in 1929.[63]

Lesser *mullas* competed for the support of and affiliation to more charismatic and powerful personalities who could greatly increase their own status and the more prominent *mullas* used their influence to back up weaker members of the line.[64] The most dramatic example of this was in 1915 when the Gujjar Mulla was killed by the Dir Levy forces and the Sandaki Mulla and Haji Turangzai led a *lashkar* of 3,000 men to confront the Dir levies and avenge his death.[65] This sort of mutual support was central to maintaining the relevance and importance of any one religious leader within the greater Tribal Areas. Drawing on internal consensus and solidarity, *mullas* within the line tried to support each other's directives in order that if excommunicated by one *mulla*, a clan was left without access to the dominant religious order of the frontier. During a time when the Halimzai Mohmand clan was ostracised by the Haji Turangzai, his decree that it was forbidden for any religious services to be performed in the Halimzai villages was reaffirmed by the Mulla Chaknawar and Mulla Babra. When a son of a Halimzai *malik* died, the *malik* had to pay an unknown *mulla* of Alingar the princely sum of 30 rupees to conduct the services on the sly.[66]

This effort to maintain a unified front and prevent religion from becoming divided and less potent was largely managed by Haji of Turangzai. He was the primary instigator and leader of meetings at Hadda, suggesting that he, more than any other, had taken on the defining leadership role among *mullas* of the Akhund Ghaffur's line. He invited parties to Hadda '*sharif* or Hadda the pure, for mediation

---

62 MPD, 1922-23.

63 Border Administration Report (hereafter BAR) 1922-3, OIOC V/10/390; KPD, 26 May 1923.

64 Two Tirah *mullas* were competing for Mulla Sayyid Akbar's support. NWFPPD, 4, 11 Sept. 1915.

65 NWFPPD, 2, 9 Oct. 1915.

66 MPD, 26 Feb. 1927.

on disputes, as in the case of the Mohmands in 1926,[67] and equally he used Hadda as a point from which to disseminate cash and ammunition to his supporters.[68]

Despite the efforts of Haji Turangzai and other *mullas* of the Hadda line to establish a single line of religious leadership across the region, there were strong and consistent opponents to the group. As discussed in chapter 2, the Mianguls of Swat under Miangul Abdul Wudud rejected their direct spiritual lineage from Akhund Abdul Ghaffur through the Hadda Mulla, and instead claimed descent from the Pir Baba of Swat (d. 1637). As well as invoking an alternate spiritual lineage, the Mianguls created a group of their own loyal *mullas*, most prominent among whom were the Pir of Manki Sharif and his son the Miyan Manki, who distanced themselves from the Hadda Mulla's ideological movement and from the political conformity demanded by the Haji Turangzai and other prominent members of Akhund Ghaffur's line.[69] The Shinwari Mulla and Miyan Manki publicly challenged the religious interpretations of the Haji Turangzai and Sandaki Mulla.[70] The Miyan of Manki Sharif was equally critical and derisive of the Hadda Mulla and his legacy, calling it a sham. He derided the rituals of prayer of the Hadda Mulla's followers, claiming that raising the forefinger during prayer was not religiously prescribed and should not be practiced.[71]

The *mullas* of the Hadda group responded to such challenges by gathering together notable intellectuals affiliated with various *masjids* and *madrasas* and issuing *fatwas* on the validity of their dictates or forcing consent through sheer intimidation. In one case a *jirga* of

---

67 MPD 1926, p. 72.

68 NWFPPD, 3 April 1915.

69 The Mulla Spinkara had been affiliated with the Hadda Mulla in 1897. He appears to have also been distanced by the rift between the Mianguls and his father on the one side, and the Hadda Mulla and his *murids* on the other. *Whos Who NWFP, 1930.*

70 NWFPPD, 13 Nov. 1915, NWFPPD, 18 Sept. 1915.

71 Quddusi, *Tazkiray*, p. 59.

renowned *mullas* of the region produced a treatise called *Haququl Muqal*, a *shari'a*-based rationalisation of the Haji's correctness in calling for military action against the British.[72] In other cases dissenting *mullas* were militarily coerced into submission to the Hadda group as in the case of the Shinwari Mulla whose supporters' houses were burnt down on the orders of the Haji Turangzai when he briefly opposed the latter.[73] Contestation of the *pirimuridi* line's religious authority and interpretation could have deeply compromised that group, but they went on to dominate religion and political action in the Tribal Areas. This was partly due to its acquiring powerful and resourceful patrons in Afghanistan and British India, events which are discussed in greater detail in the following chapter. But the dominance of the line was more directly linked to the coercive powers of the mullas and their militarisation.

The militarisation of religious authority

Diplomatic initiatives and social dictates by *mullas* were strategically backed up by their *lashkars*. These armies were manned by both 'regulars'—the *shaikhs* or deputies and the *talibs* or students—and irregulars—Pakhtun villagers participating in specific missions—and were used to demonstrate his popularity and generate enthusiasm for the *mullas'* decisions as well as being used to crush dissent and enforce punishments. Descriptions of military mobilisations by *mullas* were the most important and detailed accounts in colonial recountings of religious leadership in the Tribal Areas. Pashtu literary and oral accounts called to mind dramatic images of the Mulla Chaknawar in white robes,[74] the Babra Mulla on his horse, the Black Sparrow,[75] and Haji Sahib Turangzai and his deputies galloping from village

---

72 Jehanzeb Khalil, *Mujahidin Movement in Malakand and Mohmand Agency* (Peshawar 2000), p. 261.

73 Khalil, *Mujahidin Movement*, p. 259.

74 Account by Syal, *Nomyali Ghazi*, pp. 23-4

75 Ahmed Yousuf, *Babray Mulla Sahib*, pp. 33-4

to village to call his devotees to battle.[76] These representations accurately suggest that the *mullas' lashkars* were the backbone of their authority.

The size of a *lashkar* was partly a measure of strength and persuasive ability as a *mulla* with great renown attracted more fighting men. Haji Sahib Turangzai, the Mulla Chaknawar and the Babra Mulla had retinues of at least 40 men each, which could be backed up by thousands of villagers.[77] The *mullas* would convene *lashkars* for three specific types of missions. The first and most important was to enforce truces or exact penalty fines on behalf of the clans that they served. In such situations, the *mullas* would lead their *lashkars* to a subject's village and have their men stand guard while the transgressor's house was destroyed.[78] Residents of the house were cleared out and then it would be set on fire while the transgressor's belongings would be appropriated by members of the *lashkar* as compensation for their trip to the village. Use of the *lashkar* could be more subtle as well. Shah described an occasion when the Mulla Babra brought his men to the house of a truce breaker and remained there for two weeks until the dissenter agreed a new settlement.[79] Custom required the 'host' to provide food and accommodation to his 'guests', the 'visit' almost bankrupting him. The convening of a *lashkar* by the *mulla* was rooted in Pakhtun cultural codes of defence, pride and the use of force to back up a clan's position. Pakhtun clansmen, even those unconnected with the dispute, supported these overt shows of strength and military organisation by *mullas* in support of their diplomatic functions among the communities. In one case Haji Turangzai led a campaign against a clan that had broken a truce made under oath on the Quran. Musa Khel clans which were uncon-

---

76 Interview Ghulam Mohammad Din 13 Aug. 2002.

77 Interview Saeed Maqsud Shah.

78 This decision would be ratified by a tribal *jirga*. The *mulla* would rarely act without the sanction of a relevant *jirga*—to neglect this would be tantamount to a declaration of war against his host clan.

79 Shah, *Azadi Ki Talash*, p. 27.

nected to the original treaty participated in this campaign. When questioned, a representative *jirga* explained that breaking the oath was an unacceptable violation of tribal codes and the sanctity of the Quran, and they were duty bound to punish the transgressors.[80] Haji Turangzai led his campaigns as a champion of Pakhtun tribal values, an agenda that was difficult to resist when it had no direct impact on the participant's interests.

The second reason for the *mullas* convening *lashkars* was to punish moral transgressors. *Mullas* would use their personal retinues to enforce punishment against those who had defied their directives by humiliating the guilty party or parties, or in most extreme circumstances burning houses and confiscating goods and valuables.[81] Haji Turangzai organised his *sheikhs* to attack the Dawezai Mohmands in 1926 on the accusation that they were 'addicted to immorality' and did not pay any heed to religious injunction.[82]

The third reason, by far the most significant for the development of religious politics over the next half century, was the use of *lashkars* by *mullas* enforcing their political directives.[83] For reasons which will be discussed in greater depth in the next few chapters, *mullas* of the Hadda line had on several separate instances opposed the British interventions in the Tribal Areas. Tribal Areas supporters of the British who were gaining a disproportionate power and wealth through their alliance, and government installations such as checkposts, communications lines and garrisons were the biggest targets in this regard. *Mullas* would gather *lashkars* and close in on a specific objective—usually an army check-post, but occasionally an entire British camp or division, or a whole clan. Attack was swift, and victory was

---

80 'Note by Deputy Commissioner Peshawar, 31 March 1927'. NWFPPA, DCOP, file 212 of 1927, vol. I.

81 Interview Malik Fazal Hadi, grandson of Malik Anmir of the Gandab Halimzai, 13 Aug. 2002.

82 MPD, 1926.

83 The Babra Mulla threatened to blacken the faces of Burhan Khel *khassadars*. NWFPPD 3 Jan. 1915.

declared when members of the attacking *lashkar* were able to enter the camp and pillage ammunition supplies and clothing stocks and get away with substantial booty.[84] These attacks, whether on the British or on local tribes, were not intended to take or hold land or positions but to destabilise adversaries in order to exact respect and consideration from them.

Militarisation of the *mullas'* authority and the increasing influence of the Hadda Mulla's line, led now by Haji Turangzai, was also crucially linked to the militarisation of the Tribal Areas population in general. The economy of arms trading in the Tribal Areas from the 1880s onwards was supported by an illegal traffic in weapons from the Persian Gulf.[85] With the creation of tribal levies in the late nineteenth century and the employment and arming of local *khassadars*, weapons captured from or surrendered by *khassadars* supplemented this supply. Local expertise in the manufacture of arms began to grow in the absence of government regulation of such enterprise, and despite efforts to control arms trade through blockades and political control, the volume of weapons traded in the Tribal Areas was sufficient to arm the majority of the Tribal Areas male population.[86] Religious militancy was as much fashioned by this illegal arms trade as it was by ideology, agnatic rivalry and the Pakhtun code of honour.

Despite the nuances in motivation behind convening a *lashkar*, both on the part of the community and the *mullas*, the fact of *mulla* leadership led the mobilisations to be referred to as *jihads*—by the *mullas*, the clansmen, and the British.[87] Trumpet calls and the beat

---

84 Ghulam Muhammad Din stated that victory was declared in the battle of Gullo Sar Jang when Haji Turangzai's *lashkar* managed to kill 4 British officers and make off with ammunition and even clothes taken from the bodies of killed or wounded British soldiers. Even the battalion flag was taken and the rich material apportioned between the participanting *maliks*. Interview Ghulam Muhammad Din, 13 Aug. 2002.

85 Baha, *NWFP Administration*, pp. 77-8, Warren, *Waziristan*, pp. 30-1.

86 See Arnold Keppel, *Gun Running and the Indian North-West Frontier* (London, 1911).

87 Syal, *Nomyali Ghazi*, p. 57.

of drums brought participants to the meeting place and the *mulla* or his deputies would lead the charge. One clansman described the gathering of a *lashkar* as he had witnessed it:

The Turangzai Baba would say—the *gora* is coming (he would call them *gora*) and we should stop him—by force—he is destroying Islam and he is destroying our laws. [Turangzai Baba] would give lectures and people would listen, and after the lectures people would join in with him. The *mulla* would announce the commencement of the *jihad*. Messengers on horses [would] designate a place where people should congregate. [This was] generally the *hujra* of a *qabila*. All the Baizai, Khwaizai, Safi and Kandahari would together designate a place where they should meet—in Nahaqqi or Safi or Kandahari or Ato Khel—something close [to the target] as a point of attack—then from there they would attack.[88]

As the *mullas'* means of raising *lashkars* and the participants demonstrated, control over the communal space of the *masjid*, the power of the sermon, and access to and recognition by different clan communities formed the foundation of religious authority. Despite the 'Islamic' leadership and anti-western rhetoric of the mobilisations, the underpinnings and mainstay of these mobilisations was the social participation of the Pakhtun *mullas* and the condition of autonomy in the region rather than specific ideological concerns.

This is not however to suggest that *mulla*-led militancy was a benign or tribally-controlled phenomenon. Although these patterns of militant mobilisation were rooted in tribal issues, they accorded *mullas* a military power and independence of action which the *mullas* could use in pursuit of personal or ideological objectives, becoming a coercive influence within the tribal set up. The instance in 1915 when the Gujjar Mulla brought his *lashkar* down to the Chakdarra government checkpost in Dir as retaliation against the Nawab of Dir's territorial encroachments and his complicity with government was such an example. The Gujjar Mulla set up camp in the village Arangi, and used this vantage point to snipe at the Nawab of Dir's

---

88 Interview Ghulam Muhammad Din 13 Aug. 2002.

*lashkar*s.[89] He operated there for some days, but was finally attacked by Dir's soldiers and killed along with four of his *shaikhs* and *talibs*.[90] Within days a *lashkar* of 100 men from Jandol led by the Haji Turangzai came down to Arangi to punish the villagers for allowing their *mulla* to be killed before them and in retaliation looted and burned the houses of the villagers.[91] While the Gujjar Mulla's original mobilisation partly served the interests of the people of Jandol, his impractical mobilisation against the Nawab of Dir, a far stronger, better equipped and richer party, was also rooted in the decision by regional *mullas* to oppose the Nawab and his aspirations to regional dominance. Haji Turangzai invoked Pakhtun cultural principles as a basis for forcing the men of Jandol to take action against the Arangi villagers in order to preserve the power and status of the *mullas* of his *pirimuridi* line.[92]

The substance and persistence of the *mullas' jihads*, which blurred the boundaries between tribal and cultural objectives and the *mullas'* own agendas, are dealt with in depth in the following chapters. With support from their local Pakhtun tribal patrons, and groups in India and Afghanistan, the Pakhtun *mullas* built up armies and pursued political agendas. These events allowed them to amass greater military and political strength, heightening the significance of their activities within the autonomous region, and their authority among the tribes.

---

89 NWFPPD, diary 37 1915.

90 NWFPPD, diary 38 1915.

91 NWFPPD, diary 39 1915.

92 *Mulla* involvement in the politics of Dir, Swat, Jandol, Khar and Nawegai— the Malakand states—is discussed in detail in chapter 5.

4
PATRONS OF THE SAINTS

Because it was outside the borders of both administered India and Afghanistan, removed from the British colonial system of controls and policing and beyond the responsibility of Afghanistan's amir, yet a crucial frontier, the Tribal Areas came to constitute a liminal space within British India with the potential to compromise the state. Although contained and segregated, the population of the region could not be entirely controlled through pressure on Afghanistan or tribal policy. During a brief period of the early twentieth century, two groups availed themselves of the possibilities it offered for striking at the government of India by using the region as a staging ground for an armed mobilisation. The first of these was a group of *'ulama* of the *madrasa* Darul Ulum Deoband near Lucknow in north-India; the other was the government of the nationalist amir Amanullah Khan in Afghanistan. Preparation for and execution of military ambitions were not undertaken independently by either group—both relied on the military capabilities of the regional *mullas* to popularise their agendas and mobilise the tribes. While the stories of these efforts in the Tribal Areas were minor incidents in both Afghan and Indian Muslim histories, the events of 1914-21 engaged the *mullas* of the Tribal Areas in such a way as to greatly increase their standing and prestige.

Darul Ulum Deoband and the Tribal Areas

Some descendents of the reformist philosopher Shah Wali Ullah developed a programme of study incorporating and stemming from his writings which began to be imparted at a *madrasa* established in the town of Deoband in 1864.[1] In rigorous debate and study at the Darul Ulum Deoband, Shah Wali Ullah's successors 'bifurcated the Sufi and revivalist tendencies' within his work—emphasising his reformist ideology but rejecting its genesis in Sufi thought and practice—and promoted programmes for the removal of heretical innovations in popular religious practice.[2] *Ulama* and students at Deoband saw themselves as being part of a tradition of interpretation and defence of Islam in increasingly hostile surroundings, and much of their religious commentary also came to focus on the definition of the Indian Muslim community and the importance of its solidarity and protection.

With the start of the twentieth century a wider debate ensued across India over the means and substance of a political consolidation of the Indian Muslim identity.[3] The idea of pan-Islamism, a universal Muslim identity, most famously articulated by the Persian political and religious philosopher Jamaluddin al-Afghani (1839-97), began to gain ground in India around 1910.[4] Pan-Islamism suggested a global solidarity that emerged from shared religious values. The inception of pan-Islamism was inseparably linked to its *alter ego*, anti-colonialism, as the former highlighted the fact that the conditions of colonial repression were shared by Muslim communities across the world. Using the Urdu press to publicise their ideas about Muslim social and political formations, many Indian Muslims voiced concerns about their own government fighting a war against the Caliph who was protector of the *Jaziratul Arab*—the sacred lands of Arabia, Palestine and Iraq.

---

1 This and all further commentary on the Darul Ulum Deoband is based on Barbara Metcalf's study *Islamic Revival in British India : Deoband, 1860-1900* (Princeton, 1982), except where otherwise stated.

2 Hermansen, *Hujjat*, p. xxxiv.

3 Mushirul Hasan (ed.), *Communal and Pan-Islamic Trends in Colonial India* (Delhi, 1981), p. vi.

4 Ira Lapidus, *A History of Islamic Societies* (Cambridge, 2002), pp. 516-18.

In 1914 Maulana Mahmudul Hasan, chancellor at Deoband, conceived a movement for the liberation of India by which armed units would be deputed to organise the Pakhtuns of the Tribal Areas, and rally support in Afghanistan in order to destabilise the British Indian government and provide a convenient point for the Turkish army to open a new front against the British. The movement was rooted in the new and exciting politics of anti-colonialism and pan-Islamism galvanised by the start of the First World War, but the founders of the movement highlighted the difference in their militaristic outlook and the politics of non-violent non-cooperation which dominated the nationalist Indian arena at that time.

Without violence [*we believed*], evicting the *angrez* from *Hindustan* was impossible. For this [violent eviction of the *angrez*] a centre, weapons and *mujahidin* were necessary. Hence, it was thought that arrangements for weapons and recruitment of soldiers should be conducted in the area of the 'free tribes'.[5]

The Tribal Areas base of the movement was chosen for its state of non-administration—conditions that would make organisation and planning a military mobilisation against the colonial government easier. Obaidullah Sindhi (1872-1944), a Sikh convert to Islam and an *alim* of the Darul Ulum Deoband who had studied and worked under Mahmudul Hasan, was one of the primary articulators of the political ideology of the movement based in the North-West Frontier. Maulana Hussain Ahmad Madni, a senior scholar at the Darul Ulum who described the frontier-based *jihad* in great detail in his autobiographical works, was another.[6] Madni's commentary was an intellectualised appraisal of the need for this movement as an integral counterpart to the political process in India. He said that Gandhi, Nehru, Maulana Bari, Dr Ansari, Maulana Muhammad Ali and

---

5   Hussain Ahmad Madni, *Naqsh-i Hayat* (Karachi, 1953) chapter 6.

6   Madni wrote *Naqsh-i Hayat* while in prison in 1942, as an account of his life and his witness to events that he felt were often misrepresented. *Tehrik-i Reshmi Rumal* was a more focused summary account of the movement of the Jamaat-i Mujahidin, probably written in the 1950s.

Maulana Shaukat Ali were all in their places at the 'headquarters' of the anti-colonial movement. Starting a complementary offensive in the Tribal Areas would re-enforce the demands of the nationalists, and because militancy was the historical prerogative of the frontier tribes, the contradiction between such a methodology and the strict non-violence propounded by Gandhi and the Congress Party was irrelevant. Obaidullah Sindhi's writings described his own beliefs that the frontier movement fulfilled the need for a party 'founded on Shah Wali Ullah's ideals' and provided a central base for organisation and mobilisation from which a political and religious agenda could be promoted.[7]

This way of thinking of the Tribal Areas and its population was reinforced by Deobandi writings on the Pakhtun Muslims as a distinct and separate population from the Muslims of British India, and on the connection between the Tribal Areas and the Muslim past in India. Highly idealised appraisals of Pakhtun society and history stressed that 'the youth of the free tribes [*azad qabail*] had always been engaged in *jihad* and were strong-willed and brave'. The Hadda Mulla's *jihads* against the British in 1893 and 1897 were emphasised as a mark of Pakhtun commitment to independence and preservation of their religious culture. Another Deobandi, Maulana Muhammad Miyan, suggested that if sufficiently re-enforced by the financial and political resources of the Deobandis, the Pakhtun would aid the pan-Islamists in their fight against the British in order to realise greater political sovereignty for themselves.[8] Obaidullah Sindhi wrote that it was their distinct nature as *paharis* or people inhabiting the mountains that separated them from Pakhtuns in the lowlands east and

---

7 Obaidullah Sindhi, '*Shah Wali Ullah Aur Un Ki Tehrik*' [Shah Wali Ullah and his Movement], introduction in Maulana Sayyid Muhammad Miyan, *Tehrik-i Sheikh-ul Hind* (Lahore, 1978), p. ii, vii. Sindhi's essay on Shah Wali Ullah was written after 1939 but Sindhi's writings on the movement compiled in *Zati Dairi* and his letters to Iqbal Shaidai were written between 1924 and 1937. These writings establish Obaidullah Sindhi's political outlook during and directly after his years of involvement with the movement of the Jamaat-i Mujahidin.

8 Ansari, *Tehrik-i Shaikh-ul Hind*, p. 73.

west of them and allowed them to accept Islam and aid Mahmud Ghaznavi and his incursions into India in the eleventh century.[9] Madni wrote even more extensively about the historic importance of Sayyid Ahmed of Rai Bareilly's *jihad* which was intended to reclaim a space and dignity for the practice of the Muslim faith, and the participation of the tribal Pakhtuns in this movement.[10] The history of the Tribal Areas produced in Deobandi texts fleshed out the map of India and its Muslim 'spaces', invoking a historical narrative of Islam in India to salvage contemporary Muslim society.

Deobandi belief in the movement was also rooted in political and social appraisals of the Pakhtun tribes. In a letter to Mahmudul Hasan, one of his deputies in the frontier said:

The independent territories lying between the Indian frontier and Afghanistan from Waziristan down to Alai near the Kashmir border is full of self-respecting high spirited Afghans who are well equipped with cartridges of every description ... these people according to the treaty between Great Britain and Afghanistan are British subjects, but owing to their innate spirit of national honour they have not recognised the sovereignty of the British or the amir [or Afghanistan] and are independent. Waziristan, Tirah and Mohmand country [do not even have] khans to rule over them.[11]

Considered as one people, fragmented and divided, without a government or political direction, yet naturally imbued with a sense of identity and desire to resist imperialism, the Pakhtuns were the perfect recruits in Maulana Mahmud's cause. The word *Yaghistan*

---

9 Sindhi, *Zaati Dairi*, p. 50.

10 Madni particularly pointed out that this programme had *Hindustan*-centred and anti-British concerns—it was not anti-Hindu. He emphasised that the movement had included Hindus and that the *jihad* was directed against Ranjit Singh, only insofar as Ranjit Singh was an extension of the East India Company's power and influence. His concluding statement on the movement was that 'the primary motive of this *jamaat* was to remove foreigners from 'Hindustan' and to establish a democratic rule in the country. See Madni, *Tehrik-i Reshmi Rumaal*, pp. 418-47.

11 Bukhari Mulla to Mahmudul Hasan, 4 Aug. 1916 in 'Afghanistan: The Silken Letter Case 1916-1918'. OIOC L/PS/10/633.

was adopted by the Jamaat-i Mujahidin in reference to the Tribal Areas, but used now to mean 'land of the free Afghan tribes'.

Maulana Obaidullah Sindhi was one of the *'ulama* sent to organise the movement in Yaghistan.[12] Along with Maulana Fazal Rabbi of Lahore and Maulana Fazal Mahmud of Peshawar, he began to re-establish Sayyid Ahmed of Rai Bareilly's old military bases of Chamarkand in the Bajaur area and Asmast in Buner as new political and military centres for the organisation of the religious warriors or the *Jamaat-i Mujahidin*.[13] Funds from India were channelled to the Chamarkand base for the purchase of arms, a printing press and other paraphernalia of revolution. The objectives of the leaders of the movement were described as being: 'to enlist volunteers', to 'create enthusiasm for confrontation' and to recruit and train the 'revolutionary' tribes into an army of liberation.[14] The Kalat and Makran tribes (of south Baluchistan) would then attack Karachi; the tribes of Ghazni (in Afghanistan) would attack Quetta; the Mohmands and Masuds (of Mohmand and Waziristan in the Tribal Areas) would attack Peshawar; and the Kohistani tribes (of upper Swat) would join with the invading Turkish army as a front line of attack when they confronted the British army.[15]

The territory that comprised this area of operation and military organisation was thoughtfully mapped by one member of the Jamaat as the interim land between the Indus River to the east and Kabul to the west, Kashmir and Bukhara to the north and Baluchistan to the south, and included Kabul and Kandahar, Peshawar, Kohat and Ba-

---

12 Madni *Naqsh-i Hayat*, chapter 6.

13 The activists in the Tribal Areas called themselves by various names including the *Jamiyyat-i Hizbullah*, the *Hindustani Mujahidin*, and the *Mujahidin-i Chamarkand*. The British referred to them as the 'Hindustani Fanatics'—a term coined during the Wahhabi trials for participants in Sayyid Ahmed of Rai Bareilly's movement. For consistency, I will refer to them as the Jamaat-i Mujahidin. Ghulam Rasul Mehr's preference for this title guides my own use of it.

14 Madni, *Naqsh-i Hayat*, chapter 6.

15 Madni, *Tehrik-i Reshmi Rumal*, chapter 9.

hawalpur, suggesting that the natural ethnic extension of *Yaghistan* had to include the Pakhtun areas east of the non-administered districts, and west of the Durand Line. The detailed heart of Yaghistan marked on the map was of the Jamaat-i Mujahidin's operation in the non-administered areas—Dir, Swat, Buner, Asmar, Shabqadar, Mohmand, Asmast, Chamarkand and Babra.

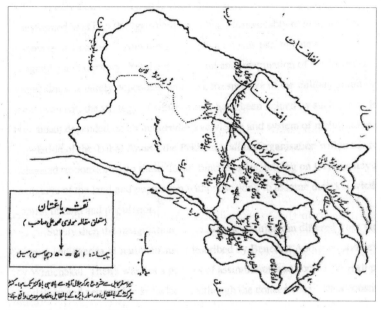

Fig. 5 Muhammad Ali Kasuri's *Naqsha-yi Yaghistan*.[16]

The appearance of the Jamaat-i Mujahidin in the Tribal Areas and their overt anti-colonial imperatives led British intelligence to believe that these 'Hindustani Fanatics' were directly organising militancy in the region.[17] However the influence of the Jamaat-i Mujahidin in the Tribal Areas was deeply dependent on the local *mullas* as the Jamaat depended on these crucial intermediaries to mobilise the Tribal Ar-

16 Kasuri, *Mushahidat*, p. i.

17 J.M. Ewart Intelligence Bureau Peshawar to Foreign and Political Department, March 1923. OIOC L/PS/11/217.

eas population. The Jamaat-i Mujahidin's organisation within the region delegated responsibility to the *mullas*, relying on their agency as mediators of the land and population without seeking to assume their knowledge and control of land and population. Madni said of the movement that:

> we were only successful insofar as we acquainted some thoughtful soldiers with the fervour of nationalism; and when Haji Turangzai and his people started the war against the British in *sarhad*, we used to supply them with important information, by which they gained a great advantage.[18]

Much was made of the importance of the *mulla* in the Deobandi writings on Pakhtun society. Madni described Pakhtuns as the ideal of a religiously observant society because *mullas* were part of their institutions of justice and social order. These *mullas* were seen as fashioning and organising society, and as the best facilitators and guides of Pakhtun *qaumiyat*, in the way that it would serve the Indian political cause and serve the Pakhtuns. Muhammad Ali Kasuri argued that the *mullas* had a central role in *Yaghistan*, and the dominant influence in the village council. He saw all social and political authority as deriving from these personalities.[19] Maulana Barkatullah applauded the role of *mullas* and *'ulama* as overseers of moral conduct, indicating their authority to burn the houses of those inclined to disobey them.[20] They maintained institutions of community dialogue and organisation that were seen to rival the British at a local level.[21] They presented not only a means of combating the British in the present, but were capable of creating a future order that would restore dignity to Islam and to indigenous custom and civilisation.

Links between the *mullas* of the Hadda line and the Deobandis of the twentieth century had been established by the Haji Turangzai in 1875 when he joined a party of *'ulama* from Deoband to perform

---

18 Madni, *Tehrik-i Reshmi Rumal*, p. 156.

19 Kasuri, *Mushahidat*, p. 30.

20 *'Ailan Muqaddas-i Dini Bay Ahali-i Pathanistan'*, appendix Mehr, *Sarguzasht-i Mujahidin*, pp. 521-33.

21 *'Ailan Muqaddas-i Dini Bay Ahali-i Pathanistan'*, pp. 542-4.

Haj.[22] Haji Turangzai went on to spend a few years in Deoband and to cement this relationship. In 1914, when Maulana Mahmud asked the Haji Sahib to move from Utmanzai into the Tribal Areas to undertake *jihad*, the Haji Sahib incorporated Maulana Mahmud's agenda into his own initiative of *islah* or social improvement and brought other members of his *pirimuridi* line to assist the movement of the Jamaat-i Mujahidin.[23] The first assistance the local *mullas* rendered was to help settle the *mujahidin* arriving in the Tribal Areas. Haji Turangzai and the Mulla Sandaki guided parties of *mujahidin* and their families into Buner and Chamarkand and negotiated the terms of their settlement with the local residents.[24] The Haji Turangzai personally guided and settled 120 families of members of the Jamaat-i Mujahidin in the Tribal Areas.[25] After Haji Turangzai's demonstration of his commitment to the movement of the Jamaat-i Mujahidin and his ability to organise their activities in the Tribal Areas, Maulana Mahmudul Hasan sent letters asking all his students and associates in the region to pledge their commitment to the Haji Sahib and follow his instructions in the *jihad*.[26] Haji Turangzai consulted with the amir of the *mujahidin* at Chamarkand to decide a date and strategy for attack.[27] The Mulla Sandaki and Mulla Babra met regularly with the Jamaat-i Mujahidin members to discuss strategy, at their new base in Chamarkand, and other times, at the *mullas'* own homes.[28] In 1915 Haji Turangzai jointly issued a *firman* with

---

22 Javed, *Haji Sahib Turangzai*, pp. 40-2.

23 Essay on the Haji Turangzai by Abdul Ghaffur Bacha, appendix Javed, *Haji Sahib Turangzai*, p. 525.

24 NWFPPD, 11 Sept. 1915.

25 Ibid.

26 Madni, *Tehrik-i Reshmi Rumal*, pp. 160-6; Between 1915 and 1916 the Jamaat-i Mujahidin sent deputations to the Haji Turangzai, Sandaki Mulla and Mulla Babra—NWFPPD 1915-6.

27 NWFPPD, 14 Aug. 1915.

28 NWFPPD, 1915-6.

the Jamaat-i Mujahidin to the local tribes calling for a war against the British.[29]

The *mullas* most deeply involved in the movement of the Jamaat-i Mujahidin were Haji Turangzai and Mulla Chaknawar in Mohmand, the Mulla Sandaki and Mulla Babra in Swat and Bajaur, Mulla Sayyid Akbar, Mulla Abdul Haleem and Mulla Mahmud Akhunzada among the Afridis[30] and Mulla Hamzullah in Waziristan.[31] These *mullas* of the *pirimuridi* line of the Hadda Mulla were referred to as the *buzurgan-i Yaghistan* or the elders of *Yaghistan* who had organised a concerted opposition to the colonial government. Tactical leadership and organisation of the military wing of the Jamaat-i Mujahidin was entirely entrusted to the local *mullas* who were responsible for organising the Mohmand, Mahsud and Kohistani Pakhtun 'tribes' into a formidable military force.[32] Moreover, the *mujahidin* themselves mostly operated under *mulla* leadership as in one instance in 1919 when 300 *mujahidin* swore *bait* at the hand of Mulla Chaknawar to fight under his command during the Third Anglo-Afghan War.[33]

Support from the Jamaat-i Mujahidin greatly increased the standing of the Tribal Areas *mullas*, not least because of the ammunition and cash supplied through Chamarkand and entrusted to the *mullas* for distribution among the 'tribes'. In just six months 3000 rupees, 50 horses and 303 rifles were sent to the Mohmands directly from the Jamaat-i Mujahidin; 30,000 Kabuli rupees were passed on the *mujahidin*'s advice from Amir Habibullah's court to the Lala Pir of Khost for onward distribution to the Wazirs and Masuds; and

---

29 NWFPPD, Sept. 1915; NWFPPD, 28 Oct. 1916.

30 Chamarkandi, *Sarguzasht-i Mujahidin*, pp. 10-30; Kasuri, *Mushahidat*, pp. 43-4; 'Ailan Muqaddas-i Dini Bay Ahali-i Pathanistan'.

31 A deputation of members of the Jamaat-i Mujahidin based in Jalalabad visited the Mulla Mahmud in 1920, presenting him with a *postin* and a sword. NWFPPD, 28 Feb. 1920.

32 Madni, *Tehrik-i Reshmi Rumal*, p. 173.

33 Extract from CID newsletter, 30 June 1919. NWFPPA, Special Branch NWFP File 403, p. 35.

30,000 rupees Kabuli were granted by Habibullah's minister to the Jamaat-i Mujahidin to distribute in Yaghistan.[34] Association with the Jamaat-i Mujahidin also heightened the profile of the *mullas* who had hitherto never used sophisticated methods of self-projection like printing presses. Impressed by the methods of the Jamaat-i Mujahidin, such as posting proclamations of *jihad* on trees through Mardan,[35] the Haji Turangzai acquired his own printing press in 1916.[36] The members of the Jamaat also spoke highly of the *mullas* in their own addresses to the local population, thereby elevating them in local estimations. In one widely distributed pamphlet, the Jamaat wrote:

With the help of the *'ulama* of the faith you will, in the lands of the *khalifat*, be able to give your progeny knowledge of the arts and sciences and you can stand shoulder to shoulder with the other progressive and civilised nations of the world in the field of success and culture.[37]

Rather than actively leading and engineering a military strategy for *Yaghistan*, the members of the Jamaat-i Mujahidin restricted themselves to funding and supporting the activities of the *mullas*. They encouraged the religious networks to mobilise militarily, but around *mulla*-directed agendas. The Jamaat-i Mujahidin invigorated the old *pirimuridi* networks by providing funding to *mulla*-led *jihads*.

With their financing, the Haji Turangzai, the Sandaki Mulla and Babra Mulla built 'coalitions' and armies, ostensibly in support of the Jamaat's cause, but really in pursuit of local agendas and politics.[38] This was demonstrated when money and ammunition supplied to the Sartor Faqir and the Sandaki Mulla in 1915 went to assist in a local

---

34 NWFPPD, 13 Nov., 30 Oct. 1915; 6 May 1916.

35 NWFPPD, 4 Sept. 1915.

36 See NWFPPD, 2 Sept. 1916.

37 'Ailan Muqaddas-i Dini Bay Ahali-i Pathanistan', p. 521-2.

38 Haji Turangzai was reported to be building a coalition of tribes to oppose the British. Around the same time he organised the Bunerwals in an attack on Dir: NWFPPD, 7, 21 Aug. 1915.

power struggle against the Nawab of Dir.[39] While involvement of the *mujahidin* in the Tribal Areas no doubt affected religious discourse and encouraged anti-colonialism, the members of the Jamaat did not direct frontier-based mobilisation around anti-colonial activities. They allowed *mullas* to put forward punishment of clans in receipt of inequitable allowances, and containing over-ambitious rulers in the region as their prime objectives. The Jamaat's support contributed more to the consolidation of the *mullas'* authority and unanimity than to the nationalist movement in India.

After a short time establishing a presence at Chamarkand and Asmast,[40] Obaidullah Sindhi and other Deobandi *'ulama* who had joined the movement—including Maulana Abdur Raziq and Maulana Saifur Rahman—moved to Afghanistan to further the movement by securing favour and financial assistance from the Afghan amir and preparing for a Turkish mobilisation through the country. Afghanistan was the most obvious place in which to politically organise because of its strong historic connections to Muslim rule in India, to Islamic nationalist and pan-Islamic movements in Turkey and Iran, and as the only contemporary sovereign Muslim state.[41] Meanwhile a party of politically disenchanted students of Government College Lahore including Iqbal Shaidai, Abdul Karim Chamarkandi and

---

39 NWFPPD, 13 March 1915. This mobilisation is explored in greater detail in chapter 5.

40 Residents at Asmast, some of whom had been born there and whose parents had been settled there from the time of Sayyid Ahmed's movement, were drawn into lending support to the newly arrived dissidents because of the historic connections between Chamarkand and Asmast activism. However it seemed their involvement was limited as the 'amir' at Asmast, Niamatullah, wrote a letter to the Commissioner at Topi denying any sympathy for the dissidents, claiming that the Asmast settlement was only ever a 'party of devotees retired from the world' and that they rejected the movement initiated by the Deoband party. Amir Niamatullah to Sahibzada Abdul Qaiyum, C.I.E. Topi, received 26 December 1916. In 'Hindustani Fanatics, 1909-1918'. National Documentation Centre Islamabad (henceforth NDC), 4 STB. II, 268.

41 Muhammad Hussain Khan, *Afghan Badshah Alihazrat Amanullah Khan Khalladullah Malka va Hukma Ki Azimulishan Chasham Deed-o-Dastan* (Lahore, 1924), pp. 190-251.

Muhammad Ali Kasuri, 'migrated' at Maulana Mahmud's invitation and joined the dissidents at Chamarkand. In 1916, the organisers at Chamarkand prepared to finally propose the plan to the Ottoman Vizir. This last initiative was the undoing of the movement as the letters sent to the Ottomans and to Maulana Mahmudul Hasan apprising him of the progress of the movement, written on pieces of silk to avoid detection, were intercepted by the Criminal Investigation Department.[42] The content of what would come to be called the 'silk letters' was enough for Maulana Mahmud and all the other Deobandis involved in the movement to be charged with sedition and for Maulana Mahmud, Maulana Madni, and Maulana Muhammad Miyan to be sent to a prison camp in Malta.

While Deobandi institutional support to the movement and the Tribal Areas *mullas* ostensibly ended with the deportation of the Deobandi *'ulama*, the Chamarkand and Asmast bases remained operative under the management of Maulana Bashir and Fazal Ilahi while Maulana Saifur Rehman and Haji Abdur Raziq became more established in Afghanistan.[43] These *'ulama* occasionally reappeared in later years as facilitators of a rapport between the Tribal Areas and the government of Afghanistan and as champions of Tribal Areas independence and the importance of its *mullas*.[44] Perhaps more

---

42 'Afghanistan: The Silken Letter Case 1916-1918'.

43 Obaidullah Sindhi was not among these. During his early years in Kabul, Obaidullah Sindhi tried to create a military compact between the Turks and Germans and Afghans. He worked closely with the Turko-German mission to Kabul in 1915, along with Maulana Barkatullah Bhopali and Raja Mahendra Pratab, members of the Indian National Party who similarly came to Afghanistan to organise anti-colonial activity. Obaidullah Sindhi's interests became deeply influenced by the Indian National Party's communist outlook and he took a different course than other *ulama* who stayed on to work in Afghanistan as religious scholars, teachers and administrators, ultimately leaving Afghanistan for Europe in 1922 (Sindhi, *Zati Dairi*, pp. 30-50). Meanwhile many of the Lahore students continued on to Afghanistan, and then on to Europe or North America, ending their connection to the Tribal Areas.

44 Indian *ulama*, particularly those of the Darul Ulum Deoband, had been welcome in Afghanistan for their excellent training in the religious sciences. They were highly sought after for their teaching credentials, and were also

importantly, the *mullas* of the Tribal Areas maintained connections with the Darul Ulum Deoband, sending later generations there to study.[45] They would later come to contribute to the organisation of the Deoband legacy in the territories which became Pakistan in 1947, issues which will be explored further in the last chapter. Ultimately the failed and ill-conceived movement of the Jamaat-i Mujahidin did a great deal more to illuminate and consolidate the geography, substance, and concerns of the *pirimuridi* networks in the Tribal Areas and to enrich the *mullas* than to promote an anti-colonial insurrection among the Pakhtun tribes.

Nationalist Afghanistan and the Tribal Areas mullas

Eastern Pakhtuns of what became the Tribal Areas had long maintained informal military ties with the Kabul amirate. Some of these ties were established directly between the Afghan government and the groups in question while others were established through political and landed intermediaries such as the Mohmand Khan of Lalpura who distributed allowances to the more easterly Mohmands on behalf of the Afghan state.[46] A common method whereby the court or its agents had communicated with and secured military or commercial commitments from the eastern Pakhtuns was through the intercession of Pakhtun *mullas* who would commit to rallying *lashkars* on behalf of the amirate in return for grants and privileges from the court—a military compact that had been demonstrated in the mobilisations of 1820-35. This relationship was disrupted with the separation of the 'independent' tribes of the Tribal Areas from Afghanistan by the terms of the Treaty of Gandamak of 1878 and

employed in the central and regional justice departments. Once they moved to Afghanistan, these *ulama* became deeply involved in affairs of the Afghan state and maintained connections to British India and Muslim nationalist politics there as Afghans. See Chamarkandi, *Sarguzasht-i Mujahid*, p. 143; and Madni, *Naqsh-i Hayat*, pp. 607-8.

45 'List of students who passed from the Dar-ul-Ulum, Deoband'. NWFPPA, Special Branch files, in 'Youth and Student Movements'.

46 This is discussed in greater detail in chapter 1.

then the demarcation of the Durand Line in 1893. By the terms of these treaties, Amir Abdur Rahman (1879-1901) was pressurised to sever relations with the trans-border tribes.

Amir Habibullah Khan (1901-19) inherited the 1878 treaty that made Afghanistan a British protectorate.[47] He received a commitment that the British would not interfere in Afghanistan's 'internal affairs' beyond the Durand Line as well as a guarantee of a permanent subsidy to be used for the payment of troops and import of munitions.[48] In return, Habibullah was asked to confirm his acceptance of the Durand Line and the termination of his own state's interests at that juncture. Habibullah's interest in formalising the Anglo-Afghan relationship was indicated by his public proclamation ratifying the Anglo-Afghan agreements in 1905.[49] However he declined any commitment to withdrawing his influence from the British-side Tribal Areas. He also declined to discuss demarcation of the still vague border between Afghanistan and India as it ran through Mohmand, Khyber and Waziristan.

The Tribal Areas formed a natural military frontier for Afghanistan against an aggressive and untrustworthy British India which, even in these late days of the Great Game, periodically threatened to invade it to counter Russian advances from the north. While Habibullah hesitated to use his connections to the Tribal Areas in the early years of his reign because he was unwilling to jeopardise his relationship with the British, members of his court—most significantly his brother Nasrullah Khan and uncle Abdul Qayyum Khan—were so harshly critical of the agreements with the British and their ramifications for the Afghans that Habibullah began to turn a blind eye

---

47 See Adamec, *Afghanistan 1900-1923*, chapters 1-2.

48 'Draft of Agreement Subsidiary to the Definitive Treaty of Friendship and Union between the British Government and His Highness Amir Habibullah Khan, 1904' in 'Afghanistan-HMG Relationship'. OIOC L/PS/10/18.

49 'History of the negotiations with his Highness the Amir Habibullah Khan at Kabul December 1904 to March 1905'. OIOC L/PS/10/17.

to his family's patronage of the Tribal Areas communities.[50] Under the direction of Nasrullah Khan, the Afghan court continued to pay allowances to tribes in Buner, Mohmand and Waziristan, using now longstanding connections to the *pirimuridi* fraternity of the Akhund Ghaffur-Hadda Mulla line to pass these on.[51]

Amir Habibullah Khan was assassinated in 1919, possibly with the connivance of Nasrullah Khan, and Habibullah's son Amanullah Khan took the throne.[52] On claiming the throne, Amanullah Khan immediately declared in an open *darbar*, in front of the British Agent to Kabul, that Afghanistan was thereafter 'as independent a state as other states and powers of the world ... no foreign power will be allowed to interfere internally and externally with the affairs of Afghanistan.'[53] On 4 May 1919, Afghan troops moved into Bagh, in Tirah, on the British side of the border. This mobilisation was Amanullah's attempt to overturn the protectorate status accorded to Afghanistan under previous Anglo-Afghan treaties. In a *firman* to the frontier tribesmen, Amanullah suggested that his declaration of war had been timed to coincide with the Indian nationalist agitations against the Rowlatt Act and the Jallianwala Bagh affair.[54] Amanullah also phrased his aggression as the Afghan response to the British efforts to move 'forward' and establish garrisons in Waziristan.[55] Amanullah's declaration of war was a highly popular move that was

---

50 Jennifer Siegel, *Endgame: Britain, Russia and the Final Struggle for Central Asia* (New York, 2002), p. 71.

51 For example Amir Habibullah Khan communicated advice to the Wazir and Mahsud clans to help them settle their internal hostilities through the Lala Pir of Khost and Mulla Hamzullah. Later, the Mahsuds were granted an audience at his court only through the intervention of the Lala Pir. See NWFPPD, 14 Aug. 1915, 8 April 1916.

52 Ludwig Adamec, *Afghanistan 1900-1923* (California, 1967) chapter 6.

53 Quoted in ibid., p. 110.

54 This was an incident where British troops opened fire on peaceful demonstrators in Jallianwala Bagh in Amritsar on 13 April, 1919. Ibid., p. 110-2. Senzil Nawid makes the same link in her study of *Religious Responses*, p. 63.

55 Adamec, *Afghanistan 1900-1923*, p. 110.

applauded by both prominent Afghan religious personalities—the Badshah of Islampur who had presided over Sardar Nasrullah Khan's *dasturbandi* came of his own accord to confirm the amirate of Amanullah Khan and his call to *jihad* against the British,[56] and statements of support from other eastern Pakhtun *mullas* soon followed[57]—and a newly emerged group of Afghan nationalists deeply influenced by the pan-Islamism of Jamaluddin al-Afghani.[58]

Fighting was organised in two separate efforts—a rising of the independent tribes in the frontier Tribal Areas, and mobilisation of Afghan regulars to the Anglo-Afghan border. The attack, conceived as two offensive waves, relied heavily on the support of the Pakhtun communities in the Tribal Areas as a means of protecting the Afghan front by disrupting the British movement through the region to the border, and as a means of diverting British troops into skirmishes. But Amanullah Khan could not directly mobilise the tribes as the force behind British will meant that Amanullah could not receive tribal representatives at his court, nor directly grant subsidies to British-side tribes to act on his behalf lest his actions be construed as expansionist instead of merely reactive and nationalistic. The only way he could rally the communities of the autonomous region was to invoke the moral, military and representative authority of the eastern Pakhtun *mullas* and employ members of the Jamaat-i Mujahidin who had moved to Afghanistan in 1917-19 as mediators. Amir Amanullah accepted a petition submitted to him in 1919 by the Jamaat-i Mujahidin and Tribal Areas *mullas* offering their services as 'representatives' of the 'frontier tribes' and as authorities in the region.

The petition bearing the stamp of the 'Jamiyatul Hizbullah' or the 'Party of the Army of God' looked to Amanullah's patronage

---

56   Ludwig Adamec, *Historical and Political Who's Who of Afghanistan* (Graz, 1975).

57   *Who's Who Afghanistan 1930.* OIOC L/PS/20/B220/2.

58   May Schinasi, *Afghanistan at the Beginning of the Twentieth Century Nationalism and Journalism in Afghanistan: A Study of the Seraj al Akhbar* (Naples, 1979), pp. 51-61.

of a 'union of the frontier tribes' under the authority of the region's *mullas*.[59] Haji Sahib Turangzai and Maulana Bashir of Chamarkand signed as regional representatives, and the 'tribal' signatories were predominantly *mullas* and included only a few *maliks*. The *mullas* who committed their support on behalf the tribes of Mohmand, Bajaur, Swat, Buner, and Dir included Mulla Abdul Hameed, representatives of Mulla Khalil and Mulla Babra, Maulvi Amiruddin, Maulvi Muhammad Yousuf and Maulvi Sahib Kama from Mohmand and Bajaur and Kaka Miyan Sahib, the Pacha Mulla, Chinar Mulla and the Tor Mulla.[60]

These *mullas* asked for recognition of their control and autonomy of action in regional affairs in return for their loyalty to the amirate saying:

we have sent an agreement signed and fingerprinted that we will be firm on our promise... Presently we will agree to obey his excellency, Amir Amanullah Khan Ghazi [conqueror] but remain independent in our internal affairs. We have a strong bond with Afghanistan in relation to our language, religion, nationality and land.[61]

The petitioners promised Amanullah that they would bring 'every single man in the area ... to fight' and committed their loyalties to the sovereign government of Afghanistan 'no matter how much the British government threatened', offering their strategic defensive position to Afghanistan in exchange for material, political and moral support from the Afghan court.[62] The petitioners promised to mobilise 20,000 armed Mohmands at Shabqadar and 40,000 Salarzai, Utmankhel and Mamund in Bajaur. The men would be led by the Mulla Babra, Haji Turangzai, Miyan Sarkanri, and the Badshah of

---

59 'Petition to Amanullah Khan from a Group of Representatives from the Frontiers [1337?]'. Appendix Muhammad Wali Zalmai, *Mujahid-i Afghan Mawlana Haji Abdar Raziq* (Kabul, 1967), p. 78-83.

60 'Petition to Amanullah Khan'.

61 A copy of affidavit sent by tribe Khwaizai [Mohmand] to Maulvi Obaidullah Khan as authorial representative to Amir Amanullah Khan. Appendix to Zalmai, *Mujahid-i Afghan*, pp. 83-5.

62 'Petition to Amanullah Khan'.

Islampur into the Swat valley to prevent access by British reinforcements through Hoti Mardan and Nowshera.

The caveat in the pledge of loyalty—that 'we will remain independent in our internal affairs' was repeated twice in the text of the petition. In return for their support, the petitioners asked Amanullah to reconise and defend the autonomy of the Tribal Areas region:

> We sent our representatives to you to clarify the fact that the people of the frontiers were always and are free now... we hope that his highness will not underestimate the gravity of the situation.[63]

This strategic and moral alliance reaffirmed the historically established precept—that neither the amir nor the frontier *mullas* and tribes were interested in including the region in the formal, bounded version of the Afghan state. It was on this premise that Amanullah accepted the offer of the Tribal Areas petitioners from Mohmand and Bajaur to rise against the British in his support. Assembling a special *darbar* in Kabul in May 1919, Amanullah called for a *jihad*, giving orders that Miyan Sahib Sarkanri, Badshah Sahib of Islampur, Mulla Sahib Chaknawar and Haji Turangzai raise forces in Mohmand.[64] General Nadir Khan, later to become Nadir Shah, amir of Afghanistan, was told by Amanullah to consult with the Babra Mulla Sahib in organising an eastern Pakhtun front from Kunar through Bajaur as he could mobilise the Charmung, Mamund and Salarzai clans.[65] Meanwhile Maulvi Sahib Kama and the new Jan Sahib Doda were appointed to protect the Afghan front from a possible offensive launched through Swat and Dir.[66]

Maintaining this strategy of indirect mobilisation in Waziristan, Amir Amanullah deputed Haji Abdur Raziq, the Deobandi member

---

63 Ibid.

64 Extract of letter from Amanullah to Haji Turangzai, 10 May 1919, 'Letter from the Viceroy to the Secretary of State for India 6 May 1919', in 'Papers Regarding Hostilities with Afghanistan'. OIOC L/MIL/17/14/61.

65 Yousuf, *Da Babray Mulla Sahib*, p. 44.

66 Amanullah Khan to the Haji Mulla Abdul Raziq Khan, 19 Shu'ban 1337, Appendix Zalmai, *Mujahid-i Afghan*, pp. 60-1.

of the Jamaat-i Mujahidin who had resettled in Jalalabad after 1916 and taken up employment as an authority on *shari'a* and a member of the local parliament, to organise the mobilisation.[67] Raziq had spent time in Waziristan as a member of the Jamaat-i Mujahidin and built up strong contacts with the local tribes and *mullas*. Amir Amanullah approved allowances to the Wazirs, to be paid out by Abdur Raziq as military salaries. Abdur Raziq managed to enlist 1,500 British trained *khassadars* among the Ahmedzai Wazirs alone using a royal sanction of 20,000 Kabuli rupees.[68] As a gifted military commander, Abdur Raziq was also entrusted with organising the risings of the tribes across the region as a whole and was given an official seal and express authority by Amanullah to oversee the union and the fighting of the *maliks* and tribes of 'Dir, Swat, Chitral and others around that area'.[69]

It was planned that the tribal *lashkars* should collect at various points across the Tribal Areas including Shabqadar and Lalpura in Mohmand, the Khyber Pass and Tirah.[70] Mulla Chaknawar arranged food to motivate the blockaded Mohmand clans, and Haji Turangzai, Badshah Gul, the Mulla Babra and Mulla Sarkanri managed to raise a *lashkar* of 40,000 men.[71] These *mulla*-led *lashkars* aided the Afghan army's advance from Dakka, the last outpost on the Afghanistan-Khyber Agency border, through the Khyber Pass towards Landi Kotal, the last British outpost on the Khyber Pass.[72] In North-Waziristan, *lashkars* of Wana Wazir clans carried out raids

---

67 Letter from Amanullah Khan to Haji Mulla Abdul Raziq, n.d., ibid.

68 S. E. Pears, Resident Waziristan, 'Memorandum on interview with the *jirgas* of the Wana and Shakai Wazirs at Tank, 25 December 1923', in 'Relations with Afghanistan, printed correspondence 1922-23'. OIOC L/PS/10/1049.

69 Firman from Amanullah Khan to the Faithful Haji Mulla Abdul Raziq Khan, 19 Shu'ban 1337. Appendix Zalmai, *Mujahid-i Afghan*, pp. 62-8.

70 Firman from Amanullah Khan to the Faithful Haji Mulla Abdul Raziq Khan, 29 Shawal 1337. Appendix Zalmai, *Mujahid-i Afghan*, pp. 68-71.

71 Nawid, *Religious Responses*, p. 56.

72 General Staff India, *Military Report Afghanistan* (Simla, 1941), p. 83.

on military posts and camps.[73] However, after first making some advances into Mohmand, Kurram and Chaman, and inflicting serious damage on the British forces in Waziristan and the Khyber Pass, the Afghan regulars were driven back beyond the Durand Line and *mulla*-led *lashkars* dispersed under attack by the British-side frontier militia and the effects of the blockade on the Mohmand clans. On 31 May, Amanullah Khan called for a cease-fire, mobilisations within the Tribal Areas were halted and the Tribal-Areas participants were rewarded for their support and asked to stand down.[74]

During the negotiations that followed, Amanullah committed early on to an Afghanistan delimited at the Durand Line and the demarcation of previously un-demarcated parts of the border running through Mohmand in order to secure British acquiescence to his rule.[75] But the Pakhtun tribal question was not settled by this acknowledgement as the British representative demanded that the Afghan government use its influence over the tribes to control 'tribal aggression' and the Afghan representative maintained that these communities and this region in all reality belonged to Afghanistan and the Afghan amir was their natural leader and protector.[76] Negotiations between the Government of India and the amirate of Afghanistan continued, amidst new fears about Bolshevik overtures to Afghanistan and Afghan fears of a British occupation of Waziristan

73 Foreign and Political Department Government of India, *A Precis on Afghan Affairs from February 1919 to September 1927* (Simla, 1928), p. 48. OIOC L/PS/20/B285.

74 Although they were cautioned against any direct aggression after the cease-fire, Nadir Khan asked the *mullas* to remain in a state of military preparedness until such a time as a suitable agreement had been reached between the two governments. Aware of the watchful British, the Afghan government managed some of its frontier military preparedness through the Jamaat-i Mujahidin who carried presents and messages between Kabul and the *mullas* of the Tribal Areas. NWFPPD, Feb.-April 1920; General Staff India, *Military Report Afghanistan* (Simla 1941), pp. 116-7.

75 Amanullah to the Viceroy 10 May 1919 in 'Papers Regarding Hostilities with Afghanistan'.

76 See Adamec, *Afghanistan 1900-1923*, pp. 126-9.

as the frontier authorities began surveys for a metalled road to Wana in South-Waziristan, and decided to establish a permanent garrison in Razmak, also in South-Waziristan.[77]

The final resolution was that both parties agreed to 'inform the other in the future of any military operations of major importance which may appear necessary for the maintenance of order among the frontier tribes residing within their respective spheres' in order that such actions not be construed as a British forward move or Afghan agression. The Afghan delegation also accepted the separation of frontier tribes and committed that Afghanistan would not maintain independent relations with them, and would 'refrain from inciting *jihad* and supplying arms on the British side of the border'.[78] Following this agreement a subsidy to the amirate was renewed along with promises of material support of telegraph technology, and the last major Anglo-Afghan treaty was ratified.[79] In 1922, Amanullah issued a *firman* declaring that he was not going to involve himself in the affairs of the frontier tribes,[80] and by 1923 the regular allowances of the sort paid to the Wana Ahmedzai Wazirs and the Mahsuds— estimated at about 70,000 Kabuli rupees to the Mahsuds and 20,000 to the Wazirs—were cut off.[81]

---

77 See *Official History of Operations on the North-West Frontier, 1920-1935* (Delhi, 1945), pp. 1-31.

78 Article XI, 'Treaty between Great Britain and Afghanistan'.

79 'Mussoorie Conference 1920'. OIOC L/PS/11/195.

80 'Pashto proclamation from Amanullah Khan to the trans-frontier tribes bearing seal of Amanullah.' March 1922, In 'Frontier Trangressions 1923-24', p. 386.

81 'Memorandum on Anti-British Conspiracy and Intrigue with Afghanistan and the Indo-Afghan Frontier', April 1922-Jan. 1923. OIOC L/PS/18/A195. After this time the only significant bequest by Amanullah to the Wazir tribes was a land grant in Birmal on the Afghan side of the border made to Wazirs from the British side of the border as a means of maintaining his social and economic commitment to these clans without undermining the Durand Line. Wazirs from the British side had to immigrate to the Afghan side of the border to take advantage of this grant. 'Memorandum by S. E. Pears, Resident Waziristan, 9 Feb. 1924', in 'Relations with Afghanistan, 1924'.

Amanullah's policies after the Wars

The early years of Amanullah's reign are badly understood because of his many apparently contradicting policies. He had been attributed with aspirations to succeeding the Ottoman Caliph, yet had strong nationalist and modernist ambitions which led him into war with the British in India and instigated two civil wars in the course of his reign; he was accused by the British of religious ambitions for his patronage of Pakhtun *mullas*, yet was clearly curtailing the authority of the *ulama* in Afghanistan. The events and Amanullah's policies of the years 1920-4 require closer examination to resolve these contradictions and establish where Amanullah stood with regards to his *ulama*, the Indian nationalists and the *mullas* in and across his eastern border region.

As the Allied Powers began negotiations over the fate of the Turks, it began to be widely felt in British India that there was a contradiction in the status of Muslim British subjects in that they owed their allegiance to the Ottoman Caliph but were bound by the foreign policies of the British government. A number of pan-Islamist Indian nationalists engineered the '*khilafat*' movement—the word both meaning 'opposition' and maintaining reference to the Caliphate. This was a country-wide campaign of political opposition to the British government because of its rejection of Muslim demands for the preservation of the Muslim holy lands and the title of the Caliph. In 1920, in the middle of the Anglo-Afghan talks, leaders of the *khilafat* movement in India called for a mass-migration or '*hijrat*' of the Muslims of India to Afghanistan on the premise that the Allied Powers had betrayed the Muslims by stripping the Caliph of his lands, hence British-ruled India was no longer *darul Islam*, a place where Muslims could abide peacefully, but rather *darul harb*, or a place of war and persecution. [82] The *fatwas* issued by leaders of the *khilafat* movement led to the migration of 30-40,000 Indian Muslims across the Durand Line, through the Khyber and Gomal Passes and

---

82   Qureshi, *Pan-Islam in British Indian Politics*, p. 181.

into Afghanistan between March and April 1920.[83] The migration was facilitated by local 'Khilafat Committees' scattered through the administered part of the NWFP, affiliated in principle though not by any organisational rigour to the national Khilafat Committee.[84]

As the migrants began to pour across the border, the misgivings of the Afghan government were first conveyed to Indians in Afghanistan including former members of the Jamaat-i Mujahidin. The Afghan General Nadir Khan asked the latter to convey to the leaders of the *hijrat* movement, the government's reservations about Afghanistan's ability to accommodate the massive influx of humanity.[85] Meanwhile Amanullah granted only 30,000 Afghan rupees to General Nadir Khan to meet the needs of the migrants, and finally closed Afghanistan's borders to the Indian Muslim migrants in August 1920.[86]

The awkward *hijrat* period, coinciding with Amanullah's war and his patronage of the Jamaat-i Mujahidin, suggested pan-Islamic motivations and even aspirations to the title of Caliph on the part of Amanullah Khan. But the amir's vision was far more pragmatic and limited than this. The conclusions of the First World War and the Third Anglo-Afghan War had greatly altered the conditions of the Tribal Areas. The brief affair between Indian anti-colonial nationalism and Afghanistan ended, as did Afghanistan's immediate need for a frontier forward zone against the British. Under British pressure to enforce the Anglo-Afghan Treaty of 1921, Amanullah tried to

---

83 Mushirul Hasan, 'Religion and Politics in India: The 'Ulama and the *Khilafat* Movement' in Mushirul Hasan (ed.), *Communal and Pan-Islamic Trends in Colonial India*. (Delhi, 1981), pp. 13-4; also see Qureshi's estimates, *Pan-Islam in British Indian Politics*, pp. 214-5.

84 The Khilafat Committees persisted even after 'failure' of the *khilafat* movement. These organisations and their importance later on will be discussed in more detail in chapter 6.

85 Shaidai says that General Nadir Khan wrote to the president of the *mujahidin* at Chamarkand, asking them to send a representative to British India in 'Fugitive Flight from Country to Country of Iqbal Shaidai'. Shaidai Collection National Archives Islamabad (hereafter SCNAI), ISA 25, p. 16.

86 Quoted in Qureshi, *Pan-Islam in British Indian Politics*, p. 210. From a Special Branch file on the 'Hijrat Movement', NDC 12/8/3.

restrict militarisation among the Tribal Areas Pakhtuns and under his own reformist agenda, he sought also to subject religion and the power of the 'ulama and pirs to the authority of the state. He recalled Abdur Raziq from Afghanistan after the latter issued new declarations of jihad against the British government in 1922.[87] In a letter to the Mulla Chaknawar, the administration at Jalalabad reminded the mulla that 'there is a covenant between the God granted government of Afghanistan and the British government [and] agreements by a God-gifted government cannot be broken' and asked that Mulla Sahib Chaknawar should desist from calling for jihad against the British and return home.[88] The directive to Mulla Sahib Chaknawar was backed up by the threat that his government granted 'estates' would be confiscated if he did not comply.[89] In an effort to centralise political and legal controls Amanullah also restricted the freedom and authority of the Afghan 'ulama over the interpretation and application of law. In another firman the amir asked that mullas in the Eastern Province desist from campaigns of tabligh and social adjudication in Afghan territory.[90]

But although Amanullah had to defuse the post-war tensions in the Tribal Areas to curb British suspicions and contain the power of ulama or the religious party in Afghanistan, he still needed a means of maintaining connections to the communities east of the Durand line. Amanullah continued to patronise the Tribal Areas mullas to preserve the peace within and integrity of the Tribal Areas as the

---

87 Proclamation of Islamic independence and the flame of revolution signed and sealed by Haji Abdur Raziq, in 'Afghanistan—Frontier Affairs—Haji Abdur Razzik'. OIOC L/PS/10/1019.

88 Letter from the Local Administration of Jalalabad to the Noble and Honourable Mulla Sahib Chaknawar dated [Aug. 1922]. Reproduced in Meera Jan Syal, Nomyali Ghazi, p. 135.

89 Ibid.

90 Royal firman from Amir Amanullah Khan received by Mulla Sahib Chaknawar, June 1926. Appendix Syal, Nomyali Ghazi, p. 129. Mulla Chaknawar was one of the few eastern Pakhtun mullas in the unusual position of serving communities on both sides of the border.

north-eastern border of Afghanistan and treated them with a great deal of generosity in order to secure their loyalties to him.[91] These *mullas* were invited as a group to attend the state *jirga* at Kabul in 1922 and organised attendance of British-side tribesmen with them to pay their respects to the amir in the national independence-day celebrations in 1923.[92] Purses of thousands of rupees were awarded to the *mullas* when they presented themselves at the Afghan court, and horses, guns and cartridges were sent to them under orders of the amir.[93] In 1927 Badshah Gul collected a sum of 12,000 Afghan Rupees on behalf of the Haji—a gift that arrived in Ghaziabad 'in silver laden on donkeys'. In addition he was given '12 rifles, 6 revolvers, and a consignment of cartridges together with robes of honour for himself and his sons'.[94] Similar gifts were conferred on Mulla Sayyid Akbar and Mulla Mahmud Akhunzada when they presented themselves at the Afghan court. Babra Mulla Sahib received 10 rifles, a pistol and 3,000 Kabuli rupees for his own personal use.[95] Mulla Sahib Chaknawar received gifts sent personally to him by Amir Amanullah, a grant of 5,000 Kabuli rupees to send him on Haj, and a pension of 1,000 Rupees for life.[96]

Aside from these personal gifts, Amanullah Khan supported the frontier *mullas* with endowments to enhance their religious prestige, but only in the Tribal Areas. Mulla Chaknawar's *masjid* at Gandab

---

91   KPD, 3 March 1923.

92   1,500 Afridis and 2,500 Mohmands accompanied their *mullas* to the the Afghan independence-day celebrations in 1923. Amanullah was estimated to have spent up to 100,000 Kabuli rupees in gifts, entertainment and preparations for these guests. Report from Minister at Kabul to Secretary of State for India, March 1923 in 'Frontier transgressions, 1923-25'; and BAR 1922-3.

93   'Anti-British Conspiracy and Intrigue with Afghanistan and the Indo-Afghan Frontier'. OIOC L/PS/18/A 195.

94   NWFPPD, 28 May 1927.

95   Ahmed Yousuf, *Da Babray Mulla Sahib*, p. 44.

96   'Firman of Amir Amanullah Khan, 1307 [1930]'. Appendix Syal, *Nomyali Ghazi*, p. 131.

was built with a 2,000 rupee grant from Amir Amanullah in 1923,[97] and the former along with the Haji Turangzai, Shahzada of Rehankot,[98] Maulvi Makhfi and the Indian Mujahidin, also received money from the Afghans to set up schools throughout the Tribal Areas.[99] These bequests could be made with political impunity as far as the British were concerned, limit religious authority over communities in Afghanistan, and still serve the amir's purposes to maintain some connection with the British-side Tribal Areas. The religious stature of these functionaries cloaked the amir's grants in the ambiguity of devotion, and allowed him to harness the political and regulatory powers of religious authority which had been refined and consolidated by the *mullas* of the Akhund Ghaffur-Hadda Mulla line in the Tribal Areas. Hence Amanullah maintained his very tenuous hold on Afghanistan and connection to his military hinterland despite the enormous pressures on him.

The revolts of 1924 and 1928 and the utility of Amanullah's patronage

In 1924, a number of religious authorities in Afghanistan declared Amanullah's constitution as contrary to *shari'a*, and Amanullah a heretic.[100] The coalition of rebels voiced its anger at state control over matters which had long been matters decided under *shari'a* and hence deemed the concern of the *'ulama*. There was also a great outcry against mandatory conscription and women's education.[101] Rebel *'ulama* fled to the Afghan Southern Province where they

---

97 'Renovation of *mosque* and school established between Ghalani and Sanger in the Gandab by the Chaknawar Mulla in 1923'. NWFPPA, DCOP, Special Reports and Files.

98 The reknowned *mulla* of Dir who acted as the Nawab's advisor on political matters.

99 'North-West Frontier: Intrigues in Dir and Bajaur etc'. OIOC L/PS/10/929; NWFPPD, April 1923.

100 Nawid *Religious Response*, pp. 100-4, 114.

101 Ibid. p. 102; Poullada, *Reform and Rebellion in Afghanistan*, pp. 160-3.

were harboured by the Mangal clans. The clans refused to hand the dissidents over to the Afghan authorities and began organising an armed mobilisation. The Mangal clans were supported by the Ahmedzai Ghilzais in Khost and headed by Abdul Karim, a claimant to the Afghan throne. A *lashkar* of 6,000 Mangals gathered in the south-east. Army troops in Khost were insufficient to counter the attacks of hostile *lashkars* on army line and posts—moreover Amanullah was not sure of the loyalty of his general Nadir Khan or of his army.[102] He issued calls for military assistance through the governors of the Eastern and Southern Provinces, summoning the Khyber Afridis and the Wazir and Mahsud clans of Waziristan to Jalalabad.[103] Supporters had only to present themselves and join the government forces and would be issued with rifles which they could retain afterwards as a reward for services rendered.[104] Amanullah appealed particularly to the *mullas* of the Tribal Areas, drawing now on his conciliatory policy towards them.

Amanullah's military summons was reiterated within the Tribal Areas by *mullas* of the Akhund Ghaffur-Hadda Mulla line, including the Haji Turangzai, Mulla Chaknawar, the Ustad of Hadda, the Akhunzada of Tagao and Lala Pir of Khost. Haji Abdur Raziq was also deputed back to Waziristan to aid this mobilisation.[105] *Lashkars* of Wazirs, Mahsuds, Mohmands and Afridis from the British-side Tribal Areas were brought in from the east to join the Afghan army at Kandahar, Jalalabad and Urghun to try to encircle the rebels.[106] A

---

102 Foreign and Political Department to Secretary of State for India, 20 April 1924, in 'Afghanistan: the Khost Rebellion'. OIOC L/PS/10/1112.

103 Maconachie, British Minister to Kabul to Secretary of State for Foreign Affairs, 29 Sept. 1924, ibid.

104 Viceroy Foreign and Political Department to British Minister at Kabul, 27 September 1924, ibid.

105 Minister at Kabul to Secretary of State for Foreign Affairs, India Office, 12 Aug. 1924, ibid.

106 NWFP Intelligence Bureau Diary (hereafter NWFPIBD), 9 Oct. 1924 in 'Khost Rebellion—British Side Participation'. OIOC L/PS/10/1081.

lashkar of 4,000 Afghan regulars supported by tribal volunteers gathered at Gardez,[107] and another 2,000 men collected at Kandahar.[108]

The agency of the eastern Pakhtun *mullas* in countering the Khost insurgency went beyond just military organisation. The Haji Turangzai, Mulla Chaknawar, the Ustad of Hadda and the Akhunzada of Tagao participated in a deputation to negotiate with the rebel leaders and initiate a dialogue between the Mangals and the Afghan government.[109] Amanullah's policy of cultivating support among these religious authorities paid dividends as the rebels began to advance towards Kabul. Mulla Sahib Chaknawar and Haji Sahib Turangzai travelled among the Pakhtun tribes of eastern Afghanistan, trying to re-establish some loyalty to the amir.

The uprising was put down by the end of the year and Afghan government authority re-established in the Southern Province. Afridis and Wazirs, and *mullas* who had assisted Amanullah were rewarded with gifts of rifles and ammunition, and honours were conferred on them. [110] Maconachie, British minister at Kabul, stated that while the assistance rendered to Amanullah by Tribal Areas parties was not desirable, he did not see that he had much choice but to solicit this assistance. Maconachie recommended that the government turn a blind eye to the Tribal Areas mobilisations in 1924, as long as Amanullah did not seek to include these parties in large public demonstrations of his power and popularity.[111] The Khost rebellion put Amanullah's frontier policy into effect and was testimony to its potential. His patronage of *mullas'* activities among the Tribal Areas

---

107 Foreign and Political Department to Secretary of State for India, 20 March 1924, ibid.

108 Minister at Kabul to Secretary of State for Foreign Affairs India Office, 27 Aug. 1924, in 'Afghanistan: Khost Rebellion'.

109 NWFPIBD, 9 Oct. 1924; 'Anti British Conspiracy and Intrigue in Afghanistan and on the Indo-Afghan Frontier'. OIOC L/PS/18/A 195.

110 'Anti British Conspiracy and Intrigue in Afghanistan and on the Indo-Afghan frontier'.

111 Maconachie, British Minister to Kabul to Secretary of State for Foreign Affairs, 29 Sept. 1924, in 'Afghanistan: Khost Rebellion'.

population allowed him to support the leadership, military capabilities and social authority of the eastern Pakhtun *mullas* without contradicting his own national policy of centralised authority and military and religious control, or unduly antagonising the British Government of India.

With renewed confidence, Amanullah pursued his agenda of reform until September 1928 when the Hafiz Sahib of Faqirabad led a revolt of the Shinwaris against his government backed up by a *fatwa* signed by 400 Afghan *ulama* accusing Amanullah of heresy.[112] The dissidents denounced him for his centralising and modernist reforms and prepared to march on Jalalabad. Discontent was growing rapidly, but the *mullas* of the Akhund Ghaffur-Hadda Mulla line set themselves apart from the dissidents and remained in support of Amanullah Khan. Mulla Chaknawar tried to rally support for Amanullah among the Mohmands, and repeatedly approached the Afghan and British-side groups for commitments of support.[113] Mulla Chaknawar and Haji Turangzai tried to reach cease-fire agreements with the rebels, issuing a *fatwa* in support of Amanullah,[114] and Haji Turangzai despatched a *lashkar* of 2,000 Safis and Kandaharis to Jalalabad under Badshah Gul.[115] A *jirga* was convened at Hadda in December 1928 to debate support to Amanullah and was attended by the Mulla Chaknawar, Akhunzada of Tagao and Badshah of Islampur as well as some government ministers. The attendees maintained their loyalty to Amanullah while recommending that he withdraw some of his proposed reforms.[116]

The situation in Afghanistan was complicated when a second rebellion broke out in the north. Habibullah, also known as Bacha-yi Saqao, was a Robin Hood character who had started as a highway

---

112 Nawid, *Religious Responses*, p. 155

113 CC NWFP to Viceroy, 24 Nov. 1928, in 'Afghanistan: Afghan Rebellion 1928-1929.' OIOC L/PS/10/1287.

114 Viceroy to Secretary of State for India, 21 Dec. 1928, ibid.

115 CC NWFP to Viceroy, 15 Dec. 1928, ibid.

116 Nawid, *Religious Responses*, p. 164.

robber from Kohistan, and quickly came to the fore of an uprising in Tagao that began as a protest against taxes and army conscription. Habibullah quickly gained the support of the Mujaddidiyya of Kabul, increasing pressure on *mullas* of the Akhund Ghaffur-Hadda Mulla line to join with him and the other rebels. Soon after the conference at Hadda, Mulla Chaknawar and the Akhunzada of Tagao declared their sympathies with the rebels and denounced Amanullah Khan as a *kafir*. Amanullah abdicated and retreated to Kandahar, leaving the throne to his uncle, Inayatullah, who was soon deposed in favour of Habibullah.[117] In Jalalabad Ali Ahmad, the former governor of Kabul staked his own claim to the throne supported by the Ustad of Hadda and the Hazrat of Charbagh.[118] The authority of the Kabul amirate was completely fractured, and the Tribal Areas response varied from watchful silence on the part of the Mohmands to booty-motivated participation by the Afridis.[119]

In efforts to consolidate authority, the three competitors to the throne appealed to Afghan *'ulama* and *mullas*. Amanullah Khan tried to regroup in Kandahar, entertaining a *jirga* of *mullas* at his residence there.[120] He sent Mulla Guldin to Wana to distribute royal proclamations and try to encourage support there.[121] Ali Ahmed at Kandahar widely advertised that he had secured the support and loyalty of the Chaknawar Mulla, the Naqib of Charbagh, and the Ustad of Hadda, and wrongly claimed that he also had the support of Haji Turangzai.[122] Habibullah, struggling to establish himself in Kabul, declared that he would reinstate allowances to all *mullas* and tribal *maliks* (presumably on both sides of the border), previously cut off

---

117 Ibid, pp. 164-73.

118 CC NWFP to Viceroy, 28 Jan. 1929, in 'Afghanistan: Afghan Rebellion'.

119 CC NWFP to Viceroy, 30 Jan. 1929, ibid.

120 Minister at Kabul to Secretary of State for Foreign Affairs, 10 Feb. 1929, ibid.

121 CC NWFP to Secretary of State for India, 24 Feb. 1929, ibid.

122 Minister at Kabul to Secretary of State for Foreign Affairs, 14 Feb. 1929, ibid.

by Amanullah Khan.[123] During this time, Nadir Khan, general of the Afghan army under Amanullah, was in Delhi and refused Amanullah's repeated requests to join him in Kandahar.[124] In March 1929, Nadir Khan independently sent an emissary to the Tribal Areas to organise support among the Mohmands, Khugianis, Shinwaris and Safis.[125] Asserting their influence over the election of the new amir, the eastern Pakhtun *mullas* arranged a *jirga* at Hadda to decide a favoured candidate for the throne. Mulla Chaknawar, Ustad Sahib Hadda, Mulla Tagao, Badshah Gul and the Haji Turangzai along with some *'ulama* from Peshawar were notable attendees at this *jirga*.[126]

In April 1929 some *'ulama* from the administered part of the North-West Frontier Province formed a deputation or *wafd* to re-establish support for Amanullah.[127] These *'ulama* were members of the Peshawar Khilafat Committee and had helped organise the *khilafat* and *hijrat* mobilisations in the 1919-21 period.[128] Because of their participation in those activities, members of the organisation had worked with the Tribal Areas *mullas* before. The *wafd* set out for the Tribal Areas to use the influence of the members and their relations with the frontier *mullas* to consolidate support for Amanullah among the tribes. They did this within a circuit covering Mohmand and Bajaur and stretching to the Afghan Eastern Province, along which stopping points and *jirgas* were arranged by regional *mullas* at which the *'ulama* could argue their case before the local Pakhtun tribes .[129] The greatest success of the *wafd* was with the Mitai Musa

---

123 Minister at Kabul to Secretary of State for Foreign Affairs, 16 Feb. 1929, ibid.

124 CC NWFP to Viceroy, 28 Feb. 1929, ibid.

125 MPD, 9 March 1929.

126 MPD, 23 March 1929.

127 Abdur Rahim Popalzai, *Afghanistan Mein Qayam-e-Aman* (Rawalpindi, 1929, reprint Peshawar, 1996), p. 8.

128 Popalzai, *Afghanistan Mein*, p. 9. The provincial Khilafat Committees are discussed in greater detail further on in this chapter.

129 Popalzai, *Afghanistan Mein*, pp. 24, 34.

Khel. Despite the clan's long-standing animosity to the Haji Turang-zai over their acceptance of British allowances, the Musa Khel defied warnings by the District Commissioner Peshawar and declared their unanimous support for Amanullah.[130]

Soon after, Amanullah's general Nadir Khan came out with his own claim to the throne, just as Habibullah was losing popularity un-der accusations of heavy-handedness and increasing concern among the Pakhtuns about his Tajik background.[131] Nadir Khan sent letters to the Haji Turangzai and Miyan Sarkanri, promising rewards for their 'pious prayers' for him. He flattered the Tribal Areas *mullas* by sending his nephew to lend weight to an inter-clan settlement being arranged by Badshah Gul and Haji Turangzai.[132] Amanullah's return to power now seemed impossible. Having failed in their efforts to reinstate him, but faced with an acceptable substitute in Nadir Khan who had served as the agent of the amir to the Tribal Areas for so many years and promised to abolish Amanullah's reforms, Badshah Gul I, the Haji Turangzai and other Tribal Areas *mullas* came out in active support of him soon thereafter. In return for their support, Nadir Khan maintained Amanullah's style of patronage, making gifts of money and guns and conferring honours on the Mulla Chakna-war, Ustad of Hadda, Miyan of Sarkanri, the son of the Badshah of the Islampur, the Haji Turangzai and Badshah Gul.[133] Nadir Khan finally began to make gains against Habibullah supported by Khu-giani, Safi and Mohmand *lashkars*, and claimed the throne at Kabul by the end of 1929.[134]

Military successes of 1919 and 1924 and Amanullah's recogni-tion of the Tribal Areas *mullas* as important allies of his state made the Tribal Areas *mullas* visible and powerful figures in the Tribal

130   CC NWFP to Viceroy, 20 Nov. 1928, in 'Afghanistan: Afghan Rebellion.'

131   MPD, 24 Aug. 1929.

132   MPD, 31 Aug. 1929.

133   MPD, 29 March 1930.

134   MPD, Aug.-Oct. 1929.

Areas in the years that followed and gave them a strong Afghan bias. Afghan patronage of the Tribal Areas *mullas* declined with Nadir Khan's death and the succession of his son Zahir Khan—known as Zahir Shah after his coronation—in 1933. However Amanullah's reign had sufficiently established that these figures could sway the fortune of any amir in Kabul and would always be a useful check on the British. Subsequently, Zahir Shah's government was careful never to try to undermine the power of, or politically discredit the *mullas*.

5
CONSOLIDATING AUTONOMY
1923-1930

Together Deobandi and Afghan engagement in the Tribal Areas enriched the Hadda Mulla's successors and the prominence of the *pirimuridi* line through the period 1915-30 to give their activities a great deal more significance. Their constant agenda to organise tribal activity within the borders of the Tribal Areas and remain a part of community and inter-tribal relations was pursued with more resources and a great deal more colonial and press attention being paid to them. But despite the hyperbole of Amanullah's nationalistic declarations and Deobandi religious idealisation regarding Pakhtun tribal society, the *mullas'* programme of securing the terms of their regional autonomy was not one of blind resistance to political absorption into British India. It was a series of inter-tribal diplomatic and military manoeuvres aimed at preserving the conditions within which their authority was established—balanced power between different tribes and preservation of governmental and social autonomy within the tribal regions. The move away from the ideology of British resistance was encouraged by changes in the climate within which the *mullas* addressed these issues after 1921. British efforts to ensure their own military preparedness up to the border region renewed the military department's and political office's interests in establishing the loyalty of the border tribes.

The Waziristan and Khyber resistances

After the Third Anglo-Afghan War which highlighted the failures in British troop mobilisations to the border region, the British began a renewed 'forward movement' into Waziristan and the Khyber. This involved the construction of roads and cantonments and the re-establishment of the North-Waziristan Tochi Scouts and the South-Waziristan Scouts, and the construction of a broad-gauge railway through the Khyber Pass. Both initiatives met with tribal resistance but only the Khyber resistance was actively taken up by the *mullas* of the Hadda line. Comparison of the two cases highlights the very important fact that the bare principle of anti-colonialism did not determine the *mullas'* actions.

In Waziristan, tribes staged strong opposition to construction and planning work for the new roads and rails, organising attacks on survey parties and condemning any clan that offered to provide *khassadars* or labourers for the schemes. The mobilisation was strongly supported by Amanullah's deputy to the region, Abdur Raziq, who had stayed on after the conclusion of the Third Anglo-Afghan War. Another Jamaat-i Mujahidin member, Maulana Bashir moved to Waziristan during this time and began publishing a newspaper called *Ghazah* (Farsi for *ghazvah* or religious war), in 1920-1.[1] Abdur Raziq encouraged the Ahmedzai Wazirs to resist British encroachment, securing large allowances for them from Amanullah's government. Afghan aid to the Ahmedzai Wazirs was eventually cut off in 1923 and Amanullah Khan recalled Abdur Raziq to Kabul, but a deputation of 30 other *mujahidin* went to Waziristan in March 1923 and remained in Makin under Maulana Bashir's direction to encourage and aid resistance to the British there.[2] Despite *mujahidin* support of the movement, only one relatively unknown *mulla* was directly involved in the mobilisation.

The Jamaat-i Mujahidin tried to popularise sentiment against the British for their campaign in Waziristan among other Tribal Areas communities.[3] They did this through the *Al Mujahid*—the newspa-

---

1 'Intelligence Branch Memo on Maulana Bashir, 1925' in 'Maulana Abdul Rahim', Special Branch NWFP, 727/45.

2 NWFPIBD, 1 March 1923.

3 Members of the Jamaat-i Mujahidin who went to Afghanistan helped to set

per of the Chamarkand colony which began to be published in 1922 and continued to run print until 1940.[4] The newspaper contained summaries of relevant news from the British, Indian and Afghan press, with editorials and commentary highlighting issues of specific regional concern such as the *khilafat* movement, Amanullah's reforms and military expenditure in the frontier. The editors emphasised that there was a unity to the Tribal Areas encapsulated in the common condition and concerns of its disparate and often warring communities.[5] The land had however been violated and 'cut to pieces' by roads, military posts, forts and camps which separated its people.[6] The ongoing military campaign in Waziristan demonstrated the heavy-handedness of the administration and the editors warned the Pakhtuns tribes and the *mullas* that:

Mind that if the enemy succeeds even a little in Waziristan no other place in the frontier will be able to make any opposition to his aggressions because roads have long ago been constructed in the directions of Chakdarra and Chitral, and the Khyber railway, Thal, Kurram and other grand roads have

---

up the *Ittehad-i Mashriqi* in the Eastern Province. Editorial staff at the *Ittehad-i Mashriqi* lent a great deal of support to the editors of *Al Mujahid* as well as covering news of Tribal Areas mobilisations. A report of the declaration of war against the British by Haji Abdur Raziq was featured in one of the first issues of the *Ittehad-e-Mashriqi*; and in 1923, the British Agent at Kabul described the editorial staff's overwhelming concern with the conditions in Waziristan and their repeated call for a cessation of the British bombardment of that area and intervention by the amir. See Chamarkandi, *Sarguzasht-e-Mujahid* p. 95; *Ittehad-e-Mashriqi* n.d. 'Abdul Raziq's Declaration of War', appendix Zalmai, *Mujahid-i Afghan*, p. 204.

4 Chamarkandi, *Sarguzasht-i Mujahid*, p. 95.

5 This newspaper and the opinions stated there developed as the legacy of the movement of the Jamaat-i Mujahidin, but also under the patronage of an Indian intelligentsia that become involved in print journalism in Afghanistan. The launch of the *Al Mujahid* led to the articulation of Deobandi nationalist and Afghan cultural influences by individuals who had chosen to remain in the Tribal Areas and involved in the religious inter-tribal politics of the region. Chamarkandi's references to *Al Mujahid* suggest that the newspaper was produced for an external readership as well—it was surreptitiously posted to dissidents in Hindustan and had a subscriber base in Afghanistan. Chamarkandi, *Sarguzasht-i Mujahid*, p. 69.

6 *Al Mujahid*, 19 April 1923. NWFPPA Special Branch NWFP, file 410.

been fortified and defended so that the whole of *Yaghistan* is in the power of the enemy.[7]

Fazal Ilahi and Maulana Bashir translated reports of expenditure and military budgets for the north-west frontier in the *Al Mujahid*. It was reported that the finance minister had submitted for a decrease in expenditure in the civil branch of administration in the North-West Frontier Province, but demanded an increase of 3.5 million rupees for Waziristan expenses to meet the requirements of different heads there. In another article Bashir liberally estimated the expenditure on frontier campaigns as 30 million in addition to half a million in subsidies and ammunition on Waziristan expeditions over the previous four years. The article highlighted that the English ministries and papers had derided the high costs of the campaign, pointing out that the Waziristan resistance was eroding public support for the newly revived 'forward policy'.[8]

While the *mullas* of the Hadda line did express moral solidarity with the Waziristan insurgency, prominent members of the line who were in Waziristan, including the new Mulla Powindah Fazl Din and Mulla Hamzullah, did not contribute militarily to the mobilisation. The British ultimately secured tribal complicity with their project through huge increases in allowances in Waziristan—from about 130,000 rupees in 1919 to almost 280,000 by 1925, in addition to which 1.9 million rupees were being paid out under the *khassadar* scheme.[9] Despite the continuing calls to arms from the *mujahidin*, Wazir border raids and attacks on military posts in the Tribal Areas had almost entirely ceased by 1925 and the remaining pockets of resistance were wiped out in aerial campaigns.[10] The *mujahidin* continued to try to 'supply information about border problems and affairs' and 'disclose the plans of the enemies … for the erosion

---

7   *Al Mujahid*, 6 Oct. 1922. NWFPPA Special Branch NWFP, file 427.

8   *Al Mujahid*, 23 March 1923. NWFPPA Special Branch NWFP, file 410.

9   Warren, *The Faqir of Ipi*, p. 56.

10   Ibid, pp. 57-9; see also Hugh Beattie, *The Imperial Frontier: Tribe State in Waziristan* (Routledge, 2001), pp. 207-8.

of independence of the border tribes',[11] to the *mullas* of the Hadda Mulla line in Mohmand, Bajaur, Khyber, Tirah, Dir and Swat but the latter did not mobilise in support of the Wazir tribes.

The failure of the network to take up the Waziristan issue on ideological grounds can only be understood if *mulla* action and tribal action are accepted as being mutually affirming in the Tribal Areas. Because the Hadda line adherent tribes, and ultimately all the tribes in Waziristan, did not see the utility in opposing the scheme once its monetary benefit accrued to them, they did not oppose the scheme. Tribes in the northern Tribal Areas certainly had no stake in the matter and their *mullas* grounded by the tribal basis for their participation, remained aloof from the scheme. The concurrent movement in the Khyber over an almost identical railway scheme was however taken up by members of the Hadda Mulla line. These *mullas* became involved on the principle of equitable apportionment of allowances to tribes in the region, not the blind principle of opposition to 'colonial penetration'. The terms of their involvement in the resistance did not ultimately oppose British access through the region. They accepted the inevitability of this and were mollified by achieving the project.

When the plan for a new broad gauge railway through the Khyber into Afghanistan was presented in 1921, there was immediately opposition raised to the project by the Afridi clans.[12] A number of clansmen launched an appeal before Mulla Sayyid Akbar asking him to forestall the government plans because the Kuki Khels Afridis, by virtue of proximity to the road, provided *khassadars* to protect the Khyber Pass and earned profits and secured contracts for the job without sharing them with other clans who claimed equal ancestral tribal proprietary rights over the road.[13] These other clans, specifically

---

11 Report on *Al Mujahid*, 28 Aug. 1923. NWFPPA Special Branch NWFP, file 410.

12 Memo from Colonel Humphrys, British Minister at Kabul, 1921. OIOC L/PS/11/180.

13 Petition 30 Dec. 1920, submitted to PA Khyber by *jirgas* of Kambar Khel, Kamalai, Sepah and Aka Khel Afridis. There had been opposition to such schemes in the past as well. Mulla Mahmud Akhunzada and Mulla Sayyid

the Aka Khel, Kambar Khel, Kamalai and Sepah Afridis, came together at a *jirga* of about 600 people at Bagh, and formally approved
the authority of the Mulla Sayyid Akbar to punish those intending
to participate in construction of the railway.[14] Accordingly, Mulla
Sayyid Akbar publicly denounced the allowances holders and other
clans like the Zakka Khel who supported the project in anticipation
of compensation. Mulla Chaknawar gave several *khutbas* scathingly
referreing to the 'iniquity of those working on the Khyber railway' in
his support.[15]

Mulla Sayyid Akbar reiterated the *mujahidin's* warnings of violation
and dismemberment of the Tribal Areas and began to isolate groups
that were friendly to the British government and had participated
in colonial road-building schemes and provided *khassadars*.[16] His efforts quickly produced desirable results for the affronted clans—the
political office sanctioned increased allowances and contracts for
construction labour to the previously excluded groups. Under this
policy, undertaken to secure the 'goodwill and cooperation of the
Afridis during construction, and good behaviour after the line had
been completed', there was a total increase in allowances of 84,000
rupees. This included special allowances of between 6,000 and 9,000
rupees each to the Kambar Khel, Kamalai, Sepah, Aka Khel and
Malikdin Khel, and 17,000 rupees in personal *lungi* allowances to
the *maliks* of these clans.[17]

Mulla Sayyid Akbar stopped speaking out against the railway
once most of the Afridis were in receipt of government allowances
demonstrating his commitment to the resistance was secondary to

---

Akbar started a campaign to prevent Afridi enlistment in the tribal levies in
1915 and 1916. OIOC L/PS/11/180.

14 KPD, 18 June 1921.

15 KPD, 18 June 1921.

16 'Note by the PA Khyber, 31 Oct. 1920' in 'Correspondence on construction
of a railway line through Khyber'. NWFPPA. Political Agent Khyber, file
215/32.

17 'Statement of Tribal Allowances, 1931'.

his commitment to the communities he served. In return, the Afridi clans did not object when he declared himself *badshah* of Tirah and the supreme religious authority there. On the other hand, Mulla Sayyid also retained his religious position, his involvement in regional arbitrations, his connections to the Afghan court and his relationship with the Jamaat-i Mujahidin and other regional *mullas* even after capitulating on the Khyber railway resistance.[18] Leadership of the Tirah resistance had been a successful enterprise for him and only heightened Afridi commitment to him and his regional reputation.

Despite the great focus by the British government and by the nationalist press in India on tribal *mulla*-led opposition to roads and railways in the Tribal Areas, the rhetoric of resistance popularised by the Jamaat-i Mujahidin was perhaps just that. Certainly the Jamaat-i Mujahidin and the *mullas* were in no position to prevent settlements with the British owing to the limitation on all other forms of economic activity, much though they may have hoped that such rapproachments would not occur. In the case of the Khyber railway, the Mulla Sayyid Akbar's prime objective was to prevent a settlement between the Kuki Khel and the British without a corresponding settlement offer to the lesser clans in order to maintain parity between clan groups. Once this was accomplished he did not pursue a course of religiously or nationalistically motivated anti-colonial resistance any further.

The valorisation of Ajab Khan Afridi

In a case which allowed the *mullas* to take up an issue on ideological grounds without needing to correlate it to tribal concerns, the *mullas* of the Hadda line, led by Haji Turangzai, championed the cause of an outlaw whom the British wanted to extradite for punishment. The *mullas* used the case to impress upon colonial representatives that they were the only authorities in the region who could force anyone to account, and that their judgements and mediations had to be ac-

---

18 NWFPPD, 1923-1927.

corded respect rather than trying to enforce collective responsibility on tribes through threats of punishment and promises of privileges.

In April 1923 Ajab Khan of the Bosti Khel clan of the Afridi tribe of Tirah entered the administered district of Kohat and broke into the house of Major Archibald Ellis with a small group of accomplices. The group murdered Mrs Ellis and abducted the couple's eighteen-year-old daughter Molly. They then returned to Tirah with Molly held to ransom. Warnings had already gone out from the political agencies to the Afridi and Orakzai tribes, stating that any tribe that gave the 'outlaws' shelter or safe passage would be held culpable for the crime itself. Hence Ajab Khan did not return to his village but went to the Mulla Mahmud Akhunzada for shelter.[19] Mulla Mahmud wrote to the political office that Ajab Khan was with him and that he could, for the price of 15,000 rupees, serve as mediator between Ajab Khan Afridi and the British.[20]

Ajab Khan was not unknown to the political office. He and his group had been responsible for a raid on a police line at Kohat in February of that year and had made off with 46 government rifles—a valuable prize—and a tribal levy had been sent into Ajab Khan's village in Tirah at the direction of the Deputy Commissioner Kohat to recover the rifles. In the period between February and April the Political Agent Khyber had been exerting pressure on the Tirah and Afridi clans to pay a penalty for their tribesman's misdemeanour, and a date had been decided to convene a *jirga* of tribes and government to decide what compensation the responsible tribes would pay for Ajab Khan's transgression.[21]

A small deputation was despatched to the Mulla Mahmud Akhunzada comprised of the Assistant Political Officer Kurram, Khan Bahadur Kuli Khan, Khan Bahadur Gulbaz Khan and a British friend

---

19 DC Kohat to CC Peshawar, 19 April 1923 in 'Murder of Mrs Ellis and abduction of her daughter, Miss Ellis'. OIOC L/PS/10/1062.

20 Extract from official report of Legislative Assembly debates, 9 July 1923, ibid.

21 Ibid.

of the Ellis family, Mrs Starr. The movement of the group was facilitated by Abdul Haq, the son of the Mulla Karbogha, who offered
a means of intercession with the Mulla Mahmud Akhunzada, and
was 'the real safeguard of the party through independent territory'.[22]
When the group reached his house, Mulla Akhunzada put forward
Ajab Khan's demands—the release of the village men captured in the
British raid on Ajab's village in February. After securing Kuli Khan's
commitment that this would happen, Mulla Akhunzada had Molly
Ellis brought to his house and handed her over to the British party.

Arbitration performed by *mullas* between antagonistic parties was
not unusual. It was, however, unusual for the arbitration to be solicited and paid for by the Government of India. Normally, the Political
Agent would bring pressure to bear on local tribes until an 'outlaw'
had been handed over. However the delicacy of this particular situation necessitated the immediate release of Molly Ellis, at whatever
cost to established policy. Moreover, the fact that Ajab Khan was not
actually in tribal territory but under the *mulla's* protection meant that
negotiations through the tribes would be a lengthy process. In the position of arbitrator, Mulla Akhunzada was able to negotiate between
Ajab Khan and the British as though they were two equal parties,
suggesting that the release of the girl was conditional on meeting
Ajab Khan's demand. Moreover, Mulla Mahmud maintained Ajab's
freedom and autonomy of the region tribes, denying that there was a
tribal 'responsibility' to hand him over for punishment.

Other regional *mullas* took up Ajab Khan's case and Mulla Mahmud's representation of the tribes as free of obligation to the British,
turning Ajab Khan into the symbol of Tribal Areas autonomy and
resistance to the British. Mulla Chaknawar took responsibility for
part of Ajab Khan's passage across the Tribal Areas after the negotiations were over and hid Ajab Khan's accomplice, Daud Shah. Mulla
Chaknawar and Haji Turangzai rallied the tribes, encouraging and
coercing them to get shelter and protection for Ajab Khan and his

---

22 'Mrs Starr's Report', ibid.

accomplices in local villages.[23] By October, Ajab Khan was taken to Chamarkand where he resided for some time with the *mujahidin*. This period at Chamarkand marked Ajab Khan Afridi's transformation into 'Ghazi Ajab Khan of *Yaghistan*'.[24] He wrote several letters from Chamarkand, relating his side of the events to the Political Agent Khyber, Khan Bahadur Kuli Khan and others involved in frontier administration, and to the government of Great Britain (through the Chief Commissioner NWFP). Ajab Khan's letters all repeated the same basic point: that his abduction of Molly Ellis had been instigated by his outrage over the British raid on his village in pursuit of the government rifles earlier in the year. He maintained that his was not a criminal act, but an act of direct retaliation against the government transgression and insult to his village in 'independent' territory.[25] Ajab Khan berated Kuli Khan and Mughal Baz Khan for their 'treachery' in helping the British, making the 'patriotic blood boil in every patriotic Afghan and self-respecting Muslim', and reiterated that his actions and their's would have great national consequence for the Pakhtuns and for British India.[26]

The Chief Commissioner NWFP authorised immediate retaliation against Ajab Khan, and the Political Agent Khyber organised an Afridi *lashkar* to enforce punishment on the gang members. The *lashkar* entered Ajab Khan's village of Jowaki and burned down the houses of Ajab Khan and his supporters. The Jowaki villagers had

---

23 MPD, 20 Feb. 1920.

24 The valorisation of Ajab Khan was directly facilitated by the remaining *mujahidin* at Chamarkand. Ajab Khan was granted the title of *sadar*, or president, of the *Anjuman-i Khudam-i Kabah Yaghistan*. (The *mujahidin* had often referred to their organisation as the Anjuman-i Khudam-i Kabah during the *khilafat* years. This 'organisation' was merely another face and agenda of the *mujahidin* and the participants corresponded exactly to what remained of the Jamaat-i Mujahidin itself.)

25 Ajab Khan Afridi to CC NWFP, 2 Oct. 1923, in 'Relations with Afghanistan—Printed Correspondence, 1921-1924'. OIOC L/PS/10/1049.

26 Ajab Khan Afridi to Khan Bahadur Kuli Khan, APO Kurram, n.d., ibid.

also to bear the burden of expense of feeding the Afridi *lashkar*.[27] The government also fought back against the *mullas'* rejection of tribal obligation to the British and new commitments to the British government were solicited from the Adam Khel and Khyber Afridis and the Orakzais. The text of the treaties reconfirmed that

Ajab Khan, Shahzada, Sultan Mir, Gul Akbar and Haidar Shah, who are enemies of our government, are our own enemies. The above-named persons and their relations shall hereafter never enter the territory of any of our tribes, the tribe concerned shall be bound to arrest them and hand them over to the government.[28]

The delicacy of the situation was understood by the political office. Mulla Mahmud had negotiated an agreement that maintained Ajab Khan's freedom, but this was now being repudiated by the British. In order to give validity to their criminalisation and persecution of Ajab Khan Afridi, the new treaties with the tribes were negotiated by two other *mullas*—Muhammad Abdul Haq who had originally conducted the British party into the Tribal Areas, and Sahibzada Abdul Hamid who happened to be the brother of Mulla Mahmud Akhunzada. An effort was being made to undermine the position taken by the Mulla Mahmud, Mulla Chaknawar and Haji Turangzai by soliciting an alternative religious position. However the weight of numbers and passion was on the side of the *mullas* supporting Ajab Khan. The tribes that agreed to extradite Ajab Khan and had provided *khassadars* to pursue the outlaws received scathing criticism from Mulla Sayyid Akbar, who called for a reprisal against the 'violators of the independence' of the Tribal Areas.[29]

The split between the allowance-holders and supporters of British policy on the one hand, and the Haji Turangzai, Mulla Chaknawar

---

27 CC NWFP to Foreign and Political Department, 19 June 1923. OIOC L/PS/10/1062.

28 'Agreements executed by (a) Afridis and Orakzai tribes at Shinawari on 13 May 1923' in CC NWFP to Foreign and Political Department, 29 June 1923, in 'Murder of Mrs Ellis and abduction of her daughter, Miss Ellis'.

29 KPD, 23 June 1923.

and Mulla Mahmud and their adherents on the other, did not lead to a major confrontation between the *mullas* and the tribes because Ajab Khan was moved in great secrecy, allowing the tribes to remain ignorant of his whereabouts. Nor were the British able to capture and prosecute Ajab Khan and undermine the position that the *mullas* had taken. In February 1924 the British exerted pressure on Amanullah Khan to use his influence in the Tribal Areas to force Ajab Khan's extradition. Amanullah Khan conducted negotiations with Ajab Khan and his accomplices through Badshah Gul and Haji Turangzai. It was finally decided that Ajab Khan would surrender for his crime, but only to the Afghan authorities. Badshah Gul and Haji Turangzai took responsibility for conveying the 'outlaws' and their families to Jalalabad where they would live under Afghan government supervision.[30] The *mullas* were paid 1,000 rupees by the amir in recognition of their services.[31]

The case of Ajab Khan Afridi became a rallying point for the *mullas* of the Akhund Ghaffur-Hadda Mulla line on two counts. The first was that Mulla Mahmud's mediation had affirmed the agency of *mullas*, while the second was that the use of the arbitration method suggested parity between the two parties—the representatives of Miss Ellis and of Ajab Khan Afridi. The British would never have been brought to the negotiating table had the matter not involved a young British girl. An Indian political officer had been kidnapped in Kurram some months earlier and a British Political Agent murdered in the Khyber in 1921 and neither incident had brought the colonial authorities to negotiate with the perpetrators of these acts in the Tribal Areas. The sensitivity of the situation in the light of Molly's age and the moral threat posed by her captivity by 'barbarous ... Pathan villains' meant that her immediate release had to be secured regardless of the political cost. Whether Ajab Khan had realised this and planned the events that followed is improbable. Yet he and the

30 KPD, 12 Jan. 1924 to 9 Feb. 1924.
31 KPD, 16 Feb. 1924.

Tribal Areas *mullas* legitimised his act as a morally and politically motivated one.

The people involved on Ajab Khan's side strongly emphasised the respect that had been accorded to both Molly Ellis and Mrs Starr. It was asserted that Ajab Khan had acted within the moral code of hospitality to his 'guest' as defined by *pakhtunwali*.[32] Mulla Mahmud presented Mrs Starr with a gold necklace as she left his house, as a 'traditional' gesture of respect.[33] Hence Ajab Khan's 'criminality' was cast as a noble act, well within the bounds of decency. Harbouring him became a political act of resistance to the British and past and later instances of outlaws being harboured with tribes and clans in the region were glamorised (although none were ever so popular or notorious as Ajab Khan).[34] Many of these cases were settled without extradition of the criminal and compensation for crimes was deducted directly from the balance of allowances payable to the clans, so while *mullas* appeared successful in their declaration of and attempts to reinforce tribal autonomy of action through the protection of outlaws, it was the British who forced through their version of tribal responsibility which inherently compromised that autonomy, and they certainly never negotiated through a *mulla* to gain access to the region again.[35]

The Mohmand blockade 1926-7

Haji Turangzai managed to secure Afghan allowances for select Mohmand clans after their support to Amanullah in the Khost rebellion.

---

32 The 'legend' of Ajab Khan Afridi that persists to this day emphasises that Molly Ellis was never treated improperly. Rather it is claimed that she long 'remembered' her Pakhtun captors with affection for the treatment accorded her. Ajab Khan Afridi's son, Naik Muhammad Ghazizuay, claimed that Mrs Starr had returned to the Khyber many years later to visit her 'old friends'. Interview, Naik Muhammad Ghazizuay, 10 Aug. 2002.

33 Mrs Starr's Report.

34 'NWFP Political Movement: Mujahidin of Chamarkand'. NDC 919.

35 'Afghanistan trans-frontier raids 1922-1930', OIOC L/PS/10/1020; 'Frontier transgressions, 1923-25', OIOC L/PS/10/1061.

When he took these to the Halimzai, Dawezai, Musa Khel and Safi Mohmands, he got a commitment from those *maliks* that as a condition of receiving this honour from the amir they would never accept British allowances again. However the new Khyber and Waziristan projects had led to a dramatic increase in British monetary support in Tribal Areas and it soon became apparent to the Mohmands that they had a chance at more secure and generous support from the British political office than from Afghanistan. Those clans closest to the British base in Shabqadar—the Halimzai, Musa Khel, Utmanzai and Dawezai Mohmands, all of whom had been stripped of their old allowances after their assistance to Amanullah in 1919—approached the Deputy Commissioner in Peshawar with commitments of *khassadar* troops and renewed pledges of loyalty.[36] The DC's office accepted the Mohmands' offer and approved allowances of more than 15,000 rupees for the Halimzai, 12,000 for the Musa Khel, almost 2,000 for the Utmanzai and 3,500 for the Dawezai.[37] When Haji Turangzai received news of this, he immediately rallied a *lashkar* to bring the *maliks* to account for having broken their oaths.[38] The *lashkar* was manned by Haji's own *shaikhs* and Safi and Mitai Musa Khel Mohmand clans who had not accepted new allowances from the political office. It entered the Dawezai, Utmanzai, Halimzai and Musa Khel villages and burned down and looted the houses of the errant *maliks*.[39] In typical style, the *lashkar* then dispersed.

Haji Turangzai's attack was seen as audacious and provocative, and a direct challenge to the British authorities. The Chief Commissioner, NWFP, was unwilling to allow it to go unchallenged and was determined that communities supporting British interests in the region had to be defended. He approved retaliatory measures against

---

36 'Report of the recent activities of the Haji Turangzai in Mohmand country, 16 April 1927'. District Officer Frontier Constabulary Shabqadar (hereafter DOFCS), 211/11.

37 'Statement of Tribal Allowances, 1931'.

38 'Report of recent activities of Haji Turangzai.'

39 Ibid.

the clans that had joined in the Haji's attack and Safi and Mitai Musa Khel clansmen settled in British territory were rounded up and jailed. Their release was subject to payment of a fine of 2,000 rupees by the clans. In Mohmand, Haji Turangzai was unwilling or unable to back down from the stand he had taken because of the penalties his supporters would have to pay. He announced to the Safi and Mitai Musa Khel that he would set out with another *lashkar* to punish those parties that had instigated the government reprisals.[40] He was aware at this point that the British response would be stronger but tried to diffuse this through the Faqir of Alingar who sent a letter to the political officer at Shabqadar claiming that the Haji's only motive in acting against the allowance-holding tribes was in defence of his own honour.

Attempting to steer the issue clear of confrontation with the British, the Haji emphasised that this was a necessary campaign of *amr-bil maruf*, but the Faqir of Alingar believed that the Haji Turangzai should use this occasion as an opportunity to call for a *jihad* against the British and rally wider support.[41] The Haji Turangzai maintained that it was an internal concern over the broken oaths and opposition posed to the Haji's mission in January, rather than the fact of payment of government allowances and resisted the Faqir's suggestions.[42] In an effort to force the Dawezai, Utmanzai and Halimzai to capitulate without the British becoming directly involved, the Haji exerted as much pressure as he possibly could under the prescriptions of *amr-bil maruf* and ordered all *mullas* to stop religious services on behalf of the oath-breakers and their supporting clans.[43] Then he sent the sons of Babra Mulla, the Faqir of Alingar and his own sons to give news of the mission among the Baizai, Khwaizai and Safi Mohmands and organise a new *lashkar*. 3,000 men volunteered and this

---

40 MPD, 2 April 1927.
41 MPD, 29 Jan. 1927.
42 MPD, Feb.-March 1927.
43 Mohmand Report, DC Peshawar, 20 April 1927. DOFCS 211/11.

army accompanied Haji Turangzai to Gandab to open talks with the Malik Anmir of the Halimzai clan.[44]

The Haji's desire to avoid military escalation led him to instruct the *lashkar* not to attack, even when some men at the Gandab village opened fire on the *lashkar* and killed one of the Haji's *shaikhs*. He was coercing Malik Anmir into moral and not military submission. Backed up of course by his formidable army, Haji Sahib asked that if the Halimzai would prefer he would henceforth have nothing to do with them and would leave the Mulla of Qasai to perform religious functions on behalf of the clan.[45] Faced with two alternatives—to categorically reject Haji Turangzai's authority, have his village burnt down and a dangerous enemy for ever after, or to humble himself and suffer the less expensive shame of capitulation, Malik Anmir accepted that he had done wrong by breaking an oath and identified a house in his village that could be burned down as penalty. Seeing the relatively stronger and better armed Halimzai's example, the Tarakzai also apologised for their oath-breaking and asked the Haji's forgiveness. In return, no doubt relieved that he had maintained his prestige and not been forced into battle with the British, Haji Sahib announced that the clans who had accepted allowances could keep them as they had already paid the price for having broken their oaths.

This would have been the end of the matter and Haji Turangzai would have succeeded in holding on to his position had the events not led to a British inquiry about the status of the Tribal Areas *mullas* and the threat posed by the Haji's relationship with the frontier tribes. Kuli Khan, the Assistant Political Officer Kurram who had helped in the recovery of Molly Ellis, was appointed officer on special duty to report on and help control the situation in Mohmand.[46]

---

44 'Report of recent activities of Haji Turangzai.'

45 Ibid.

46 CC NWFP to Foreign Secretary, Government of India, 27 April 1927. DOFCS file 5 B.

In his report Kuli Khan warned of the serious consequences of the confrontation between Malik Anmir and Haji Turangzai:

The events of the last ten days have convinced me that the influence of the *mullas* has developed from a religious to an authoritarian one. They can coerce any Mohmand [as though] a ruler rather than a *mulla* ... influence and fear of the *mullas* had increased considerably [and the clans] have been feeling the authority and fear of the *mullas*. It is therefore most important that the *mullas* should not be supported in any *amr-i maruf* against allowance-holders.[47]

Kuli Khan also pointed out that it was not all Tribal Areas *mullas*, but specifically *mullas* who were followers of the Haji Turangzai who threatened the government's interests. The sort of compliance these *mullas* demanded from their communities gave the *mullas* too much control and compromised colonial authority. Kuli Khan advised that clans in receipt of allowances be asked to make a commitment that they would not join in or assist any *lashkar* led by a *mulla* or join in any campaign of *amr-bil maruf* because it allowed the *mullas* to accumulate and exercise power.[48] The allowance-holding clans were asked to deposit 25,000 rupees each with the political officer at Shabqadar, a sum that would go forfeit if any clan was found to be participating in the *mullas' doras*.

Having narrowly escaped a major military confrontation, the Haji Turangzai did not respond to the colonial demands of the allowance-holding tribes. But he could not prevent the less predictable and more confrontational Faqir of Alingar from demanding a local retaliation against the criminal outlawing of religious authority. It was rumoured among the Faqir's supporters that he had had visions that convinced him of the necessity to attack the Frontier Constabulary post; and it was laughed about among his detractors that he had gone mad and believed that he had an army of invisible ghosts fol-

---

47   Report of Khan Bahadur Kuli Khan, officer on special duty, 29 April 1927. NWFPPA DCOP file 212 of 1927.
48   Note Shabqadar Fort, 13 May 1927, Ibid.

lowing him.[49] Despite internal dissent Faqir raised a *lashkar* to attack Shabqadar. Haji Turangzai, despite his best efforts to dissuade the Faqir, was forced under the pressure of his fraternal commitment and his personal stake in the issue to join the Faqir's *lashkar* with 600 Safi men.[50]

The DC Peshawar announced that the movement of the *lashkar* would be halted by aerial bombing, and any Mohmand clan allowing the Faqir's *lashkar* to pass through its territory would be considered complicit in the mobilisation and would not be spared the same treatment.[51] The Faqir's mobilisation immediately clarified the implications of the Mohmand allowances. These clans could not remain neutral in the face of *mulla*-led mobilisations because they were required to hold an inner line on behalf of the colonial administration by the provision of *khassadars* and intelligence and passivity and inaction in the face of offensive mobilisations towards the administered border were deemed as punishable as complicity and participation. The Mohmand allowance-holders formed a barrier between the *lashkar* and the administered districts. Supported by provisions and arms from the British, they held this line against the *lashkar*, preventing its progress and cutting off supplies to the clans beyond that had supported the mobilisation.[52]

Haji Turangzai tried to arrange a settlement between the lower allowance-holding or 'assured' Mohmands and the upper clans in order to break the blockade. He wrote letters to some of the Halimzai *maliks* asking them to attend a *jirga* along with all other 'elders and notables' among the Mohmand, Shinwari, Utmankhel, Safi, Mamund, Salarzai and Charmung sections, at his home in Ghaziabad in June 1927. He noted that he was doing the Halimzais a service by inviting them to Ghaziabad because of the great cost and inconven-

---

49   MPD, 27 May 1927.

50   MPD, 4 June 1927.

51   DC Peshawar to Secretary CC NWFP, 9 June 1927. DCOP file 212, 1927.

52   Ibid.

ience of the alternative, the Halimzais hosting Badshah Gul and his large retinue.[53] In return he demanded immediate attendance by the Halimzai—'come soon so a decision can be made. The *maliks* summoned from all sections are coming today.'[54] When the assured clans failed to attend, Haji Turangzai and the Mulla Chaknawar perfomed *doras* among local clans, both those directly involved in the blockade and neutral parties, to call for reprisals against the Musa Khel and Halimzai[55] and Haji Turangzai convened a jirga of 60 *mullas* from the Mitai Musa Khel area and asked them to impose severe punishment on the errant clans.[56] Trying to employ other tactics, Haji Turangzai and Mulla Chaknawar wrote repeatedly to the Hakim of Jalalabad and finally gained permission to offer a financial concession from the Afghan amirate to the Musa Khel to undermine their suport for the British.[57]

The blockade was taking a tremendous toll on the Musa Khel and the Halimzai clans as they withstood sniper attacks, severely curtailed freedom of movement in the Tribal Areas, personal insecurity, religious and social condemnation and pressure from the Afghan amirate.[58] But the greater threat posed by the British combined with a recommendation from Kuli Khan that the Commissioner increase allowances to the Halimzai as a reward for their commitment led the *maliks* to reject the *mullas'* appeals.[59] The *mullas* and their *lashkar* were forced to disperse which they eventually did because the sup-

---

53   Haji Turangzai to Malik Inayatullah Khan Mohmand (Halimzai), 18 Zilhaj, 1345 (17 June 1927), ibid.

54   Ibid.

55   Political Office Mohmand to CC NWFP, 17 Dec. 1927, in 'Mohmand Situation Reports 1927'. NWFPPA Tribal Research Cell 37/3 FRP.

56   NWFPPD, 21 Jan. 1928.

57   DC NWFP to CC NWFP, 14 Feb. 1928, in 'Mohmand Situation Reports 1927'. NWFPPA Tribal Research Cell 37/3 FRP.

58   Halimzai Mohmand *maliks* to DC Peshawar, 20 June 1927. NWFPPA DCOP file 212, 1927.

59   Note APA Kuli Khan, June 1927, ibid.

porting tribes could no longer withstand the shortage of food and other necessities created by the blockade.

The failed mobilisation of the Haji Turangzai and the Faqir of Alingar and the political office's response now forced Mohmand religious politics to centre on the question of British allowances, directly pitting the *mullas* against tribes accepting colonial support. Subsequent to the blockade, Haji Turangzai and Mulla Chaknawar regularly entered Gandab and burned houses of the disloyal *maliks* in such consistent and violent attacks that a Gandab villager bitterly stated 'the Haji Turangzai was fighting his entire *jihad* against Malik Anmir.'[60] The politics of the colonial incentive system to the tribes had long made it apparent to the *mullas* in Mohmand that their position was only guaranteed in the absence of British control in the region. With the dramatic increase in British allowances to clans that had previously been outside the net after 1920, the *mullas* were deeply threatened but unable to resist. It was not until the start of the nationalist movement in the NWFP after 1930, which will be discussed in chapter 6, that they would take a concerted stand against the central government, their antagonism encouraged by nationalists in the administered NWFP.

Containing the Malakand states

Swat's politics had been a pivot for regional religious organisation since the time of the Akhund of Swat. This political centrality was reinforced when the Khan of Dir, Nawab Aurangzeb Khan whose father had been briefly ousted by Umra Khan in 1895, marched on Swat and annexed the northern territories of Nikpi Khel tribe in Swat in 1908.[61] The young Mianguls were incapable of organising opposition to Dir and turned to *mullas* of the Hadda Mulla line—the Sartor Faqir, along with the Gud Mulla, Sandaki Mulla and the old Jan Sahib Doda in Dir and Bajaur. The *mullas* organised the only

---

60 Interview Ghulam Muhammad Din, Gandab, 13 Aug. 2002.

61 This history was discussed briefly in chapter 2. See Khan, *The Story of Swat*, p. 32

effective defence against the Nawab of Dir's incursions and their successes made them the strongest authorities in Swat at the time. Sandaki Mulla received a gift of 20,000 rupees for his military and diplomatic services from the clans of Swat a few years later.[62]

Opposition to Dir grew, nurtured by the Sandaki Mulla and his favoured candidate for the throne of Swat, Sayyid Jabbar Shah, descendant of Akbar Shah. By 1914 Sayyid Jabbar Shah's control began to extend down towards Saidu and the Babuzai and to threaten the Mianguls' control to the extent that they joined with the Nawab of Dir in opposition to Sayyid Jabbar Shah and the Sandaki Mulla.[63] With the continued efforts of the Sartor Faqir and the then newly-arrived Haji Turangzai, the region began to polarise around the Swat-Dir tensions. The Mulla Chaknawar, the Babra Mulla, Sayyid Jan Badshah of Islampur, the Gujjar Mulla, Makhrani Mulla, the Jan Sahib of Doda and, most important, the Shahzada of Rehankot who was *pir* of the Nawab of Dir, joined in the opposition to the Mianguls and Dir.[64]

The Shahzada of Rehankot's engagement in the dispute on the side of the Sandaki Mulla in 1915 demonstrated that the *pirimuridi* fraternity of the Hadda Mulla's line overrode loyalties of patronage and property. In desperation Nawab Aurangzeb of Dir sent his favourite wife to dissuade the Shahzada from joining Sayyid Jabbar Shah's faction, then threatened to burn the houses and confiscate the property of 'any *mulla, shaikh* or *talib*' who acted against him.[65] Yet the Shahzada maintained his allegiance and went on to warn members of the Dir levies to leave the Nawab's service, or risk excommunication from their home villages.[66]

By 1916 the *khans* of the small states of Khar, Jar, Jandol and Nawegai were involved in the dispute, with Khar rendering crucial

---

62 *Whos Who 1914*; NWFPPD, 17 April 1915.
63 Khan, *The Story of Swat*, pp. 34-6.
64 NWFPPD 1915-6.
65 NWFPPD, 11 Sept. 1915.
66 NWFPPD, 16 Oct. 1915.

strategic help to the Nawab of Dir, and the Khans of Jar, Jandol and Nawegai siding with the Sandaki Mulla.[67] In 1917 the rumour began to spread that Sayyid Abdul Jabbar Shah was secretly a *Qadiyani*—a Muslim sect considered heretical by many orthodox groups. This suspicion led the Sandaki Mulla to grudgingly denounce Sayyid Abdul Jabbar Shah and accept the Mianguls' claim to the Swat throne and their alliance with Dir. An uneasy truce was reached, but this peace ended abruptly when Miangul Shirin Badshah was murdered at Dir's instigation in 1918 and the Nawab of Dir renewed his claims to the left bank of Swat.[68]

Sandaki Mulla, together with the younger Mianguls, declared that he would avenge the ruler's death, renewing his commitment to the Mianguls and his opposition to Dir.[69] The Swat tribes led by the Sandaki Mulla engaged the Nawab of Dir's forces in open hostilities and other clans in the region including the Mohmands, Mamunds and Salarzai and the states of Khar, Jandol and Nawegai took up arms on behalf of their favoured party. As tensions spread among the communities served by the *mullas* of the Hadda line, Haji Sahib Turangzai and the young Jan Sahib Doda attempted to open dialogue between the warring groups. Haji Turangzai convened a *jirga* between the pro-Dir Salarzai and Mamunds and the anti-Dir Mohmand factions at the house of the Babra Mulla Sahib to discuss a settlement.[70] In recognition of their role as intermediaries and their ability to drive a settlement, Nawab Aurangzeb of Dir tried to win over these *mullas* by offering them allowances[71] and sent a *jirga* of *mullas* loyal to him to try to convince the Babra Mulla to support him.[72] But the *mullas* opposed the Nawab's heavy handedness at the

---

67 NWFPPD 1915-6.

68 NWFPPD, 13 July 1918.

69 NWFPPD, 7 Sept. 1918.

70 NWFPPD, 5 Jan. 1918.

71 NWFPPD, 16 Feb. 1918.

72 This *jirga* comprised of the Mulla Sahib Markhani, Gul, son of Baba Sahib of Dir and the Siar Shaikh Sahib. NWFPPD, 14 Jan. 1919.

expense of smaller clans and and led *lashkars* in attacks against the Nawab's army.[73]

In 1924 the Khan of Khar, supported by the new ruler of Dir, Shahjahan Khan, tried to annex the territories of the Khan of Nawegai in Bajaur.[74] In Swat, Miangul Shirin's son and successor, Miangul Abdul Wudud, was trying to consolidate his position and began to draw the upper Swat-Kohistan tribes, who had previously had a tax amnesty, into his tax net. Mulla Sandaki started a movement opposing the direct taxation of the Painda Khel by the Mianguls. His vociferous denunciation of the Miangul's policy led him to be expelled from upper Swat. In Bajaur, Haji Turangzai called for a *jihad* against the Khan of Khar and mobilised a Mohmand *lashkar* to help the Khan of Nawegai respond to Khar's threatening posture.[75] Badshah Gul led this *lashkar* to attack and annex the Khar fort in 1926, following which Haji Turangzai secured his advantage by rallying another *lashkar* to force a boundary demarcation by the Khan of Khar in favour of the Khan of Nawegai.[76] Haji Sahib Turangzai declared the Khan of Khar a *kafir* or heretic to emphasise his opposition to the Khan's leadership.[77] Yet his hostility to the Khan of Khar's ambitions was clearly not personal or ideological. In the midst of rallying *lashkars* to counter the Khan's advances, Haji Turangzai made a conciliatory gesture towards him, saying he would himself secure an allowance from Kabul for Khar if the Khan ceased to seek support from the British.[78]

---

73 In the late summer of 1918, the Haji Turangzai and Babra Mulla led a *lashkar* against Dir. In 1920 Babra Mulla, Doda Jan Sahib, Haji Turangzai and Pakhli Maulvi called for *jihad* against Khar and Jar who had created an alliance. NWFPPD 36-41, 1918; 10 April 1920.

74 In 1924, Haji Turangzai encouraged the Khan of Nawegai to take action against the Khan of Khar. BAR, 1924-5.

75 NWFPPD, 25 April 1925.

76 NWFPPD, 4 July, 2 Sept. 1926.

77 NWFPPD, March 1916, 10 March 1917.

78 The Khan immediately communicated this proposal to the PA Malakand and requested an increase in his allowance from the British in order to make

With the increasing complexity of relations between *mullas*, states and tribes, the alliances arising lost consistency. The Sandaki Mulla retreated to Dir where he entered into negotiations with the Nawab of Dir, encouraging him to attack Swat.[79] In his efforts to force the Nawab of Dir's support for the Painda Khel of Swat, the Mulla Sandaki willingly arranged a secret meeting between the Nawab of Dir and the Khan of Khar to try to solicit the latter's support for an invasion of Swat.[80] Meanwhile, although the Haji Turangzai and Sandaki Mulla had declared themselves bitterly hostile to the Miangul regime, the Mulla Mahmud Akhunzada solicited the help of Miangul Abdul Wudud of Swat to resolve internal problems in Orakzai.[81] Tensions and conflicts between clans and states across Malakand continued unavoidably over the next century, and along side the *mullas* remained deeply involved in the fluctuating petty politics that they engendered. The one constant factor behind religious involvement in the Malakand state politics was in the mutual efforts by *mullas* to prevent the over-accumulation of power by any one ruler, whether the Nawab of Dir, the Khan of Khar or the Miangul of Swat. The *mullas* brought together individually weak and disparate groups—the Safi, and Kandahari clans and the Khans of Jar and Nawegai—who were independently incapable of taking on the Nawab of Dir, his accomplice the Khan of Khar, or the Mianguls, but with support and organisation were able to defend their own interests and resist expansionism by the ambitious rulers of local states.

Badshah Gul I summarised the dangers of such an accumulation of power as it affected the *mullas* in a speech to the Charmungis in Bajaur, saying 'if the Khan of Khar gets possession of Kotkai [in Bajaur] he will next attack Nawegai and openly espouse the cause of

---

him better able to counter the insidious activities of Haji Turangzai in Bajaur. NWFPPD, 27 Nov. 1927.

79 NWFPPD, 16 May 1925.

80 NWFPPD, 21 Aug. 1926.

81 NWFPPD, 15 Jan. 1927.

the government, turning out the *mullas* from Bajaur'.[82] His concern
was not misplaced. The Political Agent Malakand met secretly with
the Khan of Khar, the Khan of Jandol and Miangul of Swat in 1926
to discuss their regional positions. The Political Agent indicated that
he would be willing to allocate the Khan of Jandol up to 100,000
rupees to help him 'establish himself' in Bajaur, to counter the position of the *mullas*.[83] Curtailing the power of any one ruler preserved
the small tribes with fewer resources and hence maintained their
patronage of the *mullas* and the inter-group political space within
which the *mullas* operated and from which they derived a function
and authority.

Mulla Mahmud Akhunzada and the Shias of Orakzai

The political office's increasing willingness to intervene in the Tribal
Areas to counter religious influence made the *mullas'* two ambitions—to preserve regional autonomy and promote their authority—essentially conflicting ends. Tremedous social and political tensions were created by their programmes of *amr bil ma'ruf*—conflicts
which gave the commissioner of Peshawar opportunities to intervene
in regional affairs. This sort of social tension was created when the
Mulla Mahmud Akhunzada, in an effort to assert his Sunni Naqshbandiyya-Mujaddidiyya ideology and his supporting clans' territorial
ambitions attacked a competing *piri* family and its supporting clans.
The Kalaya *sayyids* of Orakzai were a Shia family claiming descent
from the Prophet and the established *pirs* of the Shia clans in Orakzai, most of which were settled in a tract of land extending from the
border of Kohat to Kurram. In 1923 Mullah Mahmud Akhunzada
led a *lashkar* consisting of Sunni Orakzai and the men of one Shia
clan, the Mani Khel Orakzai, to evict the Kalaya *sayyids* from Orak-

---

82 As paraphrased in NWFPPD, 15 Sept. 1928.
83 NWFPPD, 24 April 1926.

zai. Most of the extended *sayyid* line moved to Kohat to take refuge with *murids* there.[84]

Between 1926-7, some Shia clans led by the Bar Muhammad Khel debated methods of bringing the *sayyids* back into the Tribal Areas. The approval and support of the District Commissioner Kohat was sought, and while the latter did not resolve the crisis, he offered Mulla Mahmud large sums of money to win his approval of a return of the Kalaya *sayyids*.[85] Unable to go back on his original stand, Mulla Mahmud refused. Finally in 1927 the Bar Muhammad Khel, emboldened by the British promises of support for the Shia Orakzai community and having won the Mani Khel clan over to their side, decided to bring the *sayyids* back to Orakzai on their own by housing a family of *sayyids* within each of their villages.[86] This move enraged Mulla Mahmud who immediately mobilised a *lashkar* against the Bar Muhammad Khel.[87] His move met with great support from Tirah Afridis and Sunni Orakzai, who were promised shares of the lands of the Shias and he managed to raise an Afridi and Orakzai *lashkar* of 20,000 to punish the Shia clans.[88] This time the conflict was clearly divided along sectarian lines. Hundreds were killed on both sides in the fighting that ensued and the confrontation ended in the eviction of almost all the Shia clans from Orakzai.

The conflict was immediately highlighted in the press as 'orthodoxy's challenge to the heretics', [89] and the mark of 'frontier barbarism'.[90] Public condemnation of the audacity of the frontier *mullas*,

---

84 Memo on fighting in Tirah between the Kalaya Sayads and the Mani Khel, supported by Mulla Mahmud Akhunzada, 6 Aug. 1923, in 'NW Frontier: Tirah Orakzai'. OIOC L/PS/10/1096.

85 NWFPPD, 2 Oct. 1926.

86 CC NWFP to Foreign Secretary Government of India, 10 March 1927, ibid.

87 NWFPPD, 20 Aug. 1927.

88 Telegram to Foreign department, 28 Aug. 1927, in 'NW Frontier: Tirah Orakzai'.

89 *Daily Telegraph*, 4 April 1929.

90 'Frontier barbarism, Shia Muslims' woes', *Hindustan Times*, 2 Sept. 1927.

both in India and at home, forced immediate attention to the crisis and strong criticism by the Chief Commissioner in Peshawar. In their own defence, the 18 Orakzai Sunni clans, Mulla Mahmud and other supporting *mullas* involved in the expedition submitted a petition explaining that the eviction of the *sayyids* of Kalaya was first necessitated by their commission of grave crimes in the area such as the kidnapping of Sunni women. The petitioners went on to say that the absolute depravity of the *sayyids* was demonstrated by their 'excesses against their own personal disciples.'[91] But the commissioner NWFP and district commissioner in Kohat had little patience for their explanations that it was a matter of internal and moral concern and not a political issue. They sanctioned supply of arms and ammunition to the Shia clans to aid their retaliation against Mulla Mahmud and the Sunni Orakzai.[92]

Mulla Mahmud looked to his traditional alliance with Afghanistan and other *mullas* of the region for support but the threat of direct British intervention as a result of Mulla Mahmud's actions elicited strong condemnation from these quarters. The Governor of Jalalabad and Amir Amanullah sent him letters warning him that if he did not allow the Shias to resettle, the British government might garrison and forcibly resettle the Orakzai tract. 'This would be a great loss to both Mulla Mahmud and the King' it was stated.[93] Haji Turangzai accused Mulla Mahmud of wantonly and 'unjustifiably' attacking his co-religionists. He added that the action had caused 'grave offence in Afghanistan'.[94] This pressure and criticism from both the Afghan government and the Haji Turangzai demonstrated that Mulla Mahmud's efforts to secure regional predominance were themselves

---

91 Orakzai's Petition, 10 July 1927, in 'NW Frontier: Tirah Orakzai'.

92 Note by PA Khyber on Memorandum on the Afridi Situation by CC NWFP, 19 July 1930, in 'Roads in Khajuri and Afridi unrest, 1930-31'. OIOC L/PS/12/3131.

93 NWFPPD, 10 Dec. 1927.

94 NWFPPD, 4 Feb. 1928.

degrading the conditions on which the Tribal Areas autonomy was maintained.

By June 1929, after two years of intermittent fighting, the Shia clans had managed to take back some land. The Chief Commissioner NWFP suggested that this was an opportune moment to support the Shia position, and the colonial government should publicly commit to support of the Shia clans, granting them allowances to raise levies and establish posts in Shia Orakzai along the lines of the Afridi *khassadari* system.[95] This announcement was met with great concern by Mulla Mahmud and an Afridi and Orakzai *jirga* was convened in Peshawar in 1929.[96] The *jirga* agreed that lands held before 1927 would be returned to the Shias, and the *jirga* would commit itself to protect the Shia clans on the condition that the British did not establish levy posts or grant special allowances to the Shia Orakzai, and would take back arms and ammunition issued and cancel *khassadari* appointments made among the Shias.

We, the Afridis and Sunni Orakzai, have heard the Government terms … On the basis of these terms we make peace with the other party (Shia Tirah). Mahmud Akhunzada, who remained joined with us, also accepts this settlement. The Shias will be restored to their lands from where they were turned out and they will be restored to the same position as [they occupied] before August 1927… [Finally] we request your honour that as soon as the Shias are restored to the lands, [the] government should withdraw its troops and constabulary within the administrative border and the Shias, as before, like other Tirah tribes may be considered independent. [97]

Mulla Mahmud had asserted the superiority of his own religious position over that of the Kalaya *sayyids*, channelling inter-tribal com-

---

95 See compiled correspondence between DC Kohat, CC NWFP and Foreign Department, 1929, in 'NW Frontier: Tirah Orakzai'.

96 'Tribal Dispute in Tirah', 29 June 1929, *Times* (London), ibid.

97 Mulla Mahmud's equal say in the final settlements was demonstrated in the *jirga* in Peshawar, at which the Sunni Orakzais refused to commit themselves to the agreement before speaking directly to the Mulla, and established his authority over the matter in the text of the commitment signed by the Sunni Afridis and Orakzai. See 'Translation of signed statement to the Chief Commissioner NWFP, 29 March 1930', in 'NW Frontier: Tirah Orakzai'.

petition and territorial ambitions into a war over doctrine. But once the British became involved this became a militarily indefensible project and had the effect of ultimately strengthening and reinforcing the Shia clans. Arms, ammunition and allowances continued to be issued to the Shia Orakzai clans and eventually Orakzai was made into the separate tribal agency of Tirah, confirming the territorial holdings and regional presence of the Shia tribes.

Communities and their *mullas* organised along tribal lines through the 1920s as they were mutually locked within the regional-ethnographic paradigm of the Tribal Areas. Agendas were popularised and *lashkars* rallied through *jirgas*, and mobilisations seemingly driven by ideological concerns were firmly oriented by tribal politics and the regional balance of power. The operations of the *pirimuridi* network of the Akhund Ghaffur-Hadda Mulla line were convoluted by the complexity of internal alliance systems and enmities, but were still evidently in effect as *mullas* communicated with each other to criticise or affirm one another's actions and maintain a unified stance. But alongside the recent history of the retreat of active Afghan involvement in the region and British efforts to politically sideline *mullas* over the Waziristan garrisons, the Khyber railway, the Mohmand allowances and Malakand politics, the case of Orakzai and Mulla Mahmud's complete defeat illuminated the serious threat to religious authority. The new British political forward policy was intended to actively counter the autonomy of religious leaders in the region, threatening the status, freedom and effectiveness of *mullas* as negotiators, military commanders, moral dictators or proponents of a political agenda. But, although this British policy was relentlessly pursued, it did not have the effect of permanently eroding the position of the Tribal Areas *mullas*. The nationalist movement began in the administered districts of the NWFP and political parties in the administered districts loudly decried British treatment of the 'free tribes' while offering *mullas* in the Tribal Areas their moral support, and transitions towards independence opened up new possibilities for the engagement of religious leadership of the Tribal Areas.

6
CONFRONTING THE NATION
1930-1950

The centres of Muslim political thought, Delhi, Lahore and Saharan-pur, had been at a great distance when the movement of the Jamaat-i Mujahidin began in 1915 and the *mujahidin* were the primary articula-tors of its principles in the Tribal Areas. But as political activity gained momentum in the North-West Frontier Province's administered dis-tricts, the influence of Indian Muslim political discourse on the Tribal Areas was redoubled as activists in Peshawar, Hazara, Bannu, Kohat and Dera Ismail Khan began to look to engage the Tribal Areas and its communities in their politics on the basis of a shared agenda of anti-colonialism. However they appealed to the tribes as accomplices not as equal participants in an organisational arena which was confined in principle to the arena of participatory legislative politics.

Administered districts politics and the Afridi mobilisation of 1930

The Jamiyatul Ulama-yi Hind (JUH) organisation of the Deobandis was a political lobby group that sought to popularise key issues among the Muslims of India in order to preserve the authority of the *'ulama* over them.[1] The Jamiyatul Ulama-yi Sarhad (JUS), the NWFP pro-

---

1 The first of these issues taken up in the NWFP was the mobilisation against the Sarda Act—central government legislature setting a minimum age for marriage—which encroached on the authority of the *ulama* to manage traditional law. Translation of article 'A judgement of the *Majlis-i tahaffuz-i namus-i shariyat*, *Al Jamiat* (Deoband), Nov. 1929, in 'Hartal against the Sarda Act'. NWFPPA DCOP, file 288.

vincial wing of this organisation, was established in 1927. The party of the Khudai Khidmatgars, Pakhtun nationalists deeply influenced by Gandhi's theory of peaceful non-cooperation and led by Khan Abdul Ghaffar Khan, was established as the NWFP branch of the All India National Congress in 1930. Both the JUS and the Khudai Khidmatgar politics were only relevant within the provincial borders, as they were primarily concerned with provincial legislative and electoral issues that did not apply in the non-enfranchised Tribal Areas. But the small size of the arena of public political activity in the NWFP united parties and individuals, even those with radically different political views and methods.

Ghaffar Khan had collaborated with Haji Turangzai to set up Azad Islamia *madrasas* as alternatives to British missionary schools in Utmanzai, Bannu and Kohat before the Haji moved to the Tribal Areas in 1914. Ghaffar Khan had also participated during the early years of Maulana Mahmudul Hasan's *tehrik*, travelling and living for a time with the Babra *Mulla* and taking *bait* at the hand of Haji Turangzai. However he disagreed with the Tribal Areas *mullas'* militancy and their charismatic authority and distanced himself from their methods.[2] Connections between the Khudai Khidmatgars and the Tribal Areas were maintained through the 1920s by the Khilafat Committees—organisations set up in the NWFP administered districts in 1919-20 in aid of the *khilafat* and then the *hijrat* movements, and which remained in existence in a state of virtual autonomy after the decline of the *khilafat* movement in 1920.[3] Members of the committees maintained connections with the Jamaat-i Mujahidin and

---

2 Khan Abdul Ghaffar Khan, *Meri Zindagi Aur Jaddo Jehed* (Lahore, n.d.), pp.1-100.

3 Members of the committees maintained loose ideological ties with the All India National Congress [AINC], and sometimes calling themselves 'Congress committees, but acting as they chose without accountability to the AINC. These committees had organised large rallies in Hazara and Bannu, and called for resignations from military posts and government positions and for a boycott of British goods. See 'Hazara Series Correspondence 1920', OIOC L/PS/10/929; and Qureshi, *Pan-Islam in British India*, pp. 195-200.

Tribal Areas *mullas* through the 1920s while also maintaining ties to the national headquarters of the AINC and the provincial Khudai Khidmatgars.[4] When JUS was established, it drew on the existing Khilafat Committees for its membership and leadership leading the organisation to also inherit the connections between NWFP *khilafat* activists, the AINC and the Tribal Areas.[5]

Both the Khudai Khidmatgars and the JUS were focused on achieving provincial-level participation in government, approaching their organisational goals in the NWFP from within the confines of the political geography of colonial India. For Ghaffar Khan, the political construct was circumscribed at the administrative border because the tribes were not capable of participation as they had 'no interest in economics, industry, agriculture or education' and were immersed 'in custom and ritual and occupied in the realm of militancy'.[6] Although he ascribed more glamour to the condition of the free tribes, the first president of the JUS also emphasised the need to keep the tribes separate from the administered NWFP in order that the latter be able to progress at their own pace in peace and security.[7] The JUS's first goal was to create a legislative council and demand native representation in provincial government on the same lines as other provinces in India.

Neither the JUS nor the Khudai Khidmatgars conceived a method that could incorporate the region that was outside governed India, so they excluded its population from their organisation. But links between the *mullas*, the Khudai Khidmatgars and JUS allowed a political affiliation between the two regions to emerge. Political concerns were being widely broadcast into the Tribal Areas from the administered districts through the Khilafat Committees. A group of old *khilafat* activists with connections to the AINC and the JUS,

---

4 MPD, May 1925.

5 'Youth and Student Movements, Darul Ulum Deoband, 1921-1937'. NWFPPA Special Branch NWFP.

6 Ghaffar Khan, *Meri Zindagi*, p. 159.

7 Maulvi Anwar Shah, *Khutba*, p. 39.

calling itself the Peshawar Congress Committee, was distributing pamphlets in Waziristan and Mohmand condemning the Sarda Act of 1927 and calling for tribal action against the government.[8] An informer claimed that the 'Khilafat and Congress Committees in Bannu' were actively trying to mobilise the Mahsuds and were using local *mullas* to organise *jirgas* to discuss the actions of the government.[9] These connections showed their potential in 1930 when simultaneous crises across the Tribal Areas and Peshawar brought the tribes, led by the *mullas*, and the NWFP political parties into active support of one another.

It had been decided some years earlier that allowances paid in the Khyber to Sunni clans were not to be increased to conciliate those offended at colonial patronage of the Shia clans, irrespective of Sunni Afridi pressure and growing discontent. Moreover, allowances to one clan, the Adam Khel Afridis, were stopped altogether.[10] The discontent at the cap on allowances was exacerbated when it became apparent that the government was not going to disarm the Shia Orakzai and had granted new allowances to these clans and appointed a Political Agent to oversee their management. Concurrently with this, a member of the Malikdin Khel Afridi tribe, Khushal Khan, decided to organise a contingent along the lines that Ghaffar Khan organised his Khudai Khidmatgars in the administered districts. He described his gesture as one of support to the Khudai Khidmatgars in the administered districts, in the hopes that the alliance would bring both sides liberation:

Our peace cannot be made separate from that of India for the original fight took place over the religion of the Muslims and Hindus of India. If anyone could bring about our peace in that no tyranny will be made over the religion and India, and if there be *zulm* then you should be satisfied that there will

8 Memorandum on unrest in Waziristan, CC NWFP, 13 May 1930, in 'Tribal Disturbances 1930-31:Peshawar and district situation'. OIOC L/PS/12/3125.

9 Ibid.

10 Foreign and Political Department to Government of India, 19 Aug. 1930 and Report of Mughal Baz Khan, APO Khyber, 13 July 1930, in 'Roads in Khajuri and Afridi unrest 1930-31'. OIOC L/PS/12/3131.

be no peace ...The *khilafat* party is ready for the fight, but they are waiting for a gesture from your side.[11]

500 Afridis attended a *jirga* wearing red sashes and the Political Agent reported that Khushal's men had been observed marching and carrying out drills in the Mohmand areas.[12] Reports came of 250 new recruits to Khushal Khan's contingent from the Shinwari areas north-west of Mohmand.[13] In Mohmand Haji Turangzai, Mulla Sahib Babra, Mulla Chaknawar and the Faqir of Alingar who were still furious about their marginalisation over the allowance issue had independently been in touch with the Peshawar Congress party through the person of Abdur Rauf, a Nowshera-based member of the Jamiyatul Ulama-yi Sarhad with Khudai Khidmatgar connections. Abdul Rauf warned the Haji of the terrible implications of the Sarda legislation.[14]

In early 1930, several people were killed in an incident of police firing on a peaceful demonstration in Qissa Khwani bazaar in Peshawar. Dozens of Congress and JUS activists were being arrested for peaceful non-cooperation.[15] As sentiments began to run high, members of the JUS and the Peshawar Congress Committee asked the Haji to mobilise the tribes with the guarantee of a strong response and support from the administered districts if he chose this time to lead an attack on the administered districts.[16] Two Bannu-based activists, Abdul Jalil and Fazal Qadir, connected to the *khilafat* and JUS groups in Peshawar, were trying to mobilise support for the same agenda in Waziristan. They held *jirgas* to this end in some

---

11   Khushal Khan Malikdin Khel Afridi to Congress Committee Hangu, 29 July 1930, in 'Congress Activities in Trans-border areas of NWFP', NWFPPA, Tribal Research Cell.

12   NWFPIBD, 30 April 1931, 9 July 1931.

13   NWFPIBD, 9 July 1931.

14   MPD, 26 April 1930; 'List of Leading Mullas on the NWFP, 1937', NWFPPA DCOP, 1439/51.

15   Jamiyatul Ulama Afghan, *Da Suba-yi Sarhad Da Ulama-o-Qurbani* (Peshawar, 1931).

16   MPD, 3 May 1930.

villages in North-Waziristan.[17] Much of the sympathy they received was rooted in tribal concerns over the British project and allowance distribution there.[18]

On 12 May 1930 a *lashkar* of 500 Afridi men, led by Sayyid Almar and Sayyid Kabir, the son and *murid* of the now deceased Mulla Sayyid Akbar, supported by Khushal Khan's army, advanced to the Khajuri plain.[19] The *lashkar* grew to 4,000 men as it advanced towards Bara on the border between the Tribal Areas and administered districts, south-west of Peshawar.[20] As soon as the full forces were gathered at Bara, the CC NWFP authorised the dispersion of the *lashkar* through aerial bombing.[21] The planes followed the retreating army for part of the way back into the Khajuri plain of Tirah, dropping bombs on the reconnoitring groups, and managed to disperse the *lashkar* entirely. A total of 604 Afridi casualties were reported in the air strikes.[22]

Meanwhile the Mohmand *mullas* had independently organised a small *lashkar* of Safis and some Mohmands from the Afghan side of the border and started marching towards Shabqadar. Inspired by the Bannu-based activists, Mulla Shah Badan and Maulvi Muhammad Guldin of North-Waziristan managed to motivate a few discontented tribesmen in Waziristan and collected a *lashkar* of 100 Wazirs.[23] The DC Peshawar took preemptive measures against the Mohmands

17 Memo C. H. Gidney DC Bannu to Secretary CC NWFP 30 Aug. 1930, in 'Waziristan: Afghan, Soviet and Congress Activities, 1930-1932'. OIOC L/PS/12/3122.

18 Maulvi Muhammad Guldin to Nadir Khan King Afghanistan, 26 July 1930, ibid.

19 Viceroy to Secretary of State for India, 13 May and 17 May 1930, in 'Tribal disturbances Afridi Country 1930-31'. OIOC L/PS/12/3131.

20 Afridi Report, 3 June 1930, ibid.

21 Ibid.

22 Note on Afridi invasion of Peshawar District. NWFPPA Special Branch NWFP, 706/44

23 Memo CC NWFP, 13 May 1930, 'Tribal Disturbances 1930-1'. OIOC L/PS/12/3125.

and called for aerial attacks to disperse the Mohmand *mullas* before they managed to consolidate their *lashkar*.[24] Close watch was kept on the Waziristan *mullas* and warnings were issued to their host tribes by the Resident Waziristan.[25]

Because of the immediate and forceful action by the political office supported by the Royal Air Force, the *lashkars* across the Tribal Areas were dispersed. However rather than easing the situation, tensions began to escalate. On June 26 it was reported that the Kambar Khel had founded a Khilafat Committee of their own, headed by Mulla Gul Badshah Kambar Khel. The committee enlisted 200 men from Malikdin Khel and Kambar Khel and the Khyber *mullas* sent out a call for a new *lashkar* to rally. The *khilafat* party arrived at a *jirga* of *maliks* and government and tried to disperse it to prevent a settlement.[26] The Khilafat Committee *lashkar* grew to 1,600 men from both Afridi clans and Sunni clans in Orakzai.[27] The Khyber and Tirah *mullas* turned to the Malakand and Waziristan *mullas* for assistance, pointing to the terrible violence of the British bombing of the Khajuri plains. Haji Turangzai, Mulla Chaknawar, Faqir of Ipi and Mulla Babra immediately started rallying support for the Afridi mobilisation, publicising it as a two pronged effort, both in retaliation against the bombing of the Khajuri plain and the violation of the Tribal Areas, and as a gesture of assistance to the people of Peshawar.[28]

In late June the Mohmand *mullas* independently led a *lashkar* down to the Shabqadar border.[29] Abdul Jalil and Fazal Qadir led an impromptu attack with their Wazir tribal retinue on a police station

---

24 Viceroy Home Dept to Sec of State for India, 17 May 1930, in 'Tribal Disturbances Mohmand, 1930-32'. OIOC L/PS/12/3126.

25 Gidney to CC NWFP, 30 Aug. 1930.

26 Afridi Reports, 26-28 June 1930 in 'Tribal disturbances Afridi country'.

27 Afridi Reports, 28-30 June 1930, ibid.

28 Mohmand Situation Reports, June 1930, in 'Tribal disturbances in Malakand 1930-31'. OIOC, L/PS/12/3124.

29 Ibid.

in Bannu and then retreated to their host tribes where they raised a *lashkar* of 300 men.[30] In South-Waziristan, the Shewa Mulla and the Badshah Khan Shakiwal organised well-armed Wazirs returning from supporting the victorious Nadir Shah to his throne in Afghanistan. They succeeded in rallying *lashkars* of 1,400 men and set out for Bannu, via Kurram.[31] In North-Waziristan, Maulvi Guldin continued to rally the Wazir, Mahsud and Bhittani clans around him. An Afridi *lashkar* almost twice the size of the May *lashkar* and thus numbering about 7,000 men, began to gather in Khajuri and to march on Peshawar. This time the leader emphasised solidarity with Muslim India but outlined a more particular objective: the destruction of the government's capacity to attack by air. A government informer returned from Bagh where he had attended a *jirga* of Afridis discussing the proposed mobilisation and reported:

The leaders of the Congress in the *jirga* … gave lectures in which they said that the Government had passed a law that every woman before her marriage would be examined by doctors and also that any man who studied the Quran Sharif in mosques or gave a call to prayer would have to pay a tax of 40 rupees a year. They added that government had killed many small children in India. … The *jirga* decided that the Afridi *lashkar* should attack Peshawar and the Orakzai *lashkar* should attack Kohat in order to destroy the Kohat airbase and aircrafts. [32]

At first the army attempted to check the progress of the Afridi *lashkar* by shelling, but had little success. The *lashkar* brought down telegraph poles and raided some villages *en route* to the administered districts. Finally air strikes were called in again, which once again dispersed the *lashkar*.[33] The Mohmand *lashkar* in Malakand made

---

30 Gidney to CC NWFP 30 Aug. 1930.

31 Assistant PA Waziristan to Razmak, 15 Aug. 1930, in 'Office of the Resident Waziristan'. NDC 618.

32 Statement by Muhammad Azam Khan son of Khan Bahadur Wali Muhammad Khan of Hangu, 23 Peshawar, 23 Aug. 1930, in 'Tribal disturbances in Afridi country, 1930-31'.

33 'Reveiew of events, Afridi attack on Peshawar', *Pioneer* (London) 25 Aug. 1930, ibid.

less progress, and was dispersed just as quickly through air strikes, and the Waziristan contingent appeared to have dispersed before it reached the border or could threaten it.[34] Yet in both Mohmand and Waziristan the *mullas* continued to take advantage of high emotions over recent events and direct minor attacks on British posts and interests until the end of the year.[35]

The Afridis involved in the mobilisation decided the terms of settlement to be presented to the Political Agent would include demands for the cancellation of the Sarda Act; the release of all political prisoners in the NWFP; and a renegotiation of the Afridi-government compact.[36] Of course the British authorities were not inclined to negotiate at all and by December plans were in place for the permanent occupation of the Khajuri plain.[37] The tribes were in no position to resist a settlement given internal dissension, the huge losses sustained in the campaign and the apparent 'betrayal' by the Congress party when there was no mobilisation in Peshawar in support of the Tribal Areas advance. The Political Agent Khyber re-established allowances to clans on strict conditions of peace, and on the guarantee that the original tribal 'rabble-rousers', particularly Khushal Khan, would be marginalized. During the garrisoning of the Khajuri plains there was a re-establishment of terms of relations between the government and the Afridis and allowances were resumed (although under the threat of repeated military action if the Afridis should mobilise again).[38]

---

34 Foreign and Political Department to Government of India, 19 Aug. 1930, in 'Roads in Khajuri and Afridi unrest 1930-31'. OIOC L/PS/12/3131.

35 An attack initiated by Maulvi Abdul Jalil's supporters in Waziristan was of particular significance as a captain of the Indian army was killed in the confrontation. See report of the incident with the Hathi Khel *lashkar*, 24 Aug. 1930', in 'Waziristan:HMG's Tribal Policy'. OIOC L/PS/12/3151

36 Report on recent Afridi *jirga* in Maidan, 16 Aug. 1930. NWFPPA Special Branch file 707/44.

37 Foreign and Political Department to Government of India, 12 Dec. 1930, in 'Tribal Disturbances Afridi 1930-31'.

38 R. R. Maconachie, 'Afghanistan, Annual Report, 1930', 7 Jan. 1931. OIOC

The 1930 mobilisations marked the largest regional movement since the Anglo-Afghan war of 1919. As with any Tribal Areas mobilisation against the British the chances of a decisive success were virtually nonexistent, but the scale of the confrontation and the scale of the British response required had demonstrated the real danger a concerted organised effort across the tribal region could pose to the administered districts. These events had injected a greater credibility into the threat posed by the *mullas* because it appeared that the centre of 'discontent' was no longer the independent territories or Afghanistan—rather it seemed the inspiration for mobilisation could come from within India by the activities of the Congress party 'assisted by an unscrupulous campaign of lies and exaggeration to excite religious fanaticism.'[39] Hence it was decided that any sort of mobilisation, whether overtly militaristic or a meeting to discuss opposition; whether directed at the British or at 'assured' clans, would be treated as an offensive movement and dealt with in the severest manner.[40]

Afridi resentment of the government measures persisted and the clans sought new allies in the administered districts to support their position. In 1936 Mohammed Ali Jinnah, president of the All India Muslim League party which sought to unite the Muslims of India as a single political group, travelled to the North-West Frontier Province. He was given permission to travel to Landi Kotal where a deputation of Afridi *maliks* met him to discuss the British occupation of Khajuri in the aftermath of Mulla Mahmud's anti-Shia movement in Orakzai and the Afridi mobilisation to the borders of Peshawar, regarding increasingly violent colonial measures in the region. The issue was taken up by Jinnah, who agreed to support the claim to the demilitarisation of the Khajuri plains on the premise that the Tribal Areas was a culturally, organisationally and geographically separate

---

L/PS/18/A 213.

39 BAR 1930-1.

40 *Afridi qaum ka paigham ahl-i Hind kay nam* NWFPPA Special Branch file 710/44.

space.[41] Jinnah's visit marked the appropriation of the case of the Tribal Areas Pakhtuns by the Muslim League from the Congress party, as an issue primarily relating to the Muslims of India. At the annual session of the Muslim League in 1938, a resolution was passed condemning the 'forced subjugation of the independent tribal belt':

This session of the All India Muslim League is firmly of the opinion that the time now has come for the British government to reconsider its Frontier Policy ... based on the universally recognised principle of self-determination. It further condemns the policy and activities of the Congress in the NWFP by which they have given indications that the tribal areas should become part of administered territory.[42]

League support grew slowly in the Tribal Areas, supported by a growing anti-Hindu sentiment. At Chamarkand, Muhammad Bashir had given the Tribal Areas the name 'Ahraristan', declaring his solidarity with the ambitions of a group called the Ahrars promoting Sunni orthodoxy through India.[43] Another pro-Muslim League group, the Khaksars, were reported to have sent their representatives to meet with the tribes through old Khilafat Committee members to inform them of the threat Hindu nationalism posed to the Muslims of India.[44] In Tirah Khushaal Khan Malikdin Khel, who had come to prominence during the Afridi mobilisation of 1930 as a staunch Congress party supporter, wrote a letter expressing his disappointment with the Congress and his sympathy for the Khaksars and Ahrars, groups propounding the unification of the Muslim nation of India against Hindu 'injustices'.[45] In Mohmand the Mulla of Spinwara began to speak out against the Congress government at Pesha-

---

41   Shah, *Ethnicity, Islam and Nationalism*, p. 98.

42   Resolution XIII, All India Muslim League 26th Session, Patna, Dec. 1938. In Sharifuddin Pirzada, *Foundations of Pakistan* (Karachi, 1970).

43   *Al Mujahid*, 25 April 1933.

44   'Khaksar Activities Against Arya Satyagarha in Tribal Territory', *Milap* (Lahore) 6 May 1939.

45   Khushaal Khan Malikdin Khel of Tirah to Badshah Sahib and Arbab Khan Khaksars 1940 (?), in 'Khaksar Movement in Tribal Territory'. NWFPPA, Special Branch.

war.[46] Badshah Gul I, who had hitherto been reported as receiving *shukrana* from Ghaffar Khan, called a *jirga* informing Mohmand tribes that Ghaffar Khan's daughter had married a Hindu and that all support should be denied him. He further warned of the threat of a possible Hindu raj over India, which would be far worse than the current British one.[47] By 1942 the governor NWFP noted that deeply anti-Congress sentiments began to dominate in the Tribal Areas thanks to the *mullas* of the region.[48]

Seeking support for their local concerns of tribal balance and the distribution of privileges in the autonomous zone, the tribes sought allies within the emerging sphere of provincial legislative politics. Underlaid by a mutual recognition of tribal and administered district separateness, Congress, JUS and eventual Muslim League alliances with the Tribal Areas inspired by the crisis in the Khajuri plain brought the region into the high drama of communal and representative politics which would some years later lead to the creation of two separate independent states of India and Pakistan. And despite the long-standing, if tangential, Tribal Areas connection to the AINC, the crisis brought the *mullas* and the tribes in touch with Muslim nationalism as it was being represented by the Muslim League and Jinnah.

The Faqir of Ipi

Under the now entrenched British policy of disproportionate retaliation, several campaigns were led against the frontier tribes and their *mullas* in the 1930s. A military column was despatched to North-Waziristan to directly punish a tribal misdemeanour in 1931.[49] In 1932, when the Faqir of Alingar and Badshah Gul and the Mulla Chaknawar's young son, Ghulam Nabi Chaknawari, collected a

---

46 MPD, 30 May 1939.

47 MPD, 12 May 1942.

48 George Cunningham, note 5 May 1942, in 'Propaganda through mullahs', OIOC, 'Cunningham Papers'.

49 Warren, *The Faqir of Ipi*, p. 104.

lashkar of 500 upper Mohmands and Safis to punish the British allowance-holders for refusing passage to a party of upper Mohmands through Gandab to Peshawar, they were treated as 'hostiles'. The Chief Commissioner NWFP was authorised by the Government of the India to 'issue warning of "such punitive action as the government may see fit to order", and on the expiry of the warning bomb the other villages without further reference to, and previous, sanction.'[50] When the Faqir of Alingar held a grand *jirga* of Malakand tribes and pronounced them all free of their obligations to the government in 1934, his 'invading' *lashkar* was bombed by the Royal Air Force.[51] British policy became so stringent on the matter that when it appeared that a hostile Mohmand *lashkar* was gathering at the instigation of Badshah Gul I and 'doing damage' to the Gandab road in 1935, in what appeared to be a self-defeating move, the RAF was called in to drop bombs close to the road to disperse the *lashkar* and prevent it doing further damage.[52]

Inspite of the stringent government response to *mulla* activity, the *mullas* of the Tribal Areas could move in small groups which usually could not be tracked and bombed. Aerial bombings were carried out in order to frighten and disperse gatherings which could potentially grow larger and more threatening. They could do little to restrict the *mulla* on his traditional *doras*—his periodic travels among the tribes to hear cases, give rewards and apply punishments such as burning the villages of the Khan of Khar for territorial violations.[53] Crucially the functions of the Tribal Areas *mullas* as arbitrators, political spokesmen and convenors of the religious congregation persisted. But because the British government was no longer willing to tolerate

---

50 NWF: Hostile Movement in Mohmand Country, March 1932, in OIOC 'Mohmand Situation, 1930-32'.

51 BAR 1934-5.

52 Mohmand Communiqué, 17 Aug. 1935, in Peshawar Archives, 'Mohmand Agency Records'.

53 Khan Khar to PA Dir Swat Bajaur, 31 July 1933, in NDCI, 'Malakand Situation 1919-60'.

any action by a *mulla* against an assured clan, the *mullas'* influences were cast as decidedly hostile and the ferocity of the government effort to undermine them through military campaigns absolutely and irrevocably turned any *mulla* voicing some sort of discontent with British policy or with allies of the British in the Tribal Areas into a confirmed enemy of the state.

This was the situation within which Mirza Ali of Ipi claimed government and public attention. Mirza Ali had received his religious training from a variety of local sources before he came into contact with the Naqib Sahib of Charbagh (himself of the Akhund Ghaffur-Hadda Mulla line) and later with *khilafat*ists in India. He returned to the Tribal Areas to settle at Ipi in the Tochi valley and was ignored as relatively innocuous until 1936. Public passions were running high in the administered districts as people followed the case of a Hindu girl who had converted to Islam under obscure circumstances and married a Pakhtun in Bannu. The girl's family accused her husband of abduction and forced conversion. The girl refused to return to her parents, but the marriage was unlawful since she was a minor and could not legally enter into a marriage of her own accord. Unable to find evidence of either abduction or legal consent to marriage, the court ruled that the girl would live with a third party until she reached the age of majority, at which time she could decide her fate for herself. The decision was heard by the Muslim community of Bannu with great anger as a government decision in favour of the Hindu community over the Muslim one.[54] The Faqir held a *jirga* to call the attention of the tribes of Daur to the government's interference in religion—a meeting that was followed by 'some hooliganism on the road' and the Daurs blocking passage through the area.[55] He appealed for and found sympathisers among other *mullas* of the Tribal Areas including the Haji Turangzai and his sons, the Faqir of Alingar, and

---

54 Summarised from Alan Warren's *Waziristan: The Faqir of Ipi and the Indian Army*, pp. 80-6

55 BAR 1936-7.

Ghulam Nabi Chaknawari.[56] The Chamarkand *mujahidin* came out in support of the Faqir's *jihad* and rumours went around that Fazal Ilahi, their president, had gone to Waziristan to live and fight with the Faqir.[57] The Faqir also managed to forge an alliance with Fazal Din, the son of his old adversary the Mulla Powindah.

After some effort the Faqir rallied a following among the Tori Khel Wazirs of Tochi, whose *maliks* had recently entered into an agreement with the British for the garrisoning of the Khaisora region of North-Waziristan. In November 1936, as a British military column began to cross Khaisora, the Faqir attacked with a *lashkar* of 2,000 men, and with the advantage of rugged and mountainous terrain forced the army to retreat. News of the *lashkar's* success brought another 1,200 Mahsud and Afghan-side Wazir men to join the Faqir, who was now credited with miraculous powers. Government pressure on the *maliks* of tribes to turn over the Faqir and to forbid him passage or any sort of assistance did not deter him or diminish support for him. In April 1937, when the worst of the winter had passed, the Tochi valley and the Faqir's *lashkar*, now numbering 4,000 men, were subjected to aerial bombardment. The army began to move in on the ground from several different directions and the *lashkar* was forced to disperse. Raids into administered territory by scattered groups of the Faqir's supporters increased dramatically but the region was kept under constant surveillance and they were not allowed to band together again.

Like many other mobilisations in the Tribal Areas, the Faqir's movement grew through his military tactical leadership, with no significant reward offered to the participants other than the hospitality of his *langarkhana* and the spoils from raids into administered territory. Alan Warren cautions against reading too deeply into his rhetoric of opposition to the *kafir* and protection of Islam in India,[58]

---

56 Interview Ghulam Nabi Chaknawari, 8 Feb. 2002.

57 'Report on Chamarkand Colony 1936, 7 Dec. 1939'. Political Officer Mohmand records, file 46.

58 Proclamations of the Faqir of Ipi in NDCI 'Waziristan Dissidents'.

arguing that his great popularity was partly Tori Khel tribal interest in preventing government penetration into the Khaisora and preserving the autonomy of the Tochi valley.[59] But this explanation does not account for the participation of Afghan Wazirs who came from across the border and the Shabi Khel Mahsuds, who did not share Tori Khel concerns over Khaisora. It was more probably the attraction of target practice against the Indian army and the promise of booty from trans-border raids that drew in many participants. Military encounter with the British was both profitable and relatively risk-free as the *lashkar* tended to snipe rather than entering into direct combat, and participants could melt so quickly and quietly away from the scene of an encounter and make their way back home through a network of villages. But despite what the Faqir may have wanted, his men were unable and unwilling to make a concerted stand against the Indian army to force religious-political concessions for India or prevent penetration of Khaisora.

The Faqir of Ipi's *jihad* highlighted the problems with established Tribal Areas policy of exerting control through the treaty system that defined the tribe as a collective, and when that failed to use aerial campaigns to subjugate insubordinate parties. Members of the Tori Khel and participant Mahsud tribesmen were clearly acting in defiance of commitments made by their *maliks* to guarantee passage to the army through the region in return for increased allowances, and Afghan-side tribesmen were violating the Anglo-Afghan treaty. But because, in the absence of personal documentation or intelligence information, identity was only linked to the tribe, individual action outside the unanimity of the tribe was an anonymous act and hence uncontrollable. Moreover if insurgent organisation remained guerrilla-style and scattered, the RAF could do little to control it. The government furore about the fanaticism of the Wazirs and their *mulla* masked a greater uneasiness and fear: that the Tribal Areas policy could only partly contain and regulate human action. Anyone able to act outside the strict system of collective property, action and

---

59 Warren, *Faqir of Ipi*, pp. 275-7.

discipline could inflict serious damage on government interests—a threat compounded by the fact that the government could only operate *through* the treaty system in the Tribal Areas. While the Tori Khel acquiesced in paying a fine for their clansmen's parts in the Faqir's uprising, British pressure to force the Tori Khel to capture the Faqir and hand him over failed entirely despite the threat of a blockade, a punitive aerial bombardment and the suspension of Tori Khel *khassadars*, and government inability to corner and extract him in itself made him a more notable and exciting figure.[60]

When the violence of government action against the Faqir and participants in his movement in 1937 had proved to be of only limited effectiveness, this had at first increased the Faqir's popularity, generating stories about his magical powers in dodging bullets and evading capture among his supporting tribes.[61] The *mujahidin* at Chamarkand printed a special edition of the *Al Mujahid* to call attention to heavy bombardments in Waziristan; Faqir and Mohmand *mullas* called for retribution for the casualties caused by British aerial campaigns through the Tribal Areas.[62] His movement was lauded as the mark of Pakhtun bravery, and British tactics condemned as demonstrative of governmental excess, by nationalists in the administered districts.[63] Over the next few years the Faqir rallied an occasional *lashkar*, encouraged his supporters to continue carrying out raids in the administered districts, and even conferred with an Italian envoy about the possibilities for foreign support.[64] But air campaigns to disperse his *lashkars*, political office pay-outs to the tribes among whom he lived, and the nationalist parties' policy of support for the government during the Second World War made his efforts relatively

---

60 BAR 1937-8.

61 Warren, *Faqir of Ipi*, p. 129.

62 CID report 7 Dec. 1939, in PA 'Chamarkand Colony 1936'; interview, Ghulam Nabi Chaknawari, Peshawar, 3 Feb. 2002.

63 See Muhammad Nawaz Khan Mahsud, *Firangi Raj Aur Ghairatmand Musalman* (Waziristan, 2000).

64 Warren, *Fakir of Ipi*, pp. 249-66.

insignificant. His capacity to mobilise the Wazirs did not become of great political consequence again until the region became a part of Pakistan in 1947.

The War and the new politics of partition

The organisation of Tribal Areas religious politics changed dramatically in the 1930s. Mulla Babra had died in 1927 and the Badshah of Islampur in 1928, Mulla Chaknawar died in 1930, Mulla Mahmud Akhunzada in 1931, the Haji Turangzai in 1937, and the Sandaki Mulla in 1939. The Haji Turangzai's three sons and the Faqir of Alingar alone were left in Mohmand; in Khyber and Tirah the Mulla Sayid Akbar's successors took his line forward; in Waziristan the Faqir of Ipi and the new Mulla Powindah Fazal Din inherited the influence of the Lala Pir of Khost and the old Mulla Powindah and contended with the rise of a new *mulla* within the line the Shewa Mulla. Internal politics like the conflicts between the Khan of Khar and the Khan of Nawegai and between the Nawab of Dir and Khan of Jandol persisted; tensions between British allowance-holders and clans without privileges continued; and *mullas* continued to oversee internal truces and settlements.[65] But the new British policy of disproportionate response appeared to dissuade these younger and less experienced *mullas* from mobilising even their own personal retinues. Badshah Gul preoccupied himself with building up an arsenal, constructing a *serai*, and consolidating influence among the Mohmands and Shinwaris in view of the opposition posed by the Khan of Khar and the assured clans. The Faqir of Alingar withdrew into his own scheme to build a fort at his base in Gari Gasht.[66] The Faqir of Ipi tried to rally support across the region with the help of his *pir* the Naqib of Charbagh, but British warnings to the Wazirs kept them from allowing him to mobilise again.[67]

---

65 Mohmand Political Records 1939-1942.

66 NWFPID, March-April 1938.

67 NWFPID, May 1938-Dec. 1939.

Politics of the Afghan court continued to be popularised by different actors in the Tribal Areas, the most significant instance of this being an attempted revolution against Nadir Shah in 1933 by the Lewanai Faqir, a man purporting to be an agent of the ex-Amir Amanullah Khan.[68] But the amirate had become far more restrained in its patronage of Tribal Areas *mullas* as Zahir Shah (who succeeded Nadir Shah in 1933) was more involved in negotiating import transit terms with the British government and recruiting and training regular armed forces than maintaining the informal eastern Pakhtun army as a strategy for consolidating the regime.[69] As their utility had diminished, *mullas* of Bajaur, the Khyber and Malakand no longer received the sorts of allowances from Kabul that they had been granted during Amanullah's tenure. Badshah Gul and the Faqir of Alingar were accused of soliciting Afghan support against the British occupation of the Khajuri plain and construction of a road through to Nahaqqi in Mohmand.[70] And it appeared that the Hakim-i Ala of Jalalabad maintained connections with the Tribal Areas *mullas* to secure tran-

---

68 A *lashkar* had gathered in North-Waziristan, supported incidentally by the Faqir of Ipi, but was repulsed by two companies of Afghan regulars, who received support from the Royal Air Force. Report PA Khyber, 15 Oct. 1933 in IOLC 'Khost Risings'.

69 This was the opinion of Fraser-Tytler, Minister to Afghanistan, expressed in a despatch to the Foreign Office, 1 October 1936 and there is little in even the most alarmist British reports from this period to suggest the contrary, see 'Afghan Interference in British Tribes in Bajaur'. Another uprising in support of Amanullah in 1939 was effectively put down with assistance from the British. A *mulla* calling himself the Shami Pir tried to rally a Mahsud *lashkar* to bring Amanullah Khan back into power. Mulla Powindah staunchly opposed this rebellion as well, but unlike the earlier times, his support was not central to putting it down, in 'Waziristan: activities of the Shami Pir and Baghdadi Pir', 1938-39'. In 1944, a revolt of the Zadran tribe in the Southern Province was put down directly by the regular Afghan army and the surrender of the leader negotiated by the War Minister himself. Minister Kabul, 29 July 1944, in 'Khost Risings'. OIOC L/PS/12/3176, 3255, 3207.

70 Report of Faqir Alingar's visit to the Hakim-i Ala Jalalabad, Intelligence Bureau Peshawar to Government of NWFP, 2 Dec. 1935; memo Chief Secretary to Government of NWFP, 17 Aug. 1935, in 'Afridi delegation to Jalalabad 1935'. OIOC L/PS/12/3147.

sit routes in the region.[71] But the government at Kabul maintained that the amounts paid to these personalities were nominal.

Most important of all was the sudden turn-around of the British administration towards the *mullas*. The Governor NWFP during the war, George Cunningham, instructed Kuli Khan, now Political Agent Khyber, to convince *mullas* of the Tribal Areas and the *'ulama* of NWFP to speak out against the Bolsheviks, and then the Germans, Italians, and Japanese as enemies of Islam.[72] While no British officer made direct contact with the *mullas*, the attitude of the government softened towards the latter as they quickly proved effective and reliable propagandists against the Axis Powers. By the end of the War some *mullas*, including Mulla Powindah Fazal Din and the Shewa Mulla, had come out to say that in the event of the War coming to India they should fight on the side of the British, not of the Germans and their *butparast* or idol-worshipping allies the Japanese who might restrict the practice of Islam.[73] Rumours about Badshah Gul's relations with the Afghan regime were regarded with indulgence and barely followed up.[74]

Meanwhile support for the frontier Congress party, the Khudai Khidmatgars, was beginning to fragment in the administered districts. The secular stance of Ghaffar Khan disparaging the involvement of religion in government and social leadership was opening the party up to criticism. The Muslim nationalist All India Muslim League party led by Muhammad Ali Jinnah began to come to the fore in the politics of the province. The Ahrars, who were deeply

---

71 The Hakim-i Ala asked Ghulam Nabi Chaknawari to use his influence to prevent Kamali Halimzai attacks on Afghan caravans to exact their own toll. Badshah Gul supported this. Badshah Gul continued to send Mohmand *maliks* to Jalalabad to collect *kharcha* or 'expenses'. See MPD 1939.

72 George Cunningham, 'Propaganda', April 1941, in 'Correspondence with the external affairs department regarding propaganda through *mullahs*, etc.'. OIOC Cunningham Papers.

73 George Cunningham, note 5 May 1942, ibid.

74 'Afghan interference with British tribes—Badshah Gul, 1935-40'. OIOC L/PS/12/3209.

concerned with maintaining a Sunni orthodox ideological unity and paramountcy in Muslim India, and the Muslim separatist Khaksars were also popularising Muslim League religious nationalism within the electorate. An NWFP Congress ministry which had been elected in 1937 resigned and was replaced by governor's rule during Congress agitations in 1939. Ghaffar Khan's accusations that the government was trying actively to undermine Congress support through the NWFP had strong foundation in the very positive sentiments of key figures like George Cunningham, and later Olaf Caroe, towards the Muslim League over the rebellious Congress.[75] From this point on the Muslim League gained a strong foothold in the province, popularising a separatist agenda for the creation of a state of Pakistan for the Muslims of India, despite deep divisions between its members. In 1943, a League ministry took power. A move of no-confidence led by Ghaffar Khan narrowly displaced the Muslim League in 1945, and while Ghaffar Khan claimed a majority in the election of 1946, the Congress ministry was bitterly contested by Leaguers who launched a civil disobedience movement against it.

In 1945 the new Pir of Manki Sharif, whose father's position and now his own were closely tied to the Miangul regime in Swat, became deeply involved in Muslim League organisation from his base in Nowshera in the administered districts of the NWFP. He brought many of his *murids* into the League as political activists and supporters, and encouraged Miangul Abdul Wudud to support Jinnah's campaign as well.[76] The Pir's most significant organisation of Tribal Areas political activity in support of the League was to rally Shinwari and Mullagori tribesmen to stage a demonstration against Nehru when the latter toured the Tribal Areas in 1946.[77] By 1947 the Pir

---

75 George Cunningham, diaries 1943-6. OIOC Cunningham Papers. Also see Shah's summary of this, *Ethnicity, Islam and Nationalism*, pp. 224-5.

76 The Wali of Swat contributed generously to the League fund and to the Pakistan fund. See Yusufi, *Yusufzai Afghan*, p. 320. See also Wiqar Ali Shah who discusses the extent of the Pir's involvement in provincial Muslim League organisation in his study, *The Muslim League in the NWFP* (Karachi, 1992).

77 Statement by APA Khyber, quoted in Shah, *Muslim League*, p. 119.

of Zakori Sharif in Bannu had also demonstrated his sympathy for League demands and popularised them in Waziristan.[78] These advocates assured the tribes 'on behalf of Pakistan' that the government would maintain allowances and that Pakistan had 'no desire whatsoever to interfere, in any way, with the traditional independence of the Tribal Areas.'[79]

In June 1947 the central committee of the Congress Party conceded to a plan for partition of the subcontinent at independence, and distribution of Indian territories between two successor states of India and Pakistan to be decided by provincial referendum. In doing so it deeply disappointed Ghaffar Khan's Khudai Khidmatgars who had hitherto supported the central Congress line on a united India. Ghaffar Khan launched a movement for the inclusion of a third option in the referendum: the creation of an independent state of Pashtunistan comprised of the administered districts and tribal regions of the NWFP.[80]

Beneath these politics of representation and nation, the position of the tribes was largely ambivalent. Olaf Caroe met the Afridis and Shinwaris in March 1947 in an attempt to gauge local responses to the independence and partition plan. He reported that:

On no account were they prepared to deal with the advisory committee of the present Constituent Assembly which they regarded as a purely Hindu body. Neither were they prepared to deal with any separate body which might seek to approach them on behalf of the Muslim League. On this point they wished it to be understood that they regarded the Muslim League as mainly representative of Moslem [sic] India only, and if they wanted to join up with any exclusively Moslem organisation they were much closer to Afghanistan.[81]

---

78 'League Leaders Discuss Civil Liberties' *Pakistan Times*, 21 Feb. 1947.

79 Press release by Jinnah, 29 July 1947, in 'Question of accommodation of tribes in New India'. OIOC L/PS/12/3280.

80 See Erland Jansson, *India Pakistan or Pakhtunistan* (Sweden, 1981), pp. 206-15.

81 Report by O. K. Caroe, Peshawar, 15 March 1947, in 'Question of accommodation of tribes in New India'.

No possibility being offered by any of the parties appealed entirely to the Tribal Areas communities or their *mullas*. The Faqir of Ipi assured the League of his support for Pakistan,[82] swayed possibly by the self-proclaimed League supporters among the Mahsud tribes.[83] But some months later he sent a letter to various tribes in Waziristan, suggesting that the 'unity of Islam' was perhaps not as important as the unity of the tribes of the frontier province.[84] Miangul Abdul Wudud and the Pir of Manki Sharif's championship of the Pakistan issue was limited in its coercive power in the Tribal Areas owing to the deep resentment of many tribes and khanates towards the Swat regime. The Nawab of Amb, who was himself bitterly hostile to the Miangul, wrote in detail to Jinnah, warning him that while he himself supported the League and Pakistan, the tribes and *mullas* of the frontier were deeply divided among themselves. He pointed out that the support of the young Pir of Manki for the Muslim League was itself alienating other parties in the Tribal Areas from the Muslim League's cause owing to old Pir of Manki's 'rivalry and enmity' with the Hadda Mulla and his followers.[85]

Confusion stemmed from the lack of clarity around the options being presented in the Tribal Areas. An Afridi *jirga* sought confirmation that the treaties which for so long had underpinned the relations of the tribes with the Government of India were to be cancelled and that the Khyber Pass and the tolls collected on it were to revert directly to the Afridis once again. A long debate ensued in official circles attempting to clarify the application of the Cabinet Mission plan for decolonisation and partition of the sub-continent to the Tribal Areas, a debate that continued into the final days of empire

---

82 Anonymous Report on Tribes of the NWFP, April 1947. Jinnah Papers (hereafter JP) I, 1.

83 See Sher Badshah Khan Mahsud to M. A. Jinnah, 21 March 1947. JP I, 1.

84 Faqir of Ipi's circular, Abu Sulaiman to Z. A. Ansari, July 1947, enclosure. JP IV.

85 Nawab of Amb to M. A. Jinnah, 3 Aug. 1947, JP IV.

and never came to any meaningful conclusions.[86] Time began to run out and the long-standing Tribal Areas relationship with Afghanistan did not throw up a feasible plan for secession to Kabul, nor was there any real proposal for administrative and nationalist re-drafting of the Tribal Areas treaty-based relationship with the administered districts. As August 1947 approached, administrators left the region parcelled with the NWFP and its fate became linked to that of the province as a whole.

Contests over political legitimacy in the provincial legislature ultimately determined the fate of the province. The question of whether the NWFP was to be included in India or in Pakistan was left to be decided in a referendum. But because Ghaffar Khan's proposed but impractical independent Pakhtunistan was never included in the referendum, he and his Khudai Khidmatgars completely boycotted it and a landslide majority vote went to the NWFP's inclusion in Pakistan. Hence the administered and non-administered districts and agencies of the NWFP were transferred to the state of Pakistan through the referendum of 1947.

Dramatic though the communalist and nationalist politics of partition had been, there was an absence of any real political creativity and pragmatism on the part of the Muslim League and Congress towards the Tribal Areas. Ghaffar Khan, at the eleventh hour, suggested that he wanted an integration of the tribal and settled regions to comprise an independent Pakhtunistan but certainly did not present a formula either for the realisation and protection of such a state, or for the integration of its parts. Moreover, he quickly dropped this idea (under extreme political pressure) once in Pakistan. The terms of the relationship between the Tribal Areas and the successor regimes to the British were as limited as the colonial relationship had always been with its north-western frontier. Clearly this relationship, like the nationalist politics of India as a whole, was constrained within

---

86 O. K. Caroe, memo on bearing of Cabinet delegation's statement on Tribal Areas and the Frontier States 1946, in 'Question of Accommodation of Tribes'.

the administrative template that underlay the transfer of power and partition plans. But the maintenance of the Tribal Areas intact past the period of independence was also a conceptual inheritance. The departing colonial administration encouraged fortifications against the Communist threat, passing on to the nation the imperial geopolitics that had originally made the north-west into a frontier.[87]

Kashmir and the first Indo-Pakistan War

Nothing demonstrated so well the continuities from the colonial to the national period in the North-West Frontier as Jinnah's appointment of George Cunningham, Governor NWFP 1936-47, as first governor of the NWFP in Pakistan; Nehru's appointment of Mountbatten as the first Governor-General of independent India; and the assistance and advice Mountbatten and Cunningham offered to manage the political and social frictions generated by decolonisation and partition. And perhaps nothing demonstrated the enormity of the break as graphically as the communalist massacres of Muslims, Hindus and Sikhs, the invasion of Kashmir by Tribal Areas Pakhtuns in October 1947, and the start of the first Indo-Pakistan war.[88]

News began to filter into the province of massacres of Muslims by Sikhs throughout the Punjab. The Governor NWFP reported news of retaliatory attacks on Sikhs and Hindus in the province in September, and it was clear that the civil and military armed forces together were insufficient to control the situation.[89] On 22 September a Mahsud *lashkar*, ostensibly inspired by communal sentiments, attacked a convoy of Sikhs and Gurkhas being evacuated from Wana.[90] With

---

87 Memos by Caroe and Mountbatten, 1946-97, ibid.

88 George Cunningham to Lord Mountbatten, 9 May 1948, and Mountbatten's response, 29 May 1948. OIOC Cunningham Papers.

89 Cunningham to Jinnah, 8 and 15 Sept. 1947, ibid.

90 Cunningham reported that there was 'no question that the motive is communal as the bodies of our Muslim scouts were allowed to pass unscathed by the *lashkar*.' However there were stray attacks on other regular troops, including Muslims, being evacuated out of Waziristan over the next month. It is fair to estimate that the motivation may have been partly communal, but was more

the change of government and political personnel in the region news was scant but reports reached the Governor's office that Badhshah Gul II was rallying for a *jihad*. Many other tribes spoke of wanting to mobilise in opposition to the Hindus and Sikhs, and in the administered district of Hazara, talk was of 'an invasion into Kashmir'.[91] On 22 October, some thousands of Mahsuds, Mohmands and Afridis moved into Kashmir to liberate it from the Hindus.[92] Of the *mullas* of the Hadda Line, it is only certain that Badshah Gul II led a *lashkar* of Mohmands through Peshawar into Kashmir, calling along the way for volunteers to supply food, clothes and money to those at the battlefront.[93]

While details of the Pakhtun mobilisation into Kashmir are obscured by lack of detail about leadership and motivation, a precedent of moral alliance between the tribes and the Muslim nationalists across the border had been established. What was entirely without precedent was that the government in the NWFP was not inclined, or in a position, to prevent the incursions beyond attempts at verbal dissuasion.[94] Pakistani government resources were stretched to breaking and even food was scarce in the administered province. These circumstances were clearly provoking the tribes, whose movements were, for the first time in over a century, unrestricted to the east, and who were suffering as much, if not more, from the shortage of grain.[95] The first entrants into Kashmir were joined by more and more tribes, including the Mangals, the migratory Powindahs, and Wazirs. At the height of the fighting, tribesmen participant in the

---

closely related to past tensions between the army and the tribes in Waziristan. Cunningham to Jinnah, 1 Oct. 1947, ibid.

91 Cunningham to Jinnah, 15 Oct. 1947, ibid.

92 Cunningham to Mountbatten, 9 May 1948, ibid.

93 Interview Badshah Gul II, Fazal Shah Badshah, in Javed, *Haji Turangzai*, pp. 383-8.

94 Cunningham to Mountbatten, 9 May 1948.

95 Cunningham to Jinnah, 2 Feb. 1948. OIOC Cunningham Papers.

movement together numbered around 20,000.[96] They were met and reinforced by Kashmiris and, by many accounts, by troops of the newly established Pakistan army, though out of uniform.[97]

It was unlikely that Pakistani 'nationalism' was so material and compelling a reality on October 22, just over two months after the creation of Pakistan, that it provoked the tribal mobilisation into Kashmir. Opportunity, bravado, and possibly hunger, shored up by massive moral and material support once they were in probably had more to do with the invasion. The Badshahs Gul I and II, who had up till this time appeared ambivalent about their commitment to Pakistan, moved to Peshawar and joined the Frontier Province Muslim League. Badshah Gul I was reported as touring villages in the administered districts in an attempt to bring the fragmented Muslim nationalist groups together into the central Muslim League party.[98] What was of note is that the Kashmir *jihad* itself generated mutual agreement on the national participation of the tribes which had not have previously existed.

Over the course of the 1947-8 Indo-Pakistan war, with many tribesmen absent from the Tribal Areas and fighting in Kashmir, the governor of the NWFP managed to convene *jirgas* with almost all the tribes and ratify new treaty-based settlements between them and the Pakistan government on the colonial model. The Pakistan government, like the British before it, accorded allowances to *maliks* to permit them to shore up their own positions internally and enforce the settlements in the face of reports that there was great discontent among many of the young Afridi men over the internal distribution of allowances.[99] All tribes of the region, other than those of Waziristan who will be discussed in greater detail below, 'unanimously pledged

---

96 Brian Cloughley, *A History of the Pakistan Army* (Karachi, 1999), p. 19.

97 Cloughley, *Pakistan Army*, p. 19.

98 'Badshah Gul I, II and III'. NWFPPA, Special Branch.

99 Cunningham to Jinnah, 17 Feb. 1948. OIOC Cunningham Papers.

their loyalty' to the government in return for allowances totalling close to 1,000,000 rupees a year.[100]

In April 1948 Jinnah thanked the tribes for their mobilisation into Kashmir as a crucial contribution to the creation of Pakistan and proclaimed that the withdrawal of all regular army presence and garrison from the region, the provision of allowances and complete regional autonomy was the state's reward to the tribes for their help, and asked them to now stand down from their militant activity.[101] This policy, which Jinnah described as designed to 'remove all suspicion in the brotherhood of Islam, of which the tribes and the Pakistan government were both members', was essentially a policy designed to not aggravate the very difficult circumstances on the border.[102] By September India had moved much better equipped army regiments into Kashmir to counter the insurgency and secure the valley. It was a strongly held belief that the Indians were trying to undermine the Pakistani position on the Kashmir border by sending money to insurgents in Waziristan. The Afghan government had also demonstrated hostility to Pakistan. British officials still in Pakistan appraised the situation confronting the government:

It would be extremely difficult to deal with serous tribal trouble with the forces now available... Now more than ever security must depend on political control of the tribes...The tribesmen would have learned from their operations in Kashmir that a large gang of several hundreds can break through a thin line of troops, spend a day or two looting, and can get away again with impunity... There might well be trouble with them if they found themselves hungry and cold when they got to their homes.[103]

---

100   Cunningham to Jinnah, Nov.-Dec. 1947, ibid.

101   Jinnah to a *jirga* of all independent tribes, quoted in Muhammad Shafi Sabir, *Qaid-i Azam aur Suba-yi Sarhad* (Peshawar, n.d.), p. 297.

102   'Announcement by George Cunningham Governor of the NWFP to the Waziristan Tribes', annexture, C.B. Duke, Deputy High Commissioner Peshawar, to Burnett, Deputy High Commissioner for UK at Karachi, 18 Dec. 1947, in 'Disturbances, Tribal Areas, 1947'. OIOC L/PS/12/3281.

103   Duke to Burnett, 29 Dec. 1947, ibid.

As a back-up, the pilots of the Pakistan Air Force were instructed to familiarise themselves with the 18 aircraft stationed at Risalpur, Peshawar and Miramshah, capable of 'close support of ground troops and for destructive action against villages'.[104]

The Pakistan administration also opened talks with the rulers of the frontier states of Dir, Swat, Chitral, and Amb who exercised control over considerable populations and lands, and whose internal politics threatened the peace and security of the region. The authority of the rulers of Swat, Chitral and Amb was being challenged by an organisation called the 'Frontier States Muslim League' which began to organise in their territories demanding representative and accountable government. To forestall their demands, the rulers of Chitral, Amb and Swat all acceded to Pakistan immediately, handing over control of all external affairs in return for ratification of their authority. The Nawab of Dir at first refused to accede on the basis that he would be required to give up control of foreign relations and external defence, liberties which he had enjoyed under the British. Later, no doubt under great pressure from Jinnah's government, he acceded but began to carry out a massive programme of aggrandisement of personal political power and of land, in communication with and supposedly with support from Kabul. In 1949 he threatened to march on Chitral where the old Mehtar had died and been succeeded his son who was regarded as a weaker ruler.[105]

Tensions with India had to some extent been contained by 1949 in talks at Karachi and indications were that a referendum would be held to decide the fate of Kashmir. Nehru had suggested that such a validation ought to be sought to confirm the Maharaja's accession, and when both countries had jointly approached the United Nations Security Council seeking arbitration of the dispute in 1948,

---

104 Ibid.

105 Summarised from the Pakistan Despatches, Office of the High Commissioner for the United Kingdom, Peshawar, May-Sept. 1949, in 'Frontier States 1949-50'. OIOC L/PS/12/3284.

that body recommended a plebiscite.[106] A UN Commission for India and Pakistan was appointed to broker a cease-fire between the two countries and moderate the acceptance of a cease-fire line.

Under these conditions, the administration of the frontier came to be of great immediate national importance. Concerned about maintaining loyalty to Pakistan and wary of Indian infiltration and insurgency in the states, the Pakistan government sought to secure the region by 'supporting' rulers of the states. Whether or not there was truth to it, the Muslim League central party leadership denied any connection with the Frontier States Muslim League, and rumours spread that this organisation was actually the Khudai Khidmatgars in disguise, fomenting revolution and insurgency on behalf of India. The Pakistan government appointed a Political Agent to Chitral to help control the situation—essentially to strengthen the position of the Mehtar and stabilise the balance of power, at least so long as the Kashmir issue was not resolved, and the threat of Indian subversion on the frontier remained.[107] Swat and Dir managed their internal affairs and reported to the political agent Malakand on issues relating to frontier defence.

The British High Commissioner posted at Peshawar suggested what he believed to be the policy of the government towards the Tribal Areas, an understanding supported by the new structure of relations between the government at Karachi and the frontier states:

I do not believe it is the policy of the Pakistan government to push ahead too fast with the introduction into these extremely backward states of modern democratic institutions. The prime minister, who retains also the portfolio of States and Frontier Regions, is well aware of the very low calibre of the local Muslim League politicians and he is not likely to be unduly precipitate in exchanging the present comparatively benevolent regime of the hereditary rules for a specious democracy.[108]

---

106 Cloughley, *Pakistan Army*, p. 21.
107 *Pakistan Despatch*, 31 May 1949.
108 Ibid., 8 Sept. 1949.

This situation altered slightly and gradually between 1950 and 1970 when the states of Dir, Swat and Chitral were gradually transformed from independent kingdoms under the Political Agent Malakand into administered districts, the states of Amb and Phulra were abolished entirely and separate agencies of Mohmand and Bajaur were created to gain better control over what had been the Malakand Agency. But except for these modifications, the conditions created by the colonial political department were re-enforced by the Pakistan government. The social segregation of the Tribal Areas population from the administered districts was maintained and control applied by means of an allowance system. When the moment finally came, religious and political identification across the border (in both directions), and the exuberance of self-government ultimately meant very little for the structure of relations between the Pakistani nation and the region outside the administrative border. For the Pakistanis, far more so than ever had been the case for the British, the frontier held the potential to threaten the very integrity of the state as the battle over Kashmir continued.

The Pakhtunistan movement

The resources and charm of Mirza Ali Khan, Faqir of Ipi, were severely depleted after 1937, but he continued to live at his base with a retinue of over 300 men, mostly Shabi Khel Mahsuds, but including some absconders from the administered districts. He organised stray incidents of sniping and raids on army bases through the period of the war, and in 1946 apparently encouraged elements among the Shabi Khel Mahsuds to kidnap the Political Agent of South-Waziristan, Major J.O.S. Donald.[109] But it was not till after 1947 that he organ-

---

109 Mahsud, *Firangi Raj*, p. 228. Retaliatory airstrikes to punish the Mahsuds after Donald was released received a lot of attention in the administered districts where the Muslim League and Congress were closely competing for the Pakhtun vote. See Parshotam Mehra, *The North-West Frontier Drama* (Karachi, 2001), pp. 66-8.

ised sufficiently to demand the serious attention of the government to the east once again.

The one region that remained ambivalent during Cunningham's reinstatement of the tribal allowances was Waziristan. Cunningham had noted earlier in the year that the Faqir of Ipi was preparing for 'something really big'.[110] This came together early in 1948 when the Faqir pulled a *lashkar* together and attacked and then occupied the Datta Khel *khassadar* post in the Tochi valley in June 1948.[111] Later that same month, the national English daily, *Dawn*, published a front-page report that the Faqir was receiving payments from the Indian government, disbursed through the Indian embassy at Kabul, as an incentive for him to start an insurrection against the Pakistan government.[112] Historians and contemporary observers questioned the veracity of the claim supported only by a letter, ostensibly from the Faqir to the Indian prime minister, and by rumours about the movements of the Faqir's emissary, Awal Hussain. What is beyond doubt is that the hostilities with the new India and the vulnerability of the newly-separated Pakistan made the Faqir's mobilisation and his possible solicitations of help from other governments deeply threatening.

In most ways the Faqir's actions were unexceptional. He had targeted the Datta Khel post, a close and desirable target, at the height of his movement in 1937 and sniper attacks on British army troops withdrawing from the region were a commonplace throughout 1947. Moreover as the tribal mobilisation began it appeared to be premised on the question of allowances. However the Kashmir war had demonstrated how relevant mobilisations in the Tribal Areas were to the new and vulnerable Pakistan's geographical integrity. A sig-

---

110 Cunningham to Jinnah, 15 Oct. 1947.

111 Pakistan Despatch, 23 June 1948, UKHC Karachi, in 'Activities of the Faqir of Ipi'. OIOC L/PS/12/3241.

112 'Ipi-Nehru Axis to Eliminate Pakistan. Faqir's emissary arrested with letters: Indian Premier promises assistance in time', *Dawn* (Karachi), 28 June 1948.

nificant report from the British High Commission indicated sternly the problems inherent in Peshawar Intelligence Bureau information-gathering tactics as they 'accepted all stories sent back without discrimination (in fact the more highly coloured they were the more likely was the informant's pay to be increased).'[113] And there is little doubt that such scaremongering was at work on the frontier. But despite this warning, the Faqir's act was seen, understood and dealt with as nothing short of a political, anti-Pakistan insurgent movement. After some political pressure to eject the Faqir and his *lashkar*, the Pakistan Air Force was sent in to deal with the situation. Bombers went in destroy the villages of participant Shabi Khel Mahsuds and to disperse the *lashkar* from its occupation of the *khassadar* post, and the Faqir was decried at a national level as a traitor and a political insurgent. Accusations of secessionism against the Faqir gathered force when the Afghan press began to express sympathy for the Faqir and concern over the aerial action of the Pakistan army and to call for the freedom of 'Pakhtunistan', thus establishing a motive which up to this point it was not at all clear the Faqir held. From being just another incident of Tribal Areas mobilisation, the Faqir of Ipi's movement became a national crisis.

Early Pakistani-Afghan relations, unavoidably read through the prism of British documentation on the subject, were deeply uncertain.[114] Internally the young Zahir Shah was largely under the influence of his ambitious uncles and then his cousin, Muhammad Daoud, who served as prime minister from 1953-63 and later overthrew the constitutional monarchy to come back as the first prime minister of the republic in 1973. His preoccupation with the eastern Pakhtun regions has been argued to have been rooted in concern for Pakhtun

---

113 G. F. Squire to Foreign Office and UKHC Peshawar, 31 Aug. 1949, in 'Afghan-Pakistan Dispute'. OIOC L/PS/12/1827.

114 Afghan political affairs from 1930 to 1970 have not been the subject of any sound historical study. The years between Amanullah's overthrow and the 'Saur Revolution' of 1978 need scholarly attention, not least to uncover the internal politics that surrounded the tensions with Pakistan.

political dominance in Afghanistan.[115] Externally the Afghans were suddenly faced with an independent 'Muslim nation' as successor to the historically contentious Pakhtun border region, challenging the Afghan position on ethnic grounds and the long-held Afghan perception of the amirate as the sole bastion for free Islam.[116] Before partition the Afghans had urgently sought and received confirmation that transit facilities from the port at Karachi through to the borders of Afghanistan would be maintained and on this basis accepted Pakistan's inheritance of the Durand treaty.[117] Soon after independence they began to query the persistence of the Durand Line on the grounds that the most recent treaty between the British government in India and Afghanistan, that of 1921, had admitted an Afghan stake in the border tribes.[118]

The first challenge from the Afghans came soon after 14 August 1947 when, following usual practice, Pakistan-side tribesmen attended the annual *jashan* at Kabul, where Zahir Shah and his prime minister spoke out against Pakistani actions in the Tribal Areas. The state-run Kabul Radio began to run a series of commentaries criticis-

---

115 Sultan Aziz, 'Leadership Dilemmas—Challenges and Responses', in Grant Farr and John Merriam (eds), *Afghan Resistance the Politics of Survival* (Boulder, CO, 1987), pp. 59-62.

116 The Pakistan and Afghan press traded jibes over each country's form of government. A Pakistan Radio commentary on the autocracy of Zahir Shah's regime and the lack of personal political liberty in that country received a reply in an editorial in the *Islah* that maladministration was endemic in Pakistan, a country which had left administration in the hands of British officers, and failed to ensure the availability of cloth and food to citizens. Editorial in *Islah*, 28 March 1948, in 'Afghan-Pakistan Relations, 1948'. OIOC L/PS/12/1826.

117 'Supply of Documents to Pakistan Government'. OIOC L/PS/12/1825.

118 This re-interpretation of the Treaty of 1921 read the abrogation of 'all previous treaties and agreements' as meaning the erasure of the Durand Line agreement signed in 1894, and pointed out that one of the annextures to the treaty distinguished the residents of the Tribal Areas from the administered districts in a reference to the shared interest of the Afghans and the British in the border tribes. See British Legation Kabul to Secretary of State for Foreign Affairs, 19 July 1947. In IOLC 'Informal Afghan Proposals'. OIOC L/PS/12/1811.

ing the actions of the Pakistani state. In September 1947 Afghanistan was the sole member-state of the UN to oppose Pakistani membership of the world body on the basis that Pakhtun political aspirations in favour of independence (as represented by Ghaffar Khan) had not been addressed. Later that year Zahir Shah sent his special envoy Najibullah Khan to Karachi to negotiate a treaty with the Pakistan government. Trade terms were readily agreed, but the government understandably refused an Afghan request to grant complete autonomy to the North-West Frontier Province and re-name it Afghania or Pathanistan on the grounds that these matters were the affair of the Constitutional Assembly and not the Foreign Ministry.[119] In March 1949 a Kabul Radio commentary on the Pakistani air action against the Faqir of Ipi was sent to all foreign missions in Pakistan by the Afghan embassy as a press note. Despite the suggestions of support for Tribal Areas 'independence', Afghanistan's bellicocity suggested to the Pakistani government a fresh competition over ownership of the Tribal Areas:

According to reliable reports received here the Pakistan Air Force has once again bombarded the independent Tribal Areas killing hundreds of innocent and undefended Afghan men, women and children. Radio Kabul added that we strongly express our hatred of and regret this unlawful act of aggression and human cruelty. It is very regrettable that these raids were carried out at the same moment that Faqir of Ipi sent a peace mission to Pakistan ... The Afghans wherever they may be will never abandon their love of liberty ... Afghanistan is bound to these innocent and independent Afghans by numerous ties of blood, race, religion, culture and language. We wish them peace and prosperity ... Afghanistan's policy is to preserve peaceful relations with all countries, especially with our neighbours. So it is our duty to advise Pakistan to take lessons from past history and not repeat the mistakes made by the British.[120]

---

119 Summary of events annexed to 'Memorandum by the Secretary of State for Commonwealth Relations, April 1949, in 'Afghanistan-Pakistan Dispute'.

120 UKHC Karachi to Commonwealth Relations Office and H.M. Ambassador, Kabul, 11 March 1949, ibid.

Tribal attendance at *jashans* in Afghanistan, hyperbole and ma-
chismo by the Afghan ruler at public events, and passionate warmth
towards the Pakhtun fraternity in the Pakhtun-controlled Afghan
national press were aspects of Afghan political culture which related to internal issues rather than necessarily indicating expansionist
design. However Zahir Shah and Muhammad Daoud's question-
ing of the legitimacy of the Pakistani state and its relations with its
Pakhtun population at an international diplomatic level suggested
that Afghanistan sought to revise its regional position alongside
Pakistan. This was proved the case when the Afghan Amir called
the nation-wide *loya jirga*—a summons which had historically been
reserved for only the most crucial moments of national self-defini-
tion—to discuss future Afghan policy towards Pakistan.[121] In June
1949 the Pakistan Air Force dropped bombs on a hostile *lashkar* on
the Afghan side of the border. Again this was not an entirely new
occurrence—such trangressions over the vague and unmarked border
had occurred during the British period as well, whether accidental or
on purpose. But the Afghan government argued that Afghan villages
had been purposefully targeted. In July 1949 the Afghan parliament,
headed by Zahir Shah's uncle Shah Mahmud,[122] formally renounced
the Durand Line and officially claimed the territories to the east of
it.[123]

Pakistan sought assurances that Britain would support it on the
basis of its Commonwealth status in the event of an Afghan attack
across the border. While a formal guarantee was not elicited, the

---

121   Minister at Kabul to Foreign Office, 5 April 1949, in IOLC, 'Afghan-
Pakistan Dispute'. Amanullah Khan had called the Loya Jirga in 1923 to try to
push through his new constitution. Nadir Shah had called a Loya Jirga on his
assumption of the amirate in 1930, and Zahir Shah's prime minister had called
a Loya Jirga in 1941 to ascertain a nation position on the War.

122   Shah Mahmud ruled as prime minister until 1953 when Muhammad
Daud, Zahir Shah's cousin took over. See Edwards, *Before Taliban*, pp. 61-3 for
a brief account of this political history.

123   Press Release, Afghanistan Embassy, Washington', 22 Aug. 1949, in
'Activities of Amin Jan'. OIOC L/PS/12/1830.

Foreign Office agreed to exert pressure on the Afghan government as necessary to prevent an attack from Afghanistan, and provided documentation to support the maintenance of the Durand Line in the event of Afghanistan referring the issue to the United Nations'.[124] By the end of the year, Pakistan withdrew many of the transit facilities provided for Afghanistan imports through the port at Karachi.[125]

Pakistani-Afghan relations oscillated over the next decade. The two governments were reconciled due to mediation by the American government, a personal visit by Vice President Nixon to Karachi and then Kabul, and the apparent openness of Pakistan to the possibility of a regional confederation consisting of Iran, Afghanistan and Pakistan, suggested by the governments of Iskander Mirza, and then Feroz Khan Noon in the 1950s.[126] When Muhammad Ali Bogra's government proposed and then instituted the One-Unit scheme designed to balance the East Pakistan majority by merging the four provinces of West Pakistan into a single province in 1955, the Afghans once again perceived a threat on their border and the Pakhtunistan issue was revived.

Propaganda promoting the creation of an independent state of Pakhtunistan comprised entirely of territories in Pakistan and not incorporating the Afghan Pakhtun regions was circulated in London and Washington by the Afghan information ministry in 1951 and then again in 1960.[127] But while the Afghan government still refused to ratify the Durand Line between the two countries, the largest direct confrontation between the two states was a five-month closure

---

124 Memorandum by the Secretary of State for Commonwealth Relations, April 1949, 'Supply of Documents to Pakistan in Event of Reference to UNO, March 1949.'

125 Military Attache to Afghanistan summaries of intelligence, 9-22 Dec. 1949, in 'Diaries of Military Attache'. OIOC L/PS/12/1852.

126 Mujtaba Razvi, *The Frontiers of Pakistan* (Karachi, 1971), pp. 156-7.

127 Pakhtunistan propaganda literature was published and distributed by the Afghan Information Ministry. See Rahman Pazhwak, *Pakhtunistan, the Khyber Pass as the Focus of the New State of Pakhtunistan* (London, n.d.), and Rahman Pazhwak, *Pakhtunistan, A New State in Central Asia* (London, 1960).

of the border from the Pakistan side following a mob attack on the Pakistan embassy at Kabul in 1955.

The Afghan government was, in the end, unwilling to take the issue to the point of direct military confrontation, but this did not preclude once again extending support to the region's *mullas* to secure their loyalties. Financial and moral support was extended to the Faqir of Ipi to assist him in 'setting up' the 'Waziristan Branch of the Pakhtunistan National Assembly'.[128] A similar organisation was encouraged in the Khyber region among the Afridis, and Kabul Radio broadcast a declaration of independence on their behalf.[129] Haji Turangzai and his descendants were depicted as heroes and as champions of Pakhtun ethnic unity,[130] Haji Turangzai's second son, Badshah Gul II, admitted that he was approached by the Afghans and offered land and money in Afghanistan to join the 'Pathanistan' movement and Badshah Gul III moved across to Afghan Kohistan with his family.[131] In 1960 a *lashkar* of 15,000 men crossed the border from the Afghan side, and the presence of a contingent of the regular Afghan army close to the point of the incursion suggested Kabul's approval, if not complicity, in the movement.[132] The object was rumoured to be an attack on the long-time enemy of the *mullas* of the Akhund Ghaffur-Hadda Mulla line: the Khan of Khar. The following spring the Pakistan army bombed dissidents in Bajaur,[133] and it was rumoured that Lakarai, the one-time seat of Haji Turangzai's power and now the inheritance of his sons, was targeted despite the Badshah Guls' subsequent denial of involvement in the Pakhtunistan movement.

---

128 Warren, *Faqir of Ipi*, p. 263.

129 Pazhwak, *Pakhtunistan, the Khyber Pass as the Focus of the New State of Pakhtunistan*, pp. 123-6.

130 Pazhwak, *Pakhtunistan, the Khyber Pass*, pp. 52-3.

131 Javed, *Haji Turangzai*, pp. 383-8.

132 Syed Abdul Quddus, *Afghanistan and Pakistan: A Geo-Political Study* (Lahore, 1982), p. 116.

133 Quddus, *Afghanistan and Pakistan*, p. 82.

The Faqir of Ipi's biographers described him as having been motivated by orthodox religious principles which were betrayed by the western-style administration established in Pakistan.[134] Afghan propaganda suggested that the *mullas* merely gave voice to an essential conflict between Pakhtun tribal culture and the Pakistani, Punjab-centred nation state. Political administrators believed that the opposition posed by the region's *mullas* was directly intended to undermine the authority of the state.[135] Between these assumptions there emerged a persistent truth—that, as during the colonial period, the claims put forward by religious leaders were not for union with Afghanistan, but for greater regional autonomy and recognition of their own positions as leaders among the tribes. Although the Faqir obligingly outlined his ambitions for the creation of an independent Pakhtun state of which he would be the head in an interview granted to an American journalist in 1950, this was comprised solely of an autonomous Waziristan; and the Badshahs Gul never demonstrated a secessionist impulse at all.[136] Pakhtunistan was an objective ascribed

---

134 Warren's study of the Faqir of Ipi ends in 1947 and he suggests vaguely that the mobilisations of the Faqir after this time were primarily inspired by his objection to the Western style of law in Pakistan. Mahsud's study similarly ends with the creation of Pakistan, but without any attempt to address the secessionist movement launched by the Faqir in 1948.

135 See the study of Noor Mohammad Wana Mulla by Akbar S. Ahmed who spent many years as an officer of the Pakistan political service in the Tribal Areas. The Wana Mulla refused to accept the 'official' announcement of the religious holiday of Eid by the state one year and insisted that it be celebrated a day later, on the day decided by him. Political patronage from the central opposition party further confirmed the *mullas*' resources and his influence, encouraging him to declare himself '*badshah* of Wana.'Details of the Wana Mulla's activities are taken from Akbar S. Ahmed's study of the Mulla Noor Muhammad, as an example of structure of Islam in tribal society in his book *Resistance and Control in Pakistan* (Cambridge, 1991), pp. 49-54. Although Ahmed argues that '*mians* and *mullahs* ought to be understood in terms of the genealogical charter which excludes them from any inherent rights except by external association', and attributes an ultimate irrelevance to their contributions to tribal organisation, the story of the Wana Mulla demonstrates the continuing relevance of the *mulla* to tribal organisation, in this case in defiance of federal authority.

136 Christopher Rand, interview with the Faqir of Ipi, 1950, quoted in Warren,

to the Faqir of Ipi and Haji Turangzai's three sons by Afghan and Indian propaganda and alarmist reports in the Pakistani press. In essence the Faqir's ambitions appear to have been to the sole right of representation of the Wazirs both to the Pakistan government and to the Afghan state.

An autonomous national frontier

The Tribal Areas had emerged out of a colonial geography of imperial containment. An accepted terrestrial notion of what constituted the Indian subcontinent underpinned its creation and its accommodation into the state of Pakistan.[137] As the central Muslim League party struggled to deal with the Indo-Pakistan war, Afghan belligerence, the Faqir's movement and general frontier management, the friendly contact initiated by the Muslim League towards the Tribal Areas was not sustained. In Peshawar Badshah Gul I parted ways with the Frontier Province Muslim League, saying that his efforts to forge a political unity were not appreciated in the face of a battle over political legitimacy across the country.[138] Meanwhile the Khudai Khidmatgars, who were most naturally placed to consolidate a Pakistani Pakhtun political position, were facing a witch-hunt and accusations of national betrayal following Afghanistan's championship of the Pakhtunistan movement, and never ended up extending the remit of their political influence into the Tribal Areas.

The British colonial and Pakistani nationalist narratives both equally confined the Tribal Areas within the firm grip of an eternally static culture. In the NWFP political 'modernity' was born as the conjoined twin of the pre-modern, tribal peoples of the non-

Faqir of Ipi, p. 263.

137 Gyan Prakash defines this as the 'nationalist confinement in the orientalist problematic', 'Writing Post-Orientalist Histories of the Third World: Perspectives from Indian Historiography' in Vinayak Chaturvedi (ed.), *Mapping Subaltern Studies and the Postcolonial* (London, 2000), p. 170.

138 Javed, *Haji Turangzai*, p. 489. Javed quotes an interview that he conducted himself with Badshah Gul I in 1951.

administered areas. Jamiyatul Ulama, the Khudai Khidmatgars and the Muslim League alike used ideas of political modernity, social advancement and progress to promote their competing claims to provincial government—a progress that was neatly defined in opposition to the tribe and the backward but noble Pakhtuns of the non-administered highlands. Hence the relationship between the Tribal Areas and the administered districts was one of accomplices rather than of shared politics and groups on both sides continued to reaffirm the terms of Tribal Areas separateness well after 1947. Tribal Areas *maliks*, maintained by the payment of subsidies by the Pakistan government, promised to provide *khassadars* and protect the roads and warned other members of their tribes that incorporation into Pakistan would mean paying exorbitant taxes and a loss of personal liberty.[139] Successive military and elected governments, instigated by political conservatism; military bravado; the expense of infrastructure development, education, law enforcement and legislation; and a belief in the intractability of the tribes, maintained systems of regional control through political agents. Pakhtun writers in the Tribal Areas and in administered Pakistan glorified political autonomy and the cultural distinctness of tribal Pakhtuns, maintaining that the Tribal Areas was the land of an independent Islam uncompromised by modernity, westernisation and urbanisation.[140]

Dissident voices from the Tribal Areas, servants of the state or the public were undiscernible. Spokesmen on all sides ignored evidence to the contrary that hundreds of young Pakhtuns were migrating from the Tribal Areas to Peshawar and Kabul in pursuit of education, business opportunities or jobs and claiming domicile in the administered districts in order to claim identity cards and passports

---

139 Nurul Islam Mian drew attention to this sentiment in his *Preliminary Economic Survey of the Tribal Areas Adjoining West Pakistan* (Peshawar, 1956), p. 3.

140 Some important examples of such literature are Gul Ayub Khan Saifi, *Bannu aur Waziristan Tarikh* (Bannu, 1969); Meera Jan Syal, *Da Pashtun Qabilo Shajaray* (Peshawar, 1988); Ahsanullah Khan, *Pakhtun Qabail* (Peshawar, nd) and Allah Baksh Yusufi, *Yusufzai Afghan* (Karachi, 1960).

without having to seek the express approval of the Political Agent.[141] So although many within the Tribal Areas may have desired the social, civic and institutional amenities available in administered districts, the strategic and cultural argument for separation of the region became part of the discourse of the Pakistani nation.

---

141 Muzaffar Syal, Ghulam Nabi Chaknawari, Ahmed Yusuf, and Obaidur Rahman all drew attention to the fact that many young men, including themselves, left the Tribal Areas in search of education and employment, and whether or not they returned to the Tribal Areas, most maintained homes in administered parts of Afghanistan or Pakistan. Dissent on the issue of Tribal Areas separation deserves a far more comprehensive and thoughtful analysis than is possible here. Unfortunately there are very few substantial writings which explore the efforts or need of Tribal Areas men and women to overcome the state, religiously and tribally-imposed segregation of the region. See Abubakar Siddique, 'Paradise Lost' *Newline* (Karachi) July 2006; 'War on Terror highlights development needs in FATA' *The Friday Times* (Lahore) 29 Jan. 2004; and 'Legal regime in Fata has outlived its utility' *The Friday Times* 2 July 2004 for some of the only publicly voiced considerations of the issue.

ISLAMISTS AND THE UTILITY OF AUTONOMOUS SPACE: FROM THE AFGHAN JIHAD TO AL-QAEDA

In 1973 Zahir Shah's constitutional monarchy was overthrown and a national parliament was established. The parliament was dominated by the more moderate faction of the communist PDPA party with Muhammad Daoud, the amir's cousin, at its head as prime minister. In Pakistan a civil-military establishment had colluded to dismiss parliament and took the country to war against India over Kashmir in 1965. Ayub Khan, Commander-in-Chief of the Army, followed by Yahya Khan, had instituted draconian measures to control East Pakistan's Bengali majority, which led to a civil war and the breakaway of East Pakistan into the independent state of Bangladesh in 1971. The constitution of the Republic of Pakistan of 1973 was written, superseding the constitutions of 1956 and 1962 and naming Islam as the religion of the state and the basis for all legislation. Zulfiqar Ali Bhutto and his Pakistan People's Party with a vote base in Sind and Punjab, formed a government in Islamabad, opposed by a coalition opposition of the National Awami Party and the Jamiyatul Ulama-yi Islam which together dominated the NWFP and Baluchistan.

Religion was being steadily regularised in both Afghanistan and Pakistan between 1963 and 1980. The press, party politics, urbanisation and government suspicion in Afghanistan increasingly marginalised traditional religious leaders during the constitutional period from 1963 to 1978. The state attempted to control the local centres of religious instruction, so much so that the old *dargah* of the Hadda

Mulla at Hadda Sharif now housed a state-run *madrasa*.[1] Faculties of religious law were set up at state universities, to bring traditional education into line with the practices of Western education. Many more traditionally inclined religious scholars left to seek instruction in Quran and *hadith* studies at institutions in India, Pakistan, Cairo and Damascus,[2] and in their place the university-trained religious leadership began to develop a theologically derived position to counter the politics of the increasingly left-leaning Afghan intelligentsia. While these university-trained theologians, the most prominent of whom were Burhanuddin Rabbani and Gulbuddin Hekmatyar, appealed to a de-tribalised middle class across ethnic lines, they were also being drawn into a wider, global religious ideology through connections with the Muslim Brotherhood in Cairo and the Jamaat-i Islami in Pakistan.[3]

In Pakistan *madrasas* and *masjids* were drawing *'ulama, mullas* and students into national and provincial organisations by promoting the idea of a national religious curriculum and the paramountcy of Sunni orthodoxy while religious parties were pressing for the enforcement of *shari'a*-based law. Religiously motivated but untrained 'Islamists', led by the formidable Abul Ala Maududi and his Jamaat-i Islami, and the scholars of Pakistan's Islam, the *'ulama*, parted ways as political allies, but each continued to affect the progression of Pakistan's Islamisation.[4]

The *'ulama* of Pakistan, dominated by several Deobandis,[5] were working to strengthen the interior domain of Islam—the *madrasas*

---

1   Edwards, *Genealogies*, p. 196.

2   Olivier Roy, 'Modern Political Culture and Traditional Resistance', in Bo Huldt and Erland Jansson, (eds), *The Tragedy of Afghanistan* (London, 1988), pp. 106-12.

3   Tahir Amin, 'Afghan Resistance: Past, Present and Future', *Asian Survey* (California, 1984), pp. 375-7.

4   Muhammad Qasim Zaman, *The Ulama in Contemporary Islam, Custodians of Change* (Princeton, 2002), pp. 102-10.

5   Namely, Shabbir Ahmed Usmani, Naseeruddin Ghorghashtavi, Syed Muhammad Yusuf Banori, Ahmed Ali Lahori and Ahtashamul Haq Thanvi.

and *masjids*—and to guard the interpretation of religion jealously. They demanded that religious commentators should have received not only a course of religious study, but the particular *dars-i nizami* of Deoband. In addition to the Deoband-modelled *madrasas* established in the urban centres of Karachi, Lahore, Gujranwala and Multan, such institutions were also established in the administered districts of the NWFP and Baluchistan. The *madrasas* of NWFP and Baluchistan began to induct and train hundreds of exiled Afghan *'ulama*[6] and Maududi's Jamaat-i Islami rallied furiously to the support of Afghan Islamists escaping persecution by Muhammad Daoud's government between 1973 and 1978.

The year 1978-9, corresponding to the millennium year 1399 in the Islamic calendar, marked the beginning of a new political era across the region. In Afghanistan Soviet-inspired officers of the Afghan national army deemed Muhammad Daoud unequal to meet the country's needs although his regime was suspicious and heavy-handed towards possible opponents of the state. His government was overthrown in what was termed the Saur Revolution, to be replaced by a pro-Soviet military regime and the country was renamed the Democratic Republic of Afghanistan (DRA). A new government was established under Nur Muhammad Taraki, but his Marxist-inspired economic and social decrees made it deeply unpopular. Widespread city-based political demonstrations took place and were put down only through Soviet military assistance. In the eastern Pakhtun tribal regions, deep resentment against land reforms, laws for women's protection and the systematic undermining of traditional religious leaders instigated a calculated tribal response beginning in the Pech-Kunar region and spreading across Nuristan and Badakshan with isolated tribal risings occurring in Paktia and Ningrahar as well. Tribal *lashkars* formed

---

6 Haqqaniyya Madrasa in Akora Khattak alone graduated at least 371 Afghan students between 1945-78. See '*Darul Ulum Haqqaniyya ka aik faizan: fazla-yi Afghanistan*'—an incomplete list of Afghan graduates of Haqqaniyya, in *Al Haq* (Abdul Haq Number, 1993), pp. 658-81. See also Gilles Dorronsoro, *Revolution Unending* (London, 2005); Amin, *Afghan Resistance*, pp. 377-80.

and attacked military targets to great effect, dispersing quickly and untraceably into the surrounding population.[7]

In an attempt to shore up public support for the regime, Taraki was removed by the Politburo and replaced by his deputy Hafizullah Amin. When Amin proved equally incapable of controlling the situation, the Soviet army entered and occupied Afghanistan in January 1980 to prop up the weak and unpopular government. Amin was executed and replaced by Babrak Karmal. Karmal's government instituted a massive depopulation campaign along the eastern border, to eliminate the cover of human habitation that the suddenly converging and quickly dispersing *lashkar* formation relied on. This marked the transfer of the majority of the Afghan eastern Pakhtun population and anti-Soviet organisation to Pakistan, and its consolidation under political management of the Afghan Islamists in Peshawar.

In Pakistan Zulfiqar Ali Bhutto was removed from power in a military coup by General Zia ul Haq and later executed. Zia ul Haq's Islamist bent led him to increase government support for (and control of) *madrasas*, to impose a mandatory *zakat* tax, implement some aspects of Islamic criminal law and increase the number of *'ulama* on the parliamentary advisory body, the 'Council of Islamic Ideology'.[8] Zia's regime was well disposed to act as patron of the resistance groups. Political organisation of the resistance in Pakistan took place

---

7 See reports in *Dawn*, March-Oct. 1979; David B. Edwards, 'Origins of the Anti-Soviet Jihad', in Farr and Merriam (eds), *Afghan Resistance*, pp. 22-50 for a close consideration of the initial resistance; and Edwards, *Before Taliban*, pp. 65-71, 132-7 for analysis of the eastern Pakhtun motivation in mobilising.

8 Most of these measures were implemented between 1977-9. It is important to note that Zia ul Haq was not the author of Pakistan's Islamic principles. The constitution of 1973 rooted the country's legislation in principles of *shari'a* and formulated the Council of Islamic Ideology as an advisory body to parliament. The controversial amendment which declared the Ahmedi community a non-Muslim minority community was added in 1974, although legislation requiring Ahmedis to declare themselves non-Muslim in order to get identity documents was passed by Zia ul Haq's regime. Zaman notes that Zia's enforcement of the Shari'a Ordinance actually restricted the power of *shari'a* courts, and thereby that of the *ulama*, by vesting 'final authority to determine questions of repugnance to the *shari'a*' in the high courts. *The Ulama in Contemporary Islam*, p. 89.

under seven primary leaders and their political parties: Gulbuddin Hekmatyar and the Hizb-i Islami; Burhanuddin Rabbani and the Jamaat-i Islami; Yunis Khalis and the Hizb-i Islami-yi Khalis; Abdal Rab Sayaf and the Ettehad-i Islami; Sebghatullah Mujaddiddi and the Jebh-i Nijat-i Milli; Sayyid Ahmed Gailani and the Mahaz-i Milli Islami; and Mulla Nabi Muhammadi and the Harkat-i Inqi-lab-i Islami. These resistance fighers who came to be known as the 'Afghan Mujahidin' and their political groups began to organise the displaced Afghan population in Peshawar and to support the sponta-neous tribal and rural mobilisations against the Afghan government and the army.[9]

Refugees pouring into Pakistan from Afghanistan entered into the Tribal Areas first. Despite Pakistani government efforts to re-settle this displaced population in refugee camps away from the border, 104 out of the 278 Refugee Tented Villages in the NWFP remained in the Tribal Areas, primarily in the Bajaur, Kurram and North-Waziristan Agencies.[10] The Tribal Areas residents aligned themselves with the resistance mobilisation and in the first months of 1979 Mohmand, Afridi, Wazir and Yusufzai clans met in a *jirga* and called for an assault on Kabul to remove the Soviets.[11] *Lashkars* in support of the Afghan Pakhtuns formed in the Pakistan Tribal Areas and attacked military columns, official convoys and any acces-sible DRA target.

While Pakistan was a willing host to refugees and anti-Soviet Mujahidin based in Peshawar, domestic concerns meant that the government could not encourage any direct offensive organisation in administered territory so Afghan Mujahidin and Pakistani patrons of the resistance fighters looked to the Tribal Areas as a crucial area for reconnaissance. Arms were secreted in the Tribal Areas by the

---

9 Amin, 'Afghan Resistance', p. 380.

10 Nancy Dupree, 'Demographic Reporting on Afghan Refugees in Pakistan, *Modern South Asian Studies* (Cambridge, 1988), p. 846.

11 David Chaffetz, 'Afghanistan in Turmoil', *International Affairs* (London, 1980), pp. 15-36.

resistance parties to arm fighters crossing into Afghanistan and support the ongoing resistance inside the country. Mujahidin would 'as a rule' conduct campaigns in the Afghan border provinces where they could easily receive reinforcements from the Pakistan side of the border and retreat back across it if they needed to. The normal lack of clear distinction between the Tribal Areas and the eastern Afghan regions was exacerbated as the region became the forward point of the Afghan *jihad* and the first point from which the resistance could take a stand.[12] Such integration of the Tribal Areas into the Afghan front was most complete in the Kunar-Mohmand-Bajaur region where the Mujahidin artillery offensive was located in Mohmand on the Pakistan side of the border, supporting Mujahidin ambushes and raids on the Afghan side.[13] In response, the DRA began to subject Bajaur, Mohmand, North-Waziristan, Khyber and Kurram on the Pakistan side of the border to the same aerial bombardments used to flush guerrilla fighters out of the eastern Afghan provinces,[14] despite objections lodged by Pakistan at the UN.[15]

As the war and the depopulation of the eastern Afghan provinces continued, refugees continued to pour in and to settle on the Pakistani side of the border. By August 1980, 90,000 Afghans were reported to be entering Pakistan each month.[16] A 'working symbiosis' began to emerge between Pakistani tribesmen and those refugees who settled in the Tribal Areas. Refugees grazed livestock on wheat stubble and offered their services at the time of harvest. In return for tolerating the refegees, Pakistani tribesmen 'got labour and fertiliser and could claim to be upholding Pakhtunwali hospitality.'[17] Just as

---

12 '3 MIGS of Afghan Air Force downed: Mujahidin's claim', *Dawn*, 12 May 1979.

13 Lelsey Grau and Michael Gress, *The Soviet-Afghan War* (Kansas, 2002), p. 62.

14 'Booby-trapped toys kill many Afghan children', *Dawn*, 5 Aug. 1980.

15 'Pakistan letter to UN: Afghan Attacks', *Dawn*, 8 Nov. 1980.

16 'Booby-trapped toys kill many Afghan children', *Dawn*, 5 Aug. 1980.

17 Andre Singer, 'Ahmed on the Afghan Refugees', *RAIN* (London, 1980), pp. 1-2.

Afghan refugees began to settle into the Pakhtun tribal subsistence farming economy, equally the Pakhtun tribesmen were inducted into the Afghan economy of resistance. Pakistan-side tribesmen were encouraged by Mujahidin leaders to farm the highly lucrative poppy crop. The poppy crop doubled from 1982-3 and by 1988 up to 200 heroin refineries had been set up in the Khyber alone.[18] Darra Adam-khel *bazaar* in the Khyber became the central transaction point for the sale of Russian weapons captured by the *mujahidin* and the trade of Chinese and American arms coming in as international assistance to the Afghan *jihad*.[19] The volume of arms and ammunition being traded in Darra supplied the Afghan resistance, and proved sufficient to also arm a number of groups from Karachi to Kashmir.[20]

By 1984 the Mujahidin gained strength and were able to take back positions on the Afghan side of the border. The offensive moved back into Afghanistan and Mujahidin returned to Pakistan only with the wounded or for supplies. Many refugees on the Pakistan side of the border began to travel seasonally to farm their land in 'free' areas of Afghanistan.[21] A number of roads and passes through the region were widened and metalled at a rate of development which was un-equalled in the Tribal Areas hundred-year history. It was during this period that evidence of friction between the Tribal Areas residents and the Afghan Mujahidin and refugees began to appear. In South-Waziristan pamphlets were distributed calling for the removal of Afghan refugees who were said to be threatening the security of the Tribal Areas after the Jandola bridge was destroyed in a DRA attack. These anti-Mujahidin sentiments were encouraged by the Kabul

---

18   Ikramul Haq 'Pak-Afghan Drug Trade in Historical Perspective', *Asian Survey* (California, 1996), p. 954.

19   Amin, 'Afghan Resistance', p. 390.

20   Arms trading in the Tribal Areas was confined in a narrow supply and demand interaction up till the start of the Afghan *jihad*. See chapter 3 for a discussion of Tribal Areas arms trading during the period of British rule.

21   Dupree, 'Demographic Reporting', p. 848.

regime, which hosted a 'High Jirgah of Frontier Tribes' in 1985.[22] Tensions between the residents of the Tribal Areas (and those of the administered districts), the Afghan refugees and Mujahidin remained through to the end of the Soviet occupation in 1988.[23] But despite increasingly negative propaganda about the refugees, rather than threatening the status of the Tribal Areas, the Afghan war enhanced local economic activity and created an inflow of wealth that reduced the previous reliance on government allowances.

The state-condoned, increasing independence of the Tribal Areas was reflected in accounts of *madrasas* providing simultaneous military and religious training through the region and engaging local Pakistan-side Pakhtuns in the industry and ideology of the Afghan *jihad*.[24] A camp called 'Maaskar Sadda' was established in the Kurram agency, run by Abal Rab Sayyaf and the Ettehad-i Islami. Sheikh Jamiur Rahman of Kunar established the camp Huzaifa Bin Yamaan in Bajaur and was reputed to have established 250 more *madrasas* through the Tribal Areas and to have controlled the Nawa Pass between Mohmand and Afghan Kunar.[25] After 1986 many Arab 'Islamists' arrived to participate in the *jihad*, setting up camps in the border region near Khost. They were there for their own reasons, and

---

22 Ibid., p. 864.

23 Marvin G. Weinbaum, Pakistan and Afghanistan: the Strategic Relationship', *Asian Survey* (California, 1991), pp. 503-5.

24 Mariam Abou Zahab and Olivier Roy, *Islamist Networks: The Afghan-Pakistan Connection* (London, 2004), p. 27.

25 Arif Jamal, 'Restart', *The News* (Karachi), 11 July 2004. This crucial (and highly politically charged) issue also receives brief attention in the following noteworthy accounts: Seyyed Vali Reza Nasr, 'The Rise of Sunni Militancy in Pakistan: The Changing Role of Islamism and the Ulama in Society and Politics', *Modern Asian Studies* (Cambridge, 2000), p. 150; Husain Haqqani, *Pakistan Between Mosque and Military* (Washington, 2005), pp. 185-90; and Frederic Gare, *Political Islam in the Indian Subcontinent* (Delhi, 2001), p. 89. It remains however that the role, location, enrolment, curriculum, and militant participation of these *madrasas* is deemed proven through a handful of journalistic accounts. This issue demands comprehensive scholarly attention.

largely uninvited,[26] but their offers of assistance were not refused. These actors adhered to a vision of a unified, borderless Muslim *ummah*, which could be created through militant means and contributed their efforts and personal wealth to the Afghan Mujahidin's resistance effort.[27] The Arab Islamists numbered in the thousands, but were organised by a core group of Arabs, including Abdullah Azzam, a Palestinian, and Osama Bin Laden, the Saudi dissident.[28] Connections between Arab and Pakistani Islamists brought Arab militant organisation and an ideology of global unification of Muslims to Pakistani *madrasas*, both in the administered districts and in the Tribal Areas.

Within Pakistan religious parties strongly supported the war, despite their growing hostility to Zia ul Haq's military regime.[29] Deeply invested now in the Pakistani nation and its progress, the *'ulama*, dominated by Deobandis, described their interest in the war as being the defence of Pakistan's borders and Pakistan's Islam.[30] The Jamiyatul Ulama particularly rallied support for the *jihad* through the influence of its member *'ulama* and their *madrasas*.[31] Pakistani Deobandis supporting the *jihad* began to establish their own bases in Wana and Mirali in North and South-Waziristan.[32]

---

26 As pointed out by David Edwards, *Genealogies*, p. 18.

27 Barry Rubin and Judith Colp Rubin, *Anti-American Terrorism and the Middle East* (New York, 2002).

28 Zahab and Roy, *Islamist Networks*, pp. 14-7.

29 See Seyyed Wali Reza Nasr on the Jamaat-i Islami and Zia ui Haq, 'Islamic Opposition to the Islamic State: The Jamaat-i Islami, 1977-88', *International Journal of Middle East Studies* (Cambridge, 1993). The Jamiyatul Ulama-yi Islam also became hostile to Zia's regime, yet maintained a vested interest in the ongoing *jihad*.

30 Abdul Qaiyyum Haqqani observed debates between Abdul Haq and the *mujahidin*, both Afghan and Pakistani, detailed in his witness account, *Sahbatay ba Ahl-i Haq* (Akora Khattak, 1990), p. 290.

31 Abdul Haq's Madrasa Haqqaniyya hosted *mujahidin* as devotees and as honoured guests. *Sahbatay ba Ahl-i Haq*, pp. 358-406.

32 Jamal, 'Restart'.

Both the Pakistani and the Arab-led Islamists contributed most of their support to the *jihad* through the Mujahidin leaders. Of these, two in particular organised resistance among the eastern Pakhtuns: Maulvi Yunis Khalis, a graduate of Haqqaniyya Madrasa who was closely linked to the Pakistani Islamists,[33] and Maulvi Abdal Rab Sayaf who spoke fluent Arabic and was a favourite in the 'eyes of the wealthy Arabs'.[34] Yunis Khalis' Hizb-i Islami particularly appealed to eastern Pakhtun tribes, hierarchies and customs, and enlisted many of the eastern Pakhtun *mullas* around Kandahar as commanders, including Maulvi Jalaluddin Haqqani, Maulvi Nizamuddin Haqqani, Mulla Ibrahim and Mulla Abdur Rahman of Zadran, Haji Abdul Qader and Mulla Malang of Kandahar, among others.[35] Abdal Rab Sayaf formed the locus of his Ettehad-i Islami around the Afghan refugee camps in Pakistan, drawing volunteers through the resources at his disposal rather than through tribal ties, Sufi networks or clerical authority. Other than these personalities, lesser Mujahidin leaders such as Maulvi Hussain of the Safi tribe in Pech established himself at a base in Bajaur, and Badshah Gul I, who organised a society of Pakhtun volunteers for the Afghan *jihad*, called *Tehrik-i Junud Allah*,[36] lived among the Pakhtuns to channel Arab funds to refugees involved in the *jihad* effort. These personalities were the primary links between the Arab-led and Pakistani Islamists and the eastern Pakhtuns of Afghanistan, and the links through which Osama Bin Laden brought in engineers and heavy machinery to help build roads and depots through the frontier territory into Afghanistan to help the their efforts.

When the Soviet troops began to leave Afghanistan in 1988, the administrative landscape of the Pakhtun regions was left relatively unaffected. Pakistan maintained the validity of the Durand Line,

---

33 Haqqani, *Sahbatay*, p. 216.

34 Edwards, *Genealogies*, p. 266.

35 As gathered from vignettes on *mujahidin* tactics in Ali Jalali and Lester Grau, *Afghan Guerilla Warfare* (London, 2001), pp. 168, 213.

36 Haqqani, *Sahbatay*, p. 214.

and of the state of non-administration of the Pakhtuns buffering its north-western frontier. But demographically, economically and socially, everything had changed. The Afghan *jihad* had provoked the movement and non-genealogically derived resettlement of people, across tribe and clan lines, in the Pakistan Tribal Areas. Just as the social insularity of the region was disrupted, the Tribal Areas economy of subsistence farming, local arms trading and allowances was transformed in a matter of years into a massive export industry of heroin and weapons. Tribal Areas residents were connected, palpably and currently, to the Afghan economy, population and politics while the policy of social and political containment and economic control of the Tribal Areas by the Pakistani government was abandoned for strategic reasons. Wealth increased dramatically in the region, although there is little doubt that this remained in the hands of a few, rather than being shared across the population.

After the Soviet withdrawal, a government of former Mujahidin took power in Kabul. Years of bitter in-fighting between them followed until the Taliban, a group of eastern Pakhtun *mullas*, veterans of the Afghan *jihad*, all having received some *madrasa* training, were provoked by the insecurity and lawlessness of post-Soviet Afghanistan to assume control and set it right themselves. They began their campaign in 1994 and by 1997 had taken control of 22 of Afghanistan's provinces. The Taliban *mullas* had almost all participated in the anti-Soviet resistance, either as commanders in their own right or as young men growing up in the refugee camps in Pakistan. But they maintained their provincial affiliation both during and after the *jihad*. Their locus of organisation during the *jihad* had been around the eastern province of Kandahar, and they returned as local *mullas* to their home villages in the same region after the Soviet withdrawal, albeit greatly strengthened through experience and stockpiles of weapons.

Mulla Omar, who was to organise and lead the Taliban, was himself the village *mulla* of Singesar in Kandahar, and was supported by friends from his home-town of Uruzgan: Mulla Ghaus, Mulla

Muhammad Rabbani, and Mulla Hassan.[37] The Taliban leaders organised wider support through other local *mullas* in the eastern Pakhtun regions, most of whom had also been *mujahidin* commanders.
Among these were Mulla Naqib of Kandahar who, it was suggested,
had been encouraged by the intelligence wing of the Pakistan army,
the ISI, to hand over control to the Taliban in 1994; Mulla Afzal of
Nuristan, who had established an 'Islamic state' in the region as early
as 1984,[38] and surrendered authority to the Taliban in 1996;[39] and
Mulla Nasrullah Mansoor of Shahikot, who played a crucial role as a
commander in the Taliban conquest of Afghanistan.[40] In addition to
organising a regional structure of Pakhtun control, the Taliban used
their control to formalise Afghanistan's position as host to Arab-led
Islamists who had come to the Pakhtun regions during the *jihad*, now
led by Osama Bin Laden who had succeeded Muhammad. These
Islamists had set up camps dedicated to training militants for a *jihad*
against the United States,[41] and a headqarters for their international
organisation, Al Qaeda.[42] Under the Taliban these connections to
Afghanistan were enhanced by strong personal commitments such
as marriages between Afghan women and Arab men.[43]

The *mullas* of the Taliban regime and its Arab-led supporters had
all along maintained ties with religious parties and figures in Pakistan, particularly those in the Pakistani Pakhtun regions. In addition,
the 3 million Afghan refugees still in Pakistan, many of whom were
dependants of Afghan men who returned to work in Afghanistan,
reinforced a trans-border Pakhtun solidarity which was increasingly
being articulated by Pakhtun nationalist groups in Baluchistan and

---

37   Ahmed Rashid, *Taliban: Militant Islam, Oil and Fundamentalism in Central
Asia* (New Haven, 2001), pp. 23-5.

38   Roy, *Globalised Islam*, p. 284.

39   Rashid, *Taliban*, pp. 28-9.

40   M. Ilyas Khan, 'Profile of Nek Mohammad', *Dawn*, 19 June 2004.

41   Zahab and Roy, *Islamist Networks*, pp. 57-63.

42   Ibid., pp. 12-8.

43   Khan, 'Profile of Nek Mohammad'.

the NWFP.[44] Hence when the Taliban began to take control, connections to Pakistani *madrasas*, military patrons and a wider Pakhtun identity immediately came into play. The Taliban *mullas* were supported by the ISI for strategic reasons, and by the Dera Ismail Khan-based Pakistani religious party Jamiyatul Ulama-yi Islam (JUI) for ideological and personal ones, as many of the JUI *ulama* and the Taliban had studied together in Pakistani Deobandi *madrasas* in the 1980s. It has been accurately pointed out by political commentators that these supporters encouraged the Taliban's consolidation of post-Soviet Afghanistan, gripped by ethnic tension, highway banditry, rural drug cultivation, and violent competition between the Mujahidin successors.[45]

But the Taliban had their own interests in Pakistan as well, demonstrating these when they refused to ratify the Durand Line.[46] Taliban officials attended a tribal *jirga* in Mohmand at which they elicited Pakistan-side Mohmand commitment to the construction of a road across the disputed Mohmand border and into the Pakistani side, by the Taliban regime.[47] Drug barons, traders, timber merchants, smugglers and arms dealers under the Taliban regime in Afghanistan targeted the Pakistani market, using the Tribal Areas as the conduit for goods into and out of their country. The Taliban saw themselves as fulfilling a religious ideal and modelled their government as a basic and replicable system of Islamic organisation, inviting *madrasa* students and religious idealists from Pakistan (and the world) to participate in their spiritual-military programme for the reorganisation of Afghanistan. The Arab-led militants in Afghanistan also cultivated their connections in Pakistan to pull in *jihadi*

---

44 Titus, *Honour the Baluch*, pp. 670-90.

45 Ahmed Rashid, 'Pakistan and the Taliban', *The Nation* (Lahore) 5 April 1998.

46 Rashid, *Taliban*, p. 187.

47 'Taliban allowed to construct road in Pakistani territory', *Frontier Post*, 15 Aug. 1998.

recruits for the Taliban, some from the Tribal Areas but many others from as far away as Karachi.[48]

Together the Taliban and the Arab-led militants presented a social-political model for Pakistan's *'ulama* Islamists, having made Afghanistan a place where the directives of the *'ulama* and the *mullas* were paramount.[49] This model was touted by the JUI as an inspiration for legislative reform before the larger Pakistani public and parliament, and it encouraged vigilante Taliban-style movements in the Pakistani Tribal Areas including one led by Maulana Sufi Muhammad which drew thousands of adherents in 1994, and had to be put down by the army.[50] The Taliban also drew young *madrasa* students from the Tribal Areas into their ranks as fighters and commanders. In 1998, 4,000 NWFP students, many of whom were from the Tribal Areas, migrated to Kabul to volunteer their military services to the Taliban.[51] Among the Pakistani Tribal Areas volunteers to the Taliban was Nek Muhammad of Wana who had studied at the Madrasa Jamia Darul Uloom Waziristan.[52]

Pakhtun-centric and eastern *mulla*-led organisation in Afghanistan once again drew the Tribal Areas, irresistibly into Afghanistan's politics now dominated by the Taliban-led ideological and military system. By the turn of the century, many *madrasas* and leaders in the Tribal Areas publicly demonstrated strong links to the Taliban regime, and privately maintained connections with the Arab-led Islamists in Afghanistan despite the fact that there was now strong international attention on and condemnation of the Taliban for

---

48 Zahab and Roy, *Islamist Networks*, pp. 57-65.

49 In an address to students and visiting *ulama* at Darul Ulum Haqqaniyya, Maulana Samiul Haq said that 'Afghanistan's human rights model was exemplary in the world'. 'Pakistan in search of new options for Afghan peace', *The Muslim* (Lahore), 9 March 1998.

50 Rashid, *Taliban*, pp. 193-4.

51 'Pak students reinforcing Taliban's ranks', *The Frontier Post* (Peshawar), 12 Aug. 1998.

52 'Profile of Nek Mohammad' *Dawn*, 19 June 2004. Also among these were Maulana Abdul Khaliq of Wana.

their excesses against women and their destruction of ancient Buddhist statues in the Bamiyan province, and of the Arab-led Islamists for their involvement in attacks on American interests around the world.

Maulana Sufi Muhammad of Swat, the militant anti-Shia leader of the group Tehrik-i Nifaz-i Shariat-i Muhammadi, who had participated in the Afghan *jihad*, staunchly supported the Taliban, calling for Pakistani diplomatic support to the new regime.[53] He invited the Arab-led Islamists in Afghanistan to the Pakistani Tribal Areas and offered them both moral support and personal hospitality and protection. Nek Muhammad, whose services to the Taliban brought him into contact with Arab-led Islamists in the country, returned to Wana as a commander with a high profile and wealth having received substantial gifts of money and military aid from them. *Madrasas* in the Tribal Areas were headed by local religious adherents to key Taliban figures like Jalaluddin Haqqani. In Waziristan this connection was particulary strong since many important self-proclaimed adherents of senior Taliban officials resided here. In addition to Nek Muhammad, these included Abdul Khaliq of Madrasa Gulshanul Ulum in Khaney Khel North-Waziristan[54] and 'Khalifa' who established the Khalifa Madrasa near Miramshah, in North-Waziristan.[55]

These independent financial, military, diplomatic and ideological relations between Tribal Areas religious activists and the Taliban and Arab-led Islamists in Afghanistan corresponded to a new articulation of Tribal Areas independence from the government to the east. *Ulama* and *mullas* of Orakzai, Khyber and North and South-Waziristan, as well as the administered territories of Hangu, Bannu and Dera Ismail Khan, called for a rejection of the government-sponsored justice system and a submission to the judicial authority of *'ulama* and *mullas*.[56] But because the religious directives were not

---

53   Rashid, *Taliban*, p. 194.

54   Owais Tohid, 'The Warrior Tribes', *Newsline* (Karachi) April 2004.

55   'Militants' den destroyed in Miramshah', *Dawn*, 16 March 2006.

56   Babar Shah, 'The myth of Talibanisation of Pakistan', *Institute of Stategic*

specifically anti-government, these articulations of autonomy were understood to be largely unobjectionable and an internal matter by the Pakhtun communities of the tribal region.

In September 2001, the ambitions of the Arab-led Islamists in Afghanistan came to immediate attention when a carefully planned attack on America was executed, and the resulting investigation identified Osama Bin Laden as its primary initiator. The Taliban refused to extradite Osama Bin Laden to the United States without proof of his involvement despite pressure from world governments and a deputation of senior political, religious and military officials from Pakistan. In Pakistan the Islamists upheld this refusal as the correct and necessary response to American pressure, and began to mobilise Pakistani recruits to reinforce the Taliban in anticipation of an American attack on Afghanistan. The militant party Lashkar-i Tayyaba, closely linked with the Tehrik-i Nifaz-i Shariat-i Muhammadi (TNSM), reported the movement of 'thousands' of Pakistani Pakhtun volunteers into Bajaur under the supervision of Maulana Sufi Muhammad, where they organised in preparation for joining with and reinforcing the Taliban militias.[57] In Khyber Afridi tribesmen demonstrated against the American ultimatum, shouting slogans in support of Osama Bin Laden.[58] By the end of October the TNSM reported that over 30,000 Pakistani activists had been sent to Afghanistan through Dir and Bajaur. Of these, 10,000 were Pakistan-side Pakhtun tribesmen, whose mobilisation had been directly solicited in an appeal from Mulla Omar.[59]

After the failure of demands to the Taliban that they hand over Osama Bin Laden and other Al-Qaeda members to the United States, US-led forces bombarded Afghanistan with a view to 'flush-

---

Studies Islamabad Online Archive.

57 'Thousand of volunteers bound for Afghanistan', reported in the official website of the *Mujahideen Lashkar-e-Taiba*, 30 Oct. 2001. Snapshot archived in the *September 11 Web Archive MINERVA project.*

58 'Taliban take to the mountains', *Online Asia Times*, 6 Oct. 2001.

59 'TNSM supporters head for Afghanistan', *Dawn*, 28 Oct. 2001.

ing out' the Arab-led Islamists. These Islamists immediately retreated into the topographic and habitational landscape of the Pakhtun borderland. Months of bombardment, satellite tracking, ground troop deployment and intelligence gathering failed to bring the Islamists to hand, and it began to be reported that the Islamists had crossed into the Pakistan-side Tribal Areas where they had taken refuge among the Pakistani Pakhtun tribes. The first major movement of Arab-led Islamists from Afghanistan was into South-Waziristan where they were said to have used their connections to immediately marry local women and to establish their belonging and disappear among the local populations. These foreign Islamists, rumoured to number up to 600 at the time, lived locally as Pakhtuns, dressing, speaking and moving indistinguishably among the local population. From this location 'some of them did farming and others *jihad*.'[60]

Links between the Arab-led Islamists and the Tribal Areas, which had once relied on Sufi Muhammad and other mediators like him in the Tribal Areas, had engendered social, economic and ideological connections which accommodated the Arab-led Islamists into the clan-based village communities. Distinguishing the new entrants from among the tribal descendants was made difficult by the Pakhtun cultural principle of according equal importance and protection to family, clan and guests. When the Pakistani government, prompted by the United States, demanded the extradition of these foreign Islamists from tribal lands, they were met with hostility and resistance, which escalated almost immediately into a full-scale military confrontation.

Much of the resistance to the Pakistani government was motivated and led by a number of local religious leaders and veterans of the Afghan *jihad* calling for the protection of the region from subjugation by the federal government and the army. In Waziristan, where ties to the Afghanistan-based Islamists were strongest, well known activists including Nek Muhammad, Maulana Abdul Khaliq, Maulvi Aziz, Maulvi Abbas, Sharif Khan and Nur Islam called for

---

60 Tohid, 'The Warrior Tribes'.

local protection to the foreign Islamists and Shahzada Pahalwan, the contemporary successor to the Mulla Powindah, decried military operations launched in pursuit of the Islamists in the Tribal Areas.[61] The organisation and success of the Muttahida Majlis-i Amal (the MMA), a coalition of religious parties led by the Jamiyatul Ulama-yi Islam, in the NWFP in the elections of 2003, added weight to these demands. Maulana Fazlur Rahman, president of the Jamiyatul Ulama and secretary-general of the MMA, took a strong position on defending Tribal Areas autonomy and sanctity, opposing American interests and condemning Pakistani military action aimed at killing or extraditing foreign Islamists from the region.[62]

Tribal Areas resistance to Pakistan government and US pressure to extradite fugitives was not only a conspiracy between Pakistani *'ulama-* Islamists and Tribal Areas *mullas*. Non-religious figures supported and reiterated the stand being taken by the *mullas* as in the case of a former Tribal Areas senator from Khyber who expressed strong criticism of pressure from a political party to encourage the hand-over of Islamists, saying that 'the heads of political parties ought to avoid interfering' in the affairs of the Tribal Areas.[63] Tribal Areas residents complained at the violations of the military action and pressure on the tribes.[64] As the Pakistan government's military campaign to hunt out elusive Al Qaeda members in South-Waziristan continued into its sixth year, a sudden overnight airstrike on a *madrasa* in Bajaur in October 2006 which killed 82 people, many of them boys under the age of 15, provoked criticism across the country.[65] Resistance to the new government policy of intervention in the

---

61 Rahimullah Yusufzai and Sailab Mahsud, 'Fighting subsides as jirga seeks truce', *The News*, 22 March 2004; 'Wana tribes asked to hand over 216 wanted men', *The News*, 20 September 2004.

62 'Wana operation to harm country: Fazl', *Dawn*, 17 September 2004.

63 'Parties warned against meddling in tribal affairs', *The News*, 4 April 2004.

64 Rahimullah Yusufzai, 'No end in sight', *Newsline*, April 2006.

65 'Bajaur dead were all militants says Musharraf', *Dawn*, 31 Oct. 2006; 'NWFP Assembly condemns Bajaur operations', *Dawn*, 31 Oct. 2006.

region was also posed more obliquely as in Khyber where the Tamache Mulla issued a *fatwa* condemning a government-sponsored polio campaign, saying that the polio drops were being administered as part of an American conspiracy.[66]

The years of the Afghan *jihad* and the Taliban had once again entrenched a culture of autonomous activity and motivation in the Tribal Areas, and brought new *wahhabi* influences to bear on religion and society. Under these influences, local *mullas* asserted a newly narrowed and increasingly rigid set of Islamic codes with a brutality that eclipsed even the early days of the *amr bil maruf* initiative. Criminal transgressors were publicly executed and their bodies left on display as an example to others. Residents were warned to obey religious injunction against music and video, non-religious festivity and alcohol, and to grow beards—a directive reinforced by the destruction of video and music shops and a radio station, and the forced closure of barbers' shops.[67] As government informers and journalists were routinely captured and executed, it became clear that the vigilantes were also warning the government to leave public morality, dispensation of justice and moral policing to be negotiated between the tribes and their *mullas*.[68]

The disjuncture created by the extraordinary events and destruction of the Afghan war disallows the drawing of direct parallels between the authority and initiatives of the early twentieth century *mullas* and the religious politics of the Tribal Areas today. However the terrain of the Tribal Areas remains outside systems of national participation and the protection accorded to the individual by state. The government pursues a policy of conciliation towards privileged elites who continually re-enforce a differentiated set of cultural and political codes and reject urban liberal critiques of criminality and disenfranchisement among the communities on cultural grounds. It

---

66 'Anti-polio campaign launched in Landi Kotal', *Dawn*, 2 September 2003

67 Zahid Hussain, 'Terror in Miramshah', *Newsline*, April 2006.

68 'Shura plans peace campaign: new military commander appointed for Waziristan', *Dawn*, 6 Nov. 2006.

is in this environment that power still accrues to religious leaders as moderators of the north-west frontier's 'tribalism'.

GLOSSARY

akhund, hazrat, Sufi, faqir	titles denoting distinction within the Sufi tradition
akhuwwat	strength
alim	Muslim religious scholar (pl. *'ulama*)
amir	ruler within the Muslim tradition
amir–badshah	ruler with temporal and religious authority
amr–bil maruf wa nahi anal munkir	prevention of vice and promotion of virtue.
azad	free
bait	pledge at the hand of a spiritual teacher or *pir*
buzurg; buzurgan	elder; pl. elders
crore	unit of measurement equal to ten million
dahshatgardi	terrorism
dak	mail
darasgahs	schools
darbar	court
dargah	Sufi shrine
darul harb	place of war or persecution
dasturbandi	coronation (lit. turban tying)
dora	preaching mission
farangi	white men
fatwa	authoritative comment by

	a religious scholar
faqir	ascetic
firman	royal pronouncements
ghairat	honour
ghazvah; ghazah	war (Urdu; Farsi)
ghazi	warrior
ghee	(cooking) oil
gora	Englishman (white person)
hadith	sayings attributed to the prophet
hafiz-i Quran	one who has memorised the Quran
haj	Muslim pilgrimage to Mecca
hijrat	migration to escape religious persecution
hujra	an area for entertaining guests
hukumat	government
ilaqa-yi ghair	Tribal Areas (lit. unrelated region)
imam;imamate	religious leader—a term often used for one that leads the prayers in the mosque; the formal office of *imam* is now only held in the Shia tradition.
inqilab	revolution
islah	reform
ittihad	Union
jagir	Estate
jamaat	gathering or congregation
jamhuri; jamhuriyyat	democratic; democracy
jihad	struggle in the cause of religion
jirga	tribal council
qafila	retinue
kafir	non-believer

khalifa (caliph)	highest temporal authority in the muslim world
khalifa	deputy; representative
khandan	family; used also for 'tribe' or 'clan'
khassadars	informal levy troops
khud mukhtar	self governing
khutba	sermon
lakh	one hundred thousand
langarkhana	almshouse
lashkar	armed retinue
loya jirga	large regional tribal council
madrasa	Muslim school of religious learning
Majlis-i Shura	Afghan state council (lit. gathering of notables)
markaz	centre
malik	head of the clan or tribe unit, whose authority is ostensibly confirmed through male consensus in the clan.
markaz	centre
masjid	mosque
maulvi; maulana	title taken by a religious scholar (*alim*)
mehmandari	hospitality
millat	religious community
muhajir; muhajirin	one who performs *hijrat*; pl.
muhtamim	head administrator
mujahid; mujahidin	one who wages *jihad*; pl.
mulk	country
mulla	generic term to refer to the leader of prayers at the *masjid*
murid	devotee of a *pir*

mustaufi	highest religious authority of Afghan state, an official position
muttahida	united
muwajib	cash award paid by amir as mark of recognition.
naib-us saltanate	chief minister of state under the Afghan amir
nizamnameh	constitution
pahari	mountainous/mountain dwelling
pakhtunwali	unwritten Pakhtun tribal code of community living
pir	spiritual guide, in the Sufi tradition
pirimuridi	the relationship between *pir* as teacher and *murid* as disciple
qabila; qabail	tribe; tribes
qaum	nation; used also for 'tribe'
qaumiyat	nationalism
qazi	judge
rais	governor
reshmi rumal	silk handkerchief
rifqa-yi jihad	companions in *jihad*
rivaj	custom
sadar	president
sadar-i mudarris	principal of a *madrasa*
sajjada nashin	heir to the *pir's* title
sayyid, shaikh and miyan	descendent of the Prophet Muhammad
shaikh	deputy
shajarah	genealogy
shari'a	Islamic law
sharif	(the) pure
shaakh	branch

sharq	east
silsila	a Sufi order
sunnah	sayings or actions attributed to the Prophet
tabligh	propagation of religion by preaching
tajdid	elucidation
talib	student
tariqa	method
tashaddud	violence
tazkirah	biography
tigah	truce
tehrik	movement
'ulama	Muslim religious scholar (sing. *alim*)
vakil	representative/lawyer
vaz	religious sermon
wafd	deputation
waqf	estates granted by the king as a religious endowment
watan	state
yaghi	rebel
zakat	charity
zikr	mystical (Sufi) chant

BIBLIOGRAPHY

I. Private Papers

Bailey Collection (papers of Lt.-Colonel Frederick Marshman Bailey, Indian Political Service, 1916-18), India Office Library and Collections, London.

Cunningham Collection (papers of Sir George Cunningham, 1888-1964).

Curzon Collection (papers of Lord Curzon, 1866-1925, Viceroy of India, 1899-1904), India Office Library and Collections, London.

Durand Collection (papers of Sir Henry Mortimer Durand, 1850-1924, Foreign Secretary Government of India, 1884-94), India Office Library and Collections, London.

Iqbal Shaidai Collection (papers of Iqbal Shaidai, Indian nationalist, 1880-1974), National Archives Islamabad.

Parsons Collection (papers of Arthur Edward Broadbent Parsons, 1884-1966, Indian Political Service, 1919-39), India Office Library and Collections, London.

Saifur Rahman Collection (papers of Maulana Saifur Rahman, Deobandi *alim*, d. 1950), Obaidur Rahman Collection, Peshawar.

II. Government Records

Peshawar Archives, Pakistan

1. Deputy Commissioner's Officer Peshawar Files:
   Diaries District Officer Frontier Constabulary, Hazara.
   Diaries Frontier Constabulary Peshawar, 1935.
   Khyber Political Diaries, 1920-40.
   Miscellaneous Diaries and Reports, 1915-40.

223

Mohmand Political Diaries, 1924-39.
North-West Frontier Province Provincial Diaries, 1920-40.
Political Diaries Police Department, 1919-30.
2. Special Branch NWFP files, 1915-50.
3. Tribal Research Cell, Home Department, 1915-35

Disctrict Officer Frontier ??
Mahmud Reports 1927-40

National Documentation Centre, Islamabad:
North-West Frontier Province Provincial Diaries, 1915-1947.
Special Branch Police Records Abstracts of Intelligence, 1911-1947.

Oriental and India Office Collection, London:
C 137-142, Memoranda and Papers laid Before the Council of India, 1874-9.
L/PO/5, Files on External Affairs, Frontier Questions, 1918-46.
L/PS/10, Political and Secret Papers, 1902-31.
L/PS/11, Political and Secret Annual Files, 1919-30.
L/PS/12, Political and Secret External Files and Collections.
L/PS/18, Political and Secret Memoranda, 1840-1947.
L/PS/20, Political and Secret Department Library and Collections.
V/10/370-389, Indian States Administration Reports, NWFP.
L/MIL/17, Military Department Records, North-West Frontier and Balochistan.
W/L/PS, Political and Secret Department Map Collection.

British Library Rare Books Collection
V/4 Parliamentary Papers
Cabinet Papers on Indian Affairs

III. Official Publications

Aitchison, Charles, *A Collection of Treaties, Engagements and Sunuds Relating to India and Neighbouring Countries*, Calcutta: Superintendent Government Printing, 1909.

Ashraf, Khalid, *Some Land Problems in the Tribal Areas of West Pakistan*, Peshawar: Board of Economic Enquiry, 1963.

Cunningham, Arthur, *Archaeological Survey of India Reports*, 5-6, 1871-3, Calcutta: Superintendent Government Printing, 1875-8.

General Staff Branch, Indian Army, *Official History of Operations on the North-West Frontier, 1920-1935*, Delhi: Superintendent Government Printing, 1945.

———, *Operations in Waziristan 1919-1920*, Calcutta: Superintendent Government Printing, 1920.

Government of India, *A Dictionary of the Pathan Tribes in the North-West Frontier of India*, Calcutta: Office of the Superintendent Government Printing, India, 1899.

——— *Gazetteer of the North-West Frontier from Bajour and the Indus Kohistan on the north to the Mari Hills on the south*, vol. II, Simla: Government of India Press, 1887.

———, *List of Leading Persons in Afghanistan 1888*, Simla: Government of India Press, 1888.

———, *Punjab Customary Law—a selection from the records of the Punjab Government*, vol. I, Calcutta: Superintendent Government Printing, 1881.

———, *Who's Who in Afghanistan 1930*, Simla: Government of India Press, 1930.

———, *Who's Who in the North-West Frontier Province, 1914*, Peshawar: North-West Frontier Government Press, 1916.

———, *Who's Who in the Peshawar District*, Peshawar: Government Printing and Stationery Office, 1931.

———, *Who's Who NWFP, 1930*, Peshawar: North-West Frontier Government Press, 1931.

———, *Who's Who NWFP, 1937*, Peshawar: North-West Frontier Government Press, 1937.

Government of the North-West Frontier Province, *List of the More Important Political and Quasi-Political Societies, Sabhas and Anjumans in the North-West Frontier Province*, Peshawar: Government Printing and Stationery Office, 1936.

Hastings, E. G.,*Genealogical Tree of the Kandahari Sardars of the Barakzai Family*, Lahore: Government Printing and Stationery Office, 1880.

———, *Genealogical Tree of the Peshawari Sardars of the Barakzai Family*, Lahore: Government Printing and Stationery Office, 1880.

Macgregor, C. M., *Central Asia: a Contribution towards the Better Knowledge of the Topography, Ethnography, Statistics and History of the North-West Frontier of British India*, vol. I, Calcutta: Office of the Superintendent Government Printing, 1873.

Mason, A. H., *Report on the Mahsud and Waziri Tribe*, Simla: Government of India Press, 1893.

Merk, W. R., *The Mohmands*, Reprint, Lahore: Sang-e-Meel, 1984.

Mian, Nurul Islam, *A Preliminary Economic Survey of the Tribal Areas Adjoining West Pakistan*, Peshawar: Board of Economic Enquiry, 1956.

Pazhwak, Rahman, *An Article on Pakhtunistan, a New State in Central Asia*, London: Royal Afghan Embassy, 1960.

———, *Pakhtunistan, The Khyber Pass as the Focus of the New State of Pakhtunistan*, London: Royal Afghan Embassy, [1960?].

Rose, H. A., *A Glossary of the Tribes and Castes of the Punjab and North-West Frontier Province*, Lahore: Superintendent, Government Printing, 1913.

Swayne, J.E. and A. Nicholls, *Tribal Tables of the Afridis, Orakzais, Mohmands and Akozai-Yusufzais*, Simla: Government of India Press, 1897.

———, *Tribal Tables of the Mahsud and Wazir Tribes*, Simla: Quarter Master General's Office, 1897.

———, *Tribal Tables of the Bunerwals and Neighbouring Tribes*, Simla: Government of India Press, 1897.

IV. Interviews

Ahmed Yousuf, nephew of the Babra Mulla, Peshawar, 14 February 2002.

Ghulam Muhammad Din, Gandab villager, Gandab, 13 August 2002.

Ghulam Nabi Chaknawari, son of the Mulla Chaknawar, Peshawar, 3 February 2002.

Ghulam Nabi Chaknawari, Peshawar, 8 February 2002.

Malik Fazal Hadi, grandson of Malik Anmir, Gandab, 13 August 2002.

Malik Muzaffar Syal Kuda Khel, Kuda Khel Malik and nephew of Meera Jan Syal, Peshawar, 12 February 2002.

Naik Muhammad Ghazizuay, son of Ajab Khan Afridi, Peshawar, 10 August 2002.

Obaidur Rahman, great-nephew of Maulana Saifur Rahman, Peshawar, 17 August 2002.

Saeed Maqsud Shah, grandson of Haji Turangzai, Ziarat Baba, Ghaziabad, 13 August 2002.

Saeed-ur Rahman, great-nephew of Maulana Saifur Rahman, 17 August 2002.

V. Newspapers and Periodicals

Al Mujahid (Chamarkand) 1922-40.
Dawn (Karachi) 1950-2006.
The Friday Times (Lahore) 2000-6.
The Frontier Post (Peshawar) 1990-2000.
Herald (Karachi) 1980-2006.
The Muslim (Lahore) 1990-2000.
The Nation (Lahore) 1995-9.
The News (Karachi) 1990-2006.
Newsline (Karachi) 1980-2006.

VI. Internet Archives

Dawn Newspaper Archives

Institute of Strategic Studies Islamabad Online Archive
Online Asia Times
September 11 Web Archive Minerva Project

VII. Urdu, Pashto, Farsi and Russian Works

Ahmed, Choudhry Habib, *Tehrik-e-Pakistan aur Nationalist Ulama*, Lahore: Al-Bayan, 1966.

Ahsanullah Khan, *Pakhtun Qabail*, Peshawar, nd.

Allen, Charles, *Soldier Sahibs*, London: John Murray, 2000.

Aibak, Zafar Hasan, *Ap Biti*, Lahore: Mansur Book House, 1964.

Akayev, V. X., *Sufizm e Vaxxabizm Na Cevernom Kavkaze*, Moscow: Instituta Etnologi e Antropologi RAN, 1999.

Azad, Abul Kalam, *Islam Ka Nazarya-i Jang*, Lahore: Basaat-i Adab, 1960.

Chamarkandi, Abdul Karim, *Sarguzasht-i Mujahid*, Lahore: Idara-yi Matbuat Sulaimani, 1981.

Fiqri, Allama Alim, *Tazkiray Auliya-i Pakistan*, vol. 1, Lahore: Shabbir Brothers, 1987.

——, *Tazkiray Auliya-i Pakistan*, vol. 2, Lahore: Shabbir Brothers, 1993.

Gandapur, Sher Muhammad Khan, *Tarikh-i Pashtun*, Karachi: Shaikh Shaukat Ali and Sons, 1991.

Habib, Muhammad, and Hussain, Sayyid Jamal, *Sultan Mahmud Ghazni*, Allahabad: Hindustani Academy, 1940.

Haqqani, Abdul Qaiyyum, *Sahbatay ba Ahl-i Haq*, Akora Khattak: Haqqaniyya, 1990.

Haqqaniyya Madrasa, *Al Haq*, Akora Khattak: Haqqaniyya Press, 1993.

Ikram, Mohammad, *Mauj-e-Kausar: Musalmanon Ki Mazhabi Aur I-ilmi Tarikh Ka Daur-i Jadid*, Karachi: Ferozesons, 1963.

Islahi, Nazimuddin (ed.), *Maktubat-i Shaikhul Islam*, vol. II, Saharanpur: Maktaba Deoband, 1950.

Jamiyyatul Ulama-yi Hind, *Ulama-yi Hind ka Muttafiqah Fatwa*, Deradun: Fakhruddin Faruqi, Khilafat Committee, 1921.

Javed, Aziz, *Haji Sahib Turangzai*, Lahore: Iadara-yi Tahqiq-o-Tasneef, 1981.

Kasuri, Muhammad Ali, *Mushahidat-i Kabul Wa Yaghistan*, Karachi: Idara-yi Anjuman-i Taraqqi-yi Urdu, n.d.

Khan, Abdul Ghaffar, *Meri Zindagi Aur Jadd-o-Jehed*, Urdu tr. Lahore: Hashim Raza Khan Advocate, n.d.

Khan, Muhammad Asif, *Tarikh-i Riyasat-i Swat*, reprint, Swat: 2001.

Khan, Muhammad Hussain, *Afghan Badshah Alihazrat Amanullah Khan Khalladullah Malka va Hukma Ki Azimulishan Chasham Deed-o-Dastan*, Lahore: Feroze Printing, 1924.

Khan, Omar Farooq, *Aik Ishtiraki Alim-i Din, Maulana Abdur Rahim Popalzai*, Peshawar: Al Jamiyat Academy, n.d..

Khattak, Khushal Khan, *Mutakhi'bat Khushaal Khan Khattak, ba Urdu Tarja'mah*, Peshawar: Pushto Academy, University of Peshawar, 1956.

Madni, Hussain Ahmad, *Tehrik-i Reshmi Rumal*, Lahore: Classic, 1966.

———, *Naqsh-i Hayat*, Karachi: Baitul Tauheed, 1953.

———, *Tehrik-i Reshmi Rumal*, Lahore, 1966.

———, *Jamiyat-i -Ulama-yi Hind Ki Chand Ehem Khidmat-i Milli Ka Mukhtasir Tazkirah*, Delhi: Jamiyatul Ulama-yi Hind, 1940.

———, *Maududi Dastur Aur Aqaid Ki Haqiqat*, Deoband: Idarah Nashara-o Isha'at, 1956.

———, *Muttahida Qaumiyat Aur Islam*, Deoband: Majlis-e Qasimulma'arif, 1941.

Mahmood-ul Hasan, *Khutba-e-Sadarat Aur Fatwa Turk-e Muvalat*, Deoband: Matba-e Qasimi, 1920.

Mahsud, Muhammad Nawaz Khan, *Firangi Raj Aur Ghairatmand Musalman*, Waziristan: Gurwek Markaz Shumali Waziristan, 2000.

Mehr, Ghulam Rasul, *Sarguzasht-i Mujahidin*, Lahore: Kitab Manzil, 1956.

Mirza, Janbaz, *Karvan-i-Ahrar, Tarikh-i Azadi-yi Barr-i Saghir*, Lahore, 1979.

Miyan, Sayyid Muhammad, *Tehrik-i Shaikhul Hind*, Delhi: Al Jamiyat Book Depo, n.d.

——, *Ulama-yi Haq Aur Un Kay Mujahidana Karnamay*, Rahimyar Khan: Mukataba Sheikhul Islam, n.d..

Mohmand, Sayyid Ahmed, *Darawabnad Mira Jan Syal, Landah Biography*, Peshawar, 1990.

Nadwi, Mahmudur Rahman, *Tarikh-i Hind Mein Jadid Inkishaf wa Inqilab*, Lahore: Kutubkhana Darul Adab, 1931.

Popalzai, Abdul Jalil, *Hurriyet Nameh-yi Bannu*, Lahore: Ishtiyarah Publishers, 1991.

——, *Suba-yi Sarhad Ki Awami Tarikh aur Imam-i Hurriyet Alama Abdur Rahim Popalzai*, Peshawar: Al Jamiyat Academy, n.d..

——, *Suba-yi Sarhad ki Inqilabi Tehrik aur Abdur Rahim Popalzai*, Lahore: Fiction House, 1991.

——, *Suba-yi Sarhad ki Inqilabi Tehrikein aur Maulana Abdur Rahim Popalzai*, Lahore: Fiction House, 1991.

Popalzai, Abdur Rahim, *Afghanistan Mein Qayam-e-Aman: Tehrik-i Khilafat kay Wafd ki Tarikhi Kahani*, Rawalpindi, 1929, reprint, Peshawar: Al Jamiat Academy, 1996.

Quddusi, Ijaz ul Haq, *Tazkiray Sufya-yi Sarhad*, Lahore: Markazi Urdu Board, 1966.

Rahmad, Fazlur, *Batal Hurriyet Faqir of Ipi*, Lahore: Institute of Pakistan Studies, 2004.

Sabir, Mohd Shafi, *Tarikh-i Suba-yi Sarhad*, Peshawar: University Book Agency, 1986.

——, *Quaid-i Azam Aur Suba-yi Sarhad*, Peshawar: University Book Agency, 1986?

Sarhadi, Asif, *Ameerul Mu'mineen, Mulla Muhammad Umar Mujahid*, Lahore: Nigar Shaat, 2000.

Sayfi, Gul Ayyub Khan, *Bannu aw da Waziristan Tarikh*, Bannu, 1969.

Shah, Miyan Akbar, *Azadi ki Talash*, Islamabad: Qaumi Idarah Bara-e-Tahqiqi-e-Tarikh wa Shaqafat, 1989.

Shahjahanpuri, Abu Salman (ed.), *Khutut-i Tahrik-i Reshmi Rumal Aur Sindh*. Lahore: Fikshan House, 1997.

——— (ed.), *Makatib Maulana Obaidullah Sindhi*, Lahore: Al Mahmud Academy, 1994.

Sindhi, Obaidullah, 'Shah Wali Ullah Aur Unki Tehrik', introduction in Miyan, Muhammad, *Tehrik-i Shaikhul Hind*, Lahore: Maktaba Mahmoodia Karim, 1978, pp. 1-17.

———, *Kabul Mein Sat Sal*, Lahore: Sind Sagar Academy, n.d.

———, *Zati Dairi*, Lahore: Makki Darul Kutab, 1995.

Syal, Meera Jan, *Da Pashtun Qabilo Shajaray*, Peshawar: University Book Agency, 1988.

———, *Momand Baba*, Peshawar: University Book Agency, 1951.

———, *Nomyali Ghazi Chaknawar Mulla Sahib*, Peshawar: Zarim Ankhor, 1999.

Tawakkali, Allama Noor Bakhsh, *Tazkiray Mashaikh-i Naqshbandiyya*, Lahore: Maruf Press, 1974.

Thackston, Wheeler, tr. *Tuzuk-i Jahangiri*, Washington: Freer Gallery of Art and Oxford University Press, 1999.

Thanesseri, Janab Maulana Muhammad Jaffer, *Kala Pani*, Lahore: Sang-e-Meel, 1981.

Ullah, Shah Wali, *Hujjat Allah ul Baligha* (Urdu tr.), Lahore: Islami Academy, 1984.

Yousuf, Ahmed, *Da Babra Mullah Sahib*, Peshawar: Al Beruni Mutba, 2001.

Yusufi, Allah Bakhsh, *Sarhad Aur Jaddo Jehed-i Azadi*, Lahore: Markazi Urdu Board, 1986.

———, *Yusufzai Afghan*, Karachi: Muhammad Ali Educational Society, 1960.

Zalmai, Muhammad Wali, *Mujahid-i Afghan: Mawlana Haji Abd-al Raziq*, Kabul: Da Pashto da Tamim aw Indishaf Sangah, 1967.

VIII. English Works

Adamec, Ludwig, *Afghanistan 1900-1923*, Berkeley: University of California Press, 1967.

——, *Historical and Political Who's Who of Afghanistan*, Graz, Austria: Akademische Druck und Verlagsanstalt, 1975.

——, *Biographical Dictionary of Contemporary Afghanistan*, Graz: Akademische Druck und Verlagsanstalt, 1987.

Ahmad, Aziz, *Islamic Modernism in India and Pakistan 1857-1964*, London: Oxford University Press, 1967.

Ahmad, Makhdum Tasadduz, *Social Organization of Yusufzai Swat*, Lahore: Punjab University Press, 1962.

Ahmad, Qeyamuddin, *The Wahhabi Movement in India*, Calcutta: Firma K. L. Mukhopadhyay, 1966.

Ahmed, Akbar, 'Religious Presence and Symbolism in Pakhtun Society' in Akbar Ahmed and David Hart (eds), *Islam in Tribal Societies*, London: Routledge & Kegan Paul, 1984.

——, 'Tribe and State in Waziristan' in Richard Tapper (ed.), *The Conflict of Tribe and State in Iran and Afghanistan*, London: Croom Helm, 1983.

——, *Religion and Politics in Muslim Society: Order and Conflict in Pakistan*, Cambridge University Press, 1983.

——, *Resistance and Control in Pakistan*, Cambridge University Press, 1991.

Ahmed, Akbar, and Hart, David (eds), *Islam in Tribal Societies*, London: Routledge & Kegan Paul, 1984.

Alder, G. J., *British India's Northern Frontier, 1865-1895*, London: Longman, 1963.

Ali, Daud (ed.), *Invoking the Past, the Uses of History in South Asia*, Delhi: Oxford University Press, 2002.

Ali, Mohammad, 'Some Important Darul Uloom in the NWFP', unpublished MA thesis, Peshawar University Pakistan Studies Centre, 1984.

Amin, Noor-ul, 'Maulana Saifur Rahman', unpublished MA thesis, Peshawar University Pakistan Studies Centre, 2000.

Amin, Tahir, 'Afghan Resistance: Past, Present and Future', *Asian Survey* (1984), pp. 373-99.

Anderson, Jon , 'Tribe and Community Among the Ghilzai Pashtun', *Anthropos*, 70 (1989), pp. 575-601.

Ansari, Humayun Khizar, *The Emergence of Socialist Thought Among North Indian Muslims 1917-1947*, Lahore: Book Traders, 1990.

Ansari, Sarah, *Sufi Saints and State Power*, Cambridge University Press, 1992.

Baha, Lal, 'Activities of the Mujahidin', *Islamic Studies*, XVIII, 2 (1979), pp. 97-168.

Baha, Lal, 'The Hijrat Movement and the North-West Frontier Province', *Islamic Studies*, XVIII, 3 (1979), pp. 230-42.

Baha, Lal, *NWFP Administration Under British Rule*, Islamabad: National Commission on Historical and Cultural Research, 1978.

Banerjee, Mukulika, *The Pathan Unarmed:Opposition and Memory in the North-West Frontier*, Karachi: Oxford University Press, 2000.

Barth, Frederik, *Political Leadership Among Swat Pathans*, London: Athlone Press, 1965.

Barth, Fredrik, *The Last Wali of Swat: an Autobiography as told to Fredrik Barth*, Oslo: Norwegian University Press, 1985.

Bayly, Christopher, *Empire and Information*, Cambridge University Press, 1996.

Beattie, Hugh, 'Tribe and State in Waziristan, 1846-1883', unpublished PhD thesis, University of London, 1997.

Bellew, H. W., *Afghanistan and the Afghans: being a brief history of the country, and account of its people*, Calcutta, 1879, reprint Delhi: Shree Publishing House, 1982.

———, *An Inquiry into the Ethnography of Afghanistan*, London: 1891.

Bellew, H. W., *Journal of a Political Mission to Afghanistan in 1857*, London: Smith, Elder, 1862.

Bhabha, Homi K. (ed.), *Nation and Narration*, London: Routledge, 1994.

———, *The Location of Culture*, London: Routledge, 1994.

Biddulph, Michael A. S., 'Chilas', *Geographical Journal*, 1, 4 (1893), pp. 342-3.

Bray, Denys and Col. Brazier-Creagh, 'The Highlands of Persian Baluchistan: Discussion' *Geographic Journal*, 78, 4 (October, 1931).

Brown, Richard Harvey, 'Cultural Representation and Ideological Domination', *Social Forces*, 71, 3 (Mar. 1993), pp. 657-76.

Buehler, Arthur, *Sufi Heirs of the Prophet: the Indian Naqshbandiyya and the Rise of the Mediating Sufi Shaykh*, University of South Carolina Press, 1998.

Chaffetz, David, 'Afghanistan in Turmoil', *International Affairs* (London, 1980) pp. 15-36.

Chatterjee, Kumkum, 'Discovering India: Travel, History and In-dentity in Late Nineteenth and Early Twentieth Century India', in Daud Ali (ed.), *Invoking the Past, the Uses of History in South Asia*, Delhi: Oxford University Press, 2002, pp. 192-231.

Chatterjee, Partha, *The Nation and its Fragments*, Princeton University Press, 1993.

Chaturvedi, Vinayak, Mapping Subaltern Studies and the Post-Colonial, London: Verso, 2000.

Christensen, R. O., 'Political Economy on the North-West Frontier' in Clive Dewey (ed.), *Arrested Development in India*, Maryland: The Riverdale Company, 1988.

———, 'Conflict and Change Among Khyber Afridis', unpublished PhD thesis, Leicester University, 1987.

———, 'Introduction', Captain A. H. Mahon and Lt. A. D. G. Ramsay, *Report on the Tribes of Dir, Swat and Bajour together with the Utman-Khel and Sam Ranizai*, Peshawar: Saeed Book Bank, 1981.

Churchill, Winston S., 'The Story of the Malakand Field Force', *Frontiers and Wars*, London: Longmans, Green & Co., 1898.

Cloughley, Brian, *A History of the Pakistan Army, Wars and Insurrections*, Karachi: Oxford University Press, 1999.

Coen, Terence Creagh, *The Indian Political Service - A Study in Indirect Rule*, London: Chatto & Windus, 1971.

Cohn, Bernard, *An Anthropologist among the Historians and Other Essays*, Delhi: Oxford University Press, 1987.

Cornford, Philip, *Marching with the Mujahideen*, Islamabad: Khursheed Printers, 1981.

Crook, Nigel (ed.), *The Transmission of Knowledge in South Asia*, Delhi: Oxford University Press, 1996.

Dale, Stephen, *Indian Merchants and Eurasian Trade*, Cambridge University Press, 1994.

——, *Islamic Society on the South Asian Frontier: The Mappilas of Malabar, 1498-1922*, Oxford: Clarendon Press, 1980.

Davies, C. C., *The Problem of the North-West Frontier*, Cambridge University Press, 1932.

De Riencourt, Amaury, 'India and Pakistan in the Shadow of Afghanistan', *Foreign Affairs*, 61, 2 (1982/83).

Devji, Faisal Fatehali, 'Gender and the Politics of Space: The Movement for Women's Reform in Muslim India, 1957-1900', *South Asia*, XIV, 1 (1991), pp. 141-53.

——, *Landscapes of the Jihad: Militancy, Morality, Modernity*. London: Hurst, 2005.

Dietrich Reetz, 'On the Nature of Muslim Political Responses: Islamic Militancy in the North-West Frontier Province' in Mushirul Hasan (ed.), *Islam, Communities and the Nation*, New Delhi: Manohar, 1998, pp. 179-200.

Dirks, Nicholas, *Castes of Mind*, Princeton University Press, 2001.

Dorronsoro, Gilles, *Revolution Unending: Afghanistan 1979 to the Present*, London: Hurst, 2005.

Dupree, Louis, 'Tribal Warfare in Afghanistan and Pakistan: A Reflection of the Segmentary Lineage System', in Akbar Ahmed and David Hart (eds), *Islam in Tribal Societies*, London: Routledge & Kegan Paul, 1984.

——, 'Demographic reporting on Afghan Refugees in Pakistan', *Modern Asian Studies* (Cambridge, 1988), pp. 845-65.

Eaton, Richard (ed.), *India's Islamic Traditions, 711-1750*, Delhi: Oxford University Press, 2003.

———, *Sufis of Bijapur*, Princeton University Press, 1978.

———, 'The Political and Religious Authority of the Shrine of Baba Farid' in Barbara Metcalf (ed.), *Moral Conduct and Authority*, Berkeley: University of California Press, 1984.

———, *The Rise of Islam and the Bengal Frontier, 1204-1760*, Berkeley: University of California Press, 1996.

Edney, Matthew, *Mapping an Empire, the Geographical Construction of British India, 1765-1843*, University of Chicago Press, 1997.

Edwards, David, 'Origins of the Anti-Soviet Jihad', in Grant M. Farr and John G. Merriam, *Afghan Resistance and the Politics of Survival*, Boulder: Westview Press, 1987.

———, 'Mad Mullahs and Englishmen: Discourse in the Colonial Encounter', *Comparative Studies in Society and History*, 31 (1989), pp. 649-70.

———, 'Summoning Muslims: Print, Politics and Religious Ideology in Afghanistan', *Journal of Asian Studies*, 52, 3 (Aug. 1993), pp. 609-28.

———, *Before the Taliban: Genealogies of the Afghan Jihad*, Berkeley: University of California Press, 2002.

———, *Heroes of the Age: Moral Fault Lines on the Afghan Frontier*, Berkeley: University of California Press, 1996.

Farr, Grant M., and John G. Merriam, *Afghan Resistance and the Politics of Survival*, Boulder: Westview Press, 1987.

Faruqi, Ziya-ul-Hasan, *The Deoband School and the Demand for Pakistan*, London: Asia Publishing House, 1963.

Fox, Richard, *Lions of the Punjab: Culture in the Making*, Berkeley: University of California Press, 1985.

Freitag, Sandria B., *Collective Action and Community: Public Arenas and the Emergence of Communalism in North India*, Berkeley: University of California Press, 1989.

———, 'Introduction', *South Asia*, XIV, 1 (1991), pp. 1-13.

Friedmann, Yohanan, 'The Attitude of the Jami'yyat al-Ulama-i Hind to the Indian National Movement and the Establishment of Pakistan', *Asian and African Studies*, 7 (1971), pp. 157-80.

———. 'The Jami'yyat al-Ulama-i Hind in the Wake of Partition', *Asian and African Studies*, 11, 2 (1976), pp. 181-211.

Gare, Frederic, *Political Islam in the Indian Subcontinent*, Delhi: Manohar, 2001.

Gilmartin, David (ed.), *Beyond Turk and Hindu*, Florida: University Press of Florida, 2002.

———, 'Democracy, Nationalism and the Public: A Speculation on Colonial Muslim Politics', *South Asia*, XIV, 1 (1991), pp. 123-40.

———, 'Partition, Pakistan and South Asian History: In Search of a Narrative', *Journal of Asian Studies*, 57, 4 (1998), p. 1076.

———, *Empire and Islam: Punjab and the Making of Pakistan*, Berkeley: University of California Press, 1988.

Gommans, Jos J. L., *The Rise of the Indo-Afghan Empire, c 1710-1780*, Delhi: Oxford University Press, 1999.

Grau, Lester and Michael Gress, *The Soviet-Afghan War*, University of Kansas Press, 2002.

Gregorian, Vartan, *The Emergence of Modern Afghanistan*, Stanford University Press, 1969.

Guha, Ramachandra, *The Unquiet Woods: Ecological Change and Peasant Resistance in the Himalayas*, Delhi: Oxford University Press, 1989.

Guha, Ranajit, 'On Some Aspects of the Historiography of Colonial India' in Ranajit Guha (ed.), *Selected Subaltern Studies*, New York: Oxford University Press, 1988, pp. 37-44.

Hamadani, Agha Hussain, *The Frontier Policy of the Delhi Sultans*, Islamabad: National Institute of Historical and Cultural Research, 1986.

Haq, Ikramul, 'Pak-Afghan Drug Trade in Historical Perspective', *Asian Survey* (California, 1996), pp. 945-63.

Haqqani, Husain, *Pakistan Between Mosque and Military*, Washington: Carnegie Endowment for International Peace, 2005.

Hardiman, David (ed.), *Peasant Resistance in India, 1858-1914*, Delhi: Oxford University Press, 1992.

Hardy, Peter, *Muslims of British India*, Cambridge University Press, 1972.

———, *Partners in Freedom, and True Muslims: the Political Thought of Some Muslim Scholars in British India, 1912-1947*, Stockholm: Scandinavian Institute of Asian Studies, 1971.

Harrison, Selig, *In Afghanistan's Shadow*, New York: Carnegie Endowment for International Peace, 1981.

Hasan, Mushirul (ed.), *Islam, Communities and the Nation*, New Delhi: Manohar, 1998.

———, (ed), *Communal and Pan Islamic Trends in Colonial India*, Delhi: Manohar, 1981.

———, 'Religion and Politics in India: The Ulama and the Khilafat Movement', in Mushirul Hasan (ed.), *Communal and Pan Islamic Trends in Colonial India*, Delhi: Manohar, 1981.

Hermansen, Marcia and Bruce Lawrence, 'Indo-Persian Tazkiras as Memorative Communications' in David Gilmartin (ed.), *Beyond Turk and Hindu*, Florida: University Press of Florida, 2002.

Hobsbawm, Eric, and Ranger, Terence (eds), *The Invention of Tradition*, Cambridge University Press, 1983, pp. 211-62.

Holdich, Thomas, 'The Geography of the North-West Frontier of India', *The Geographic Journal*, XVII (May, 1901), pp. 461-75.

Huldt, Bo and Erland Jansson (eds), *The Tragedy of Afghanistan*. London: Croom Helm, 1988,

Hunter, William Wilson, *Our Indian Musalmans*, Lahore, 1872, reprint, Lahore: Premier Book House, 1964.

Hussain, Rizwan, *Pakistan and the Emergence of Islamic Militancy in Afghanistan*, Vermont: Ashgate, 2005.

Isby, David C., *War in a Distant Country*, London: Arms and Armour Press, 1989.

Jalal, Ayesha, *Self and Sovereignty: Individual and Community in South Asian Islam since 1850*, London: Routledge, 2000.

Jalali, Ali Ahmad and Lester W. Grau, *Afghan Geurrilla Warfare in the Words of the Mujahideen Fighters*, London: Compendium Publishing, 2001.

Jansson, Erland, *India, Pakistan or Pakhtunistan: The Nationalist Movements in the North-West Frontier Province, 1937-47*, Uppsala, 1981.

Kabbani, Shaykh Muhammad Hisham, *The Naqshbandi Sufi Way: History and Guidebook of the Saints of the Golden Chain*, Chicago: Kazi Publications, 1995.

Kaiser, Robert, *The Geography of Nationalism in Russia and the USSR*, Princeton University Press, 1994.

Kaviraj, Sudipta (ed.),*Politics in India*, Delhi: Oxford University Press, 2002.

Keppel, Arnold, *Gun-Running and the Indian North-West Frontier*, London: John Murray, 1911.

Khalid, Adeeb, 'Printing, Publishing and Reform in Tsarist Central Asia', *International Journal of Middle East Studies*, 26, 2 (May 1994), pp. 187-200.

———, *The Politics of Muslim Cultural Reform: Jadidism in Central Asia*, Oxford University Press, 2000.

Khalil, Jehanzeb, *Mujahideen Movements in Malakand and Mohmand Agencies, 1900-1940*, Peshawar: Area Studies Centre, 2000.

Khaliquzzaman, Chaudhry, *Pathway to Pakistan*, Karachi: Ferozesons, 1961.

Khan, Abdullah, *Mawlana Ubayd Allah Sindhi's Mission to Afghanistan*, Peshawar: Area Studies Centre, 1998.

Khan, Muhammad Asif, *The Story of Swat, as told by the founder*, Peshawar: Ferozesons, 1963.

Khan, Sultan Mahomed, *The Life of Abdur Rahman, Amir of Afghanistan*, vol. II, London: John Murray, 1900.

Lambert-Hurley, Siobhan, 'Princes, Paramountcy and the Politics of Indian Muslim Identity: the Begam of Bhopal on the Indian National Stage, 1901-1926', unpublished paper, 2003.

——, 'Contesting Seclusion: the Political Emergence of Muslim Women in Bhopal', PhD thesis, University of London, 1998.

Landau, Jacob, *The Politics of Pan-Islam: Ideology and Organisation*, Oxford: Clarendon Press, 1994.

Lapidus, Ira M., 'State and Religion in Islamic Societies', *Past and Present*, no. 151 (May 1996), pp. 3-27.

——, *A History of Islamic Societies*, Cambridge University Press, 2002.

Liebeskind, Claudia, *Piety on its Knees*, Delhi: Oxford University Press, 1998.

Lindholm, Charles (ed.), *Frontier Perspectives*, Karachi: Oxford University Press, 1996.

——, 'Images of the Pathan: The Usefulness of Colonial Ethnography' in Charles Lindholm (ed.), *Frontier Perspectives*, Karachi: Oxford University Press, 1996.

Lindholm, Cherry, 'The Swat Pakhtun Family As a Political Training Ground' in Charles Lindholm (ed.), *Frontier Perspectives*, Karachi: Oxford University Press, 1996.

Lindisfarne, Nancy, and Richard Tapper, 'Possession, Insanity, Responsibility and Self among Durrani Pashtuns in Northern Afghanistan' in Richard Tapper (ed.), *Conflict of Tribe and State in Iran and Afghanistan*, London: Croom Helm, 1983.

Ludden, David, 'History Outside of Civilisation and the Mobility of South Asian Culture', *South Asia*, XVII, 1 (1994), pp. 1-23.

Ludwig Adamec, *Historical and Political Who's Who of Afghanistan*, Graz: Akademische Druck und Verlagsanstalt, 1975.

Mahon, Captain A. H., and Lt. A. D. G. Ramsay, *Report on the Tribes of Dir, Swat and Bajour together with the Utman-Khel and Sam Ranizai*, Superintendent Government Printing India, 1901, reprint, Peshawar: Saeed Book Bank, 1981.

Maley, William, 'Political Legitimation in Contemporary Afghanistan', *Asian Survey* (California, 1987), pp. 705-25.

Malik, Muhammad Aslam, *Allama Inayatullah Mashriqi: A Political Biography*, Karachi: Oxford University Press, 2000.

Marwat, Fazal-ul-Rehim, and Shah, Sayed Wiqar Ali (eds), *Afghanistan and the Frontier*, Peshawar: Emjay Books, 1993.

Mazumder, Rajit, *The Indian Army and the Making of the Punjab*, Delhi: Permanent Black, 2003.

McChesney, Robert, 'Waqf at Balkh: A Study of the Endowments at the Shrine of 'Ali Ibn Abi Talib', PhD thesis, Princeton University, 1973.

Mehra, Parshotam, *The North-West Frontier Drama*, Karachi: Oxford University Press, 2001.

Metcalf, Barbara, 'Meandering Madrasas: Knowledge and Short-Term Itinerancy in the Tablighi Jamaat', in Nigel Crook (ed.), *The Transmission of Knowledge in South Asia*, Delhi: Oxford University Press, 1996, pp. 49-62.

———, *Islamic Revival in British India: Deoband, 1860-1900*, Princeton University Press, 1982.

Meyer, Karl E. and Shareen Blair Brysac, *Tournament of Shadows*, Washington DC: Counterpoint, 1999.

Minault, Gail, *The Khilafat Movement: Religious Symbolism and Political Mobilisation in India*, New York: Columbia University Press, 1982.

Moaddel, Mansoor and Kamran Talatoff (eds), *Modernist and Fundamentalist Debates in Islam*, New York: Palgrave Macmillan, 2000.

Morison, J. L., *From Alexander Burnes to Frederick Roberts: A Survey of Imperial Frontier Policy*, London: British Academy, 1936.

Muhammad, Wali, 'Maulana Abdur Rahim Popalzai: a Profile', Unpublished MA thesis, Peshawar University Pakistan Studies Centre, 1996.

Munphool, Meer Moonshee, 'On Gilgit and Chitral' in *Proceedings of the Royal Geographic society of London*, 13, no. 2 (1868-9), pp. 130-3.

Nasr, Seyyed Vali Reza, 'Islamic Opposition to the Islamic State: The Jamaat-i Islami, 1977-88', *International Journal of Middle East Studies* (Cambridge, 1993), pp. 261-83.

———, 'The Rise of Sunni Militancy in Pakistan: The Changing Role of Islamism and the Ulama in Society and Politics', *Modern Asian Studies* (Cambridge, 2000) pp. 1139-80.

Nawid, Senzil, *Religious Response to Social Change in Afghanistan 1919-1929*, California: Mazda Publishers, 1998.

Nichols, Robert, *Settling the Frontier: Land, Law and Society in the Peshawar Valley, 1500-1900*, Karachi: Oxford University Press, 2001.

———, *The Frontier Tribal Areas, 1840-1990*, Pennsylvania: The Afghanistan Forum, 1995.

Niemeijer, A. C., *The Khilafat Movement in India, 1919-1924*, The Hague: Martinus Nijhoff, 1972.

Nizami, Khaliq Ahmed, *Akbar and Religion*, Delhi: Idarah-i-Adabiyat-i-Delli, 1989.

Noelle, Christine, *State and Tribe in Nineteenth-Century Afghanistan*, London: Curzon, 1997.

Ortner, Sherry B., 'Resistance and the Problem of Ethnographic Refusal', *Comparative Studies in Society and History*, 37, 1 (Jan. 1995), pp. 173-93.

Orywal, Erwin, 'Periphery and Identity: Process of Detribalisation among the Baloch of Afghanistan', *Marginality and Modernity*, in Paul Titus (ed.), *Marginality and Modernity*, Karachi: Oxford University Press, 1996.

Ozdalga, Elisabeth, *Naqshbandis in Western and Central Asia: Change and Continuity*, Istanbul: Economic and Social History Foundation of Turkey, 1999

Paget, W. H., *Record of the Expeditions against the North-West Frontier Tribes since the Annexation of the Punjab*, London: Whiting, 1884.

Pinch, William, *Peasants and Monks in British India*, Berkeley: University California Press, 1996.

Pirzada, Shariufuddin, *Foundations of Pakistan*, Karachi: Oxford University Press, 1970.

Plowden, Trevor, *Translations of the Khalid-i Afghani*, Lahore: Central Jail Press, 1875.

Poullada, Roland, *Reform and Rebellion in Afghanistan 1919-1929*, New York: Cornell University Press, 1973.

Powell, Avril, 'Perceptions of the South Asian Past: Ideology, Nationalism and School History Text Books', in Nigel Crook (ed.), *The Transmission of Knowledge in South Asia*, Delhi: Oxford University Press, 1996, pp. 190-229.

Prakash, Gyan, 'Writing Post-Orientalist Histories of the Third World: Perspectives from Indian Historiography', *Comparative Studies in Society and History*, 32, 2 (Apr., 1990), pp. 383-408.

Pratap, Raja Mahendra, *Reminiscences of a Revolutionary*, Delhi: Books India International, 1999.

Prescott, J. R. V., *Map of Mainland Asia by Treaty*, Carlton: Melbourne University Press, 1975.

Priestly, Henry, *Afghanistan and its Inhabitants*, London: Longman, 1874.

Quddus, Syed Abdul, *Afghanistan and Pakistan A Geo-Political Study*, Lahore: Ferozesons, 1982.

Qureshi, Naeem, *Pan Islam in British Indian Politics: A Study of the Khilafat Movement, 1918-1924*, Leiden: Brill, 1999.

Ranger, Terence, 'The Invention of Tradition in Colonial Africa', in Terence Ranger and Eric Hobsbawm (eds)., *The Invention of Tradition*, Cambridge University Press, 1983.

Rashid, Ahmed, *Taliban: Militant Islam, Oil and Fundamentalism in Afghanistan*, New Haven: Yale University Press, 2001.

Raverty, H. G., 'The Geographical Terms "Tirah" and "Afghanistan"', *Geographical Journal*, 13, 1 (1899), pp. 83-4.

Razvi, Mujtaba, *The Frontiers of Pakistan: A Study of Frontier Problems in Pakistan's Foreign Policy*, Karachi: National Publishing House, 1971.

Reetz, Dietrich, 'In Search of the Collective Self: How Ethnic Group Concepts were Cast Through Conflict in Colonial India', *Modern Asian Studies*, 31, 2 (May 1997), pp. 285-315.

Rittenberg, Stephen Alan, 'The Independence Movement in India's North-West Frontier Province, 1901-1947', PhD thesis, Columbia University, 1977.

Robb, Peter G., 'Muslim Identity and Separatism in India: The Significance of M. A. Ansari', *Bulletin of the School of Oriental and African Studies*, University of London, 54, 1 (1991), pp. 104-25.

Robinson, Francis, 'Islam and the Impact of Print', in Francis Robinson (ed.), *Islam and Muslim History in South Asia*, Delhi: Oxford University Press, 2001, pp. 66-104.

——, 'Religious Change and the Self in Muslim South Asia Since 1800', *South Asia*, XXII, special issue (1999), pp. 13-27.

——, *The Ulama of Farangi Mahal and Islamic Culture in South Asia*, London: Hurst, 2002.

——, 'The Muslims of Upper India: Islam and Muslim History in South Asia', in Francis Robinson (ed.), *Islam and Muslim History in South Asia*, Delhi: Oxford University Press, 2001, pp. 138-55.

Robson, Brian, *The Road to Kabul—the Second Afghan War 1878-1881*, London: Arms and Armour Press, 1986.

Roy, Olivier, *Islam and Resistance in Afghanistan*, Cambridge University Press, 1986.

——, 'Modern Political Culture and Traditional Resistance' in Bo Huldt and Erland Jansson (eds), *The Tragedy of Afghanistan*, London: Croom Helm, 1988.

——, *Globalised Islam: The Search for a New Umma*, London: Hurst, 2004.

Royal Geographical Society, 'Geography of the North-West Frontier—Discussion', *The Geographic Journal*, XVII (May, 1901), p. 476.

Rubin, Barry and Judith Colp Rubin, *Anti-American Terrorism and the Middle East: A Documentary Reader*, New York: Oxford University Press, 2002.

Sanyal, Usha, *Devotional Islam and Politics in British India*, Delhi: Oxford University Press, 1996.

Sareen, Anuradha, *India and Afghanistan*, Delhi: Seema Publications, 1981.

Schinasi, May, *Afghanistan at the Beginning of the Twentieth Century: Nationalism and Journalism in Afghanistan, a study of the Seraj ul-Akhbar 1911-1918*, Naples: Istituto Universitario Orientale, 1979.

Shah, Sayed Wiqar Ali, *Ethnicity, Islam and Nationalism - Politics of the Frontier, 1937-45*, Karachi: Oxford University Press, 1999.

Shaikh, Farzana, *Community and Consensus in Islam: Muslim Representation in Colonial India*, Cambridge University Press, 1989.

Shakir, Moin, *Khilafat to Partition: A Survey of Major Political Trends Among Indian Muslims, 1919-1947*, Delhi: Kalamkar Prashan, 1970.

Sheh-re-Yar, 'Haji Sahib Turangzai and his Works', unpublished MA thesis, Peshawar University Pakistan Studies Centre, 1999.

Siegel, Jennifer, *Endgame: Britain, Russia and the Final Struggle for Central Asia*, New York: I. B. Tauris, 2002.

Singer, Andre, 'Ahmed on the Afghan Refugees' *RAIN* (London, 1980), pp. 1-2.

Singer, Wendy, *Creating Histories: Oral Narratives and the Politics of History Making*, Delhi: Oxford University Press, 1997.

Skaria, Ajay, *Hybrid Histories*. Delhi: Oxford University Press, 1999.

Smith, Wilfred Cantwell. 'The Ulama in Indian Politics' in C. H. Philips, ed., *Politics and Society in India*. London: George Allen & Unwin, pp. 39-51.

Sokefeld, Martin. 'Rumours and Politics on the Northern Frontier: The British, Pakhtun Wali and Yaghestan', *Modern Asian Studies* 36, 2 (2002), pp. 299-340.

Swidler, Nina. 'Beyond Parody: Ethnography engages Nationalist Discourse', in Paul Titus, ed., *Marginality and Modernity*. Karachi: Oxford University Press, 1996.

Tapper, Richard, ed. *Conflict of Tribe and State in Iran and Afghanistan*. London: Croom Helm, 1983.

Titus, Paul, and Nina Swidler, 'Knights Not Pawns: Ethno-Nationalism and Regional Dynamics in Post-Colonial Balochistan', *International Journal of Middle Eastern Studies*, 32 (2000), pp. 47-69.

Titus, Paul (ed.), *Marginality and Modernity*, Karachi: Oxford University Press, 1996.

———, 'Honour the Baloch, Buy the Pushtun: Stereotypes, Social Organisation and History in Western Pakistan', *Modern Asian Studies* (Cambridge, 1998), pp. 657-87.

Utas, Bo, 'Scholars, Saints and Sufis in Modern Afghanistan', in Bo Huldt and Erland Jansson (ed.), *The Tragedy of Afghanistan*, London: Croom Helm, 1988.

———, 'The Naqshbandiyya of Afghanistan on the Eve of the 1978 Coup d'Etat' in Elisabeth Ozdalga (ed.), *Naqshbandis in Western and Central Asia: Change and Continuity*, Istanbul: Economic and Social History Foundation of Turkey, 1999, pp. 117-28.

Vail, Leroy, *The Creation of Tribalism in Southern Africa*, London: James Currey, 1989.

Van der Veer, Peter, *Religious Nationalism: Hindus and Muslims in India*, Berkeley: University of California Press, 1994.

Warren, Alan, *Waziristan: The Faqir of Ipi and the Indian Army: The North-West Frontier Revolt of 1936-37*, Karachi: Oxford University Press, 2000.

Wazir, Waris Muhammad, *Afghanistan's Destiny and Eastern Pashtoons 1880-1980*, Peshawar, 1998.

Weinbaum, Marvin G., Pakistan and Afghanistan: the Strategic Relationship', *Asian Survey* (California, 1991), pp. 496-511.

Weiss, Anita M.. 'Much Ado about Counting: The Conflict Over Holding a Census in Pakistan', *Asian Survey* (California, 1999), pp. 679-93.

Werbner, Pnina, *Pilgrims of Love: The Anthropology of a Global Sufi Cult*, London: Hurst, 2004.

Winichakul, Thongchai, *Siam Mapped - A History of the Geo-Body of a Nation*, Chiang Mai: Silkworm Books, 1995.

Yapp, Malcolm E. , *Strategies of British India*, Oxford: Clarendon Press, 1980.

———, 'Tribes and States in the Khyber', in Richard Tapper (ed.), *The Conflict of Tribe and State in Iran and Afghanistan*, London: Croom Helm, 1983.

Zahab, Mariam Abou, and Olivier Roy, *Islamist Networks: The Afghan-Pakistan Connection*, London: Hurst, 2004.

Zaidi, Z. H., *The Jinnah Papers*, vols I-VI. Islamabad: National Archives of Pakistan, 1993-2001.

Zaman, Muhammad Qasim, 'Commentaries, Print and Patronage: 'Hadith' and Madrasas in Modern South Asia', *Bulletin of the School of Oriental and African Studies*, 62, 1 (1999), pp. 60-81.

———, *The Ulama in Contemporary Islam, Custodians of Change*, Princeton University Press, 2002.

INDEX

Abdul Ghaffur, Akhund, *see also* Akhund Ghaffur-Hadda Mulla line 33, 35, 39-47, 50, 52, 56, 62, 84
Abdul Haleem, Mulla 100
Abdul Karim 118
Abdul Wahab, Hazrat 44
Abdur Rahman Khan, Amir 15-20, 30, 38, 64, 105
Abdur Raziq, Haji 110, 115, 126
Afghan Wars, First and Second 6-8, 11; Third (1919) 106-12, 114, 125-6
Afghani, Jamaluddin al- 92, 107
Afghanistan 6-21, 30-1, 37-8, 39-41, 44, 56, 63-4, 83, 91, 92, 100-24, 125-7, 129, 136-8, 143, 151, 162, 173, 178, 182, 183, 187-95, 197-215
Afridis 10, 11, 22, 27, 77, 79, 81, 83, 100, 118-19, 129-35, 149, 150, 152, 158-64, 165, 176, 177, 181, 192, 201, 212
Ahmed, Akbar S. 26, 193n
Ahmed of Rai Bareilly, Sayyid 40, 42-3, 44, 45, 55, 95, 96
Ahmed Shah Abdali 37, 41
Ahmedzai Wazirs 110, 112, 126
Ahrars 165, 174-5
air attacks 128, 142, 160-2, 167, 169, 170, 171, 183, 187, 189, 190, 202
Ajab Khan 132-7
Akbar Shah, Sayyid (of Swat) 40-1, 44, 145

Akbar, Mulla Sayyid 100, 116, 130-1, 135, 160
Akhund Ghaffur-Hadda Mulla line, *see also* Hadda Mulla line; Hadda Mulla
Najmuddin 51-9, 61, 63-4, 68-9, 117, 118, 120, 153, 168, 177, 192, 197-8
Akhunzada, Mulla Abubakar 44, 53
Akhunzada, Mulla Mahmud 79-80, 81, 116, 132-3, 135, 148, 149-53, 172
Al Qaeda 3, 208, 212-14
Alingar, Faqir of 77, 82, 83, 139, 141-2, 144, 159, 167, 168-9, 172, 173
All India Muslim League 164-6, 174-8, 194-5
All India National Congress (Congress Party) 94, 156-66, 174-8
allowances to tribes 13, 22, 23, 27-8, 38, 104, 106, 110, 112, 116-17, 128-30, 137-8, 141-4, 158, 163, 186
Amanullah Khan/Shah, Amir 106-24, 126-7, 136-8, 151, 173
Amb 177, 183
Amin, Hafizullah 200
Anmir, Malik 140-1, 144
Arab 'Islamists' 204-5, 209-13
Arangi 90
arms manufacture and trade 88, 203
Asmast 102-3